Sir Thomas 'British Tommy' Armstrong and the War Between the States

Barry Tighe

Published by

Can Write Will Write

Cambridge Lodge
Wanstead England

ISBN 978-0-9563028-6-1

http://www.canwritewillwrite.com

Printed in the USA and UK by
Amazon

Typeface Georgia
12 Points
Margins 2.2 & 1.9
Width 22.86 & 15.24

Thank You

I wish to thank Cas Peace, Louise Comb and Marti Atkins for their practical help, positive criticism and all-round encouragement.

I wish to thank Richard Mooney for editing and pointing out Armstrong's grammatical and spelling mistakes, and my typing errors. Any remaining typos are mine.

A special thank you to General Robert E. Lee, for keeping the war going long enough for Armstrong to get seriously involved. Also Union General George McClellan for the same reason.

Cover: Tredegar Iron Works, Richmond Virginia.

BIOGRAPHICAL NOTE

SIR THOMAS ARMSTRONG, VC. Hero of the British Empire.
Known to all as *British Tommy*, Sir Thomas began his military career in 1840 and served with the British Army in Afghanistan, the Crimea, India and China. He distinguished himself in all his campaigns, enrapturing the British public and proving to all that Britons never will be slaves.
Six foot two inches tall, fourteen stone of muscle and sinew, *British Tommy* exemplified all that was finest in Victorian Britain.

In this volume of his memoirs, he recounts being shanghaied from Singapore just after the China campaign. Landing in San Francisco, he found himself in a nation on the verge of rebellion.

Sir Thomas 'British Tommy' Armstrong and the War Between the States

Chapter One

I never truly cottoned to Jeff Davis. Lord knows I should have done, for in his stand-offish, nose-peering way he was trying to be helpful, taking time out from his misbegotten cause to set me to rights. Leastways, he never sent me up country with a gun in my back, stuffed full of lies and moonshine as a sacrificial goat for his beloved Confederacy. Unlike his opposite number in Washington; aye and that scotch scoundrel Pinkerton egging him on as revenge for my oppressing his downtrodden mill hands back in Scotland. Pinkerton the workers' champion my arse, his spy agency broke strikes for cash, framed strikers and had them hanged before breakfast. That's by-the-by, what matters is that he and Lincoln hoodwinked me into risking life, liberty and military reputation just to help save his precious Union. Then again, I always liked Honest (hah!) Abe, which was perverse considering the trouble he caused me what with one thing and another, but then Abe Lincoln was a hard man to dislike.

I met both presidents, you see, during that monumental disaster for the Anglo-Saxon race, the war between the Northern and Southern American States. It was the most idiotic, tragic and avoidable conflict in history, not excluding Cromwell against the paddies or even the present farce brewing across the channel, and just my infernal luck to find myself cast right into the thick of it, conscripted by both sides (well, what army wouldn't conscript the famous Tommy?).

Time enough to get to my encounters with the rival presidents, always assuming good liquor and newsboys praising plucky little Belgium don't send me on to my reward first, so I shall set up shop like the historians do and give you chapter and verse in chronological order.

I have no strong views on the peculiar institution, as the Southern gentlemen call slavery, as long as it doesn't harm me. Mankind has always treated the weak like slaves, and always will, shackles or no. Southern plantation owners treated their slaves - most of the time - as well as or better than Northern factory owners, who would chain their labourers to thunderous limb-breaking machinery till their ears bled, then spit them out into the street the instant they could no longer turn a profit. Well, the slaveholders had to keep their slaves hale and hearty to do a good days work, of course, and you never saw an unemployed or homeless slave now did you? Slavery will always exist while there are weak and strong, call it slavery or Adam Smith free market or what you will, and devil take the hindmost.

I'll have plenty to say on the causes of America's crazy war on itself later, but this memoir is mainly concerned with the most important aspect of this war, namely Tommy's part in it, and how I came out with laurels from both sides. The war itself will jog along merrily behind.

For me, the War Between the States began in a restaurant-come-brothel in Singapore, where I was taking my soldiers' reward for valiant service in bringing the Chinese to heel at the Summer Palace in late 1860. Unfortunately, the Chinks weren't the only folk who knew how to fix a drink, and the madam who ran the joint and who I'd been dallying with - she owned it with her husband, a clergyman would you believe - puggled my glass and had my unconscious carcass robbed and then unceremoniously escorted off the premises, leaving me to wake up God knows how long later in the hold of an ageing brigantine, feeling like a Scotsman on January 2nd.

This was the third (and hopefully last) time I have been Shanghaied, and if I say it was least unpleasant of the three, still it brought me slap bang into the American lunacy, so I bar it as much as the others. At the very least I missed the England team setting off to Australia to teach the convicts cricket. Aye, and if only the Yankees and Butternuts had bothered to learn how to hit a solid ball with cricket willow instead of playing rounders, why, they might have grown civilised enough to settle their differences peaceably.

It was due to the Gold Rush, you understand. Since 1849, California had been full to bursting with miners, pockets a' brim with gold dust and nary a wench to bless themselves with. They naturally attracted the trash that follows loose money about; petty thieves, con-merchants, burglars, cutthroats, murderers and all the dross of the levee. They attracted smarter trash too. Yankee sharps, as is their second and first nature, sought to fill the miners' need for relaxation after a hard day at the diggins', and their own pockets while they were about it, by transporting Chinese girls to the San Francisco knocking shops. And weren't too particular about how they got them. After buying or stealing girls some as young as ten from inland China - the coastal tarts were too wise and poxed up to qualify - the slavers needed crew, and who better than a stalwart likely lad temporarily rendered unconscious, like poor Tommy?

As I say, I awoke below deck with a foul head and temper to match. Someone helped me up, fed me some water - it was all I could stomach - and with a smirk introduced himself as Charlie Badger, First Mate, and welcomed me aboard the good ship Venus, which I suspect was not its real name. Neither was mine, as I responded to his questioning by giving my name as George Jeffreys, a name of blessed memory (Judge Jeffries hanged my forebear and namesake). After my usual confusion, fear and nausea, I recollected my last thoughts before unconsciousness had claimed me, cursed the human race and my own susceptibilities and clambered unsteadily above to get my bearings.

The Captain was part-Dago American greaser, tall, wearing a French naval coat I doubt he was qualified for, and sporting a scar on his left cheek that suggested he did more than ferry day-trippers around the lighthouse. He didn't deign to talk to me, but Charlie the bucko Mate with his stomach hanging over his belt like foam over a jug of ale, soon brought me up to speed. We were sailing to San Francisco where (he told me with a wink) I would be well paid for my work and set on my way. I'd heard that one before; like enough I'd be cast ashore penniless or kept on board for the return journey. We'd see about that, but in the meantime it was all hands to the pumps, and time to think of the future when we hit dry land. #Note_1

The ship had started out from Shanghai, which seemed appropriate, with a cargo of girls for the Frisco brothels and crimps. She sailed to Singapore to pick up provisions and crew members for the Pacific journey. I wasn't the only one carted unwillingly aboard, by the way; at least half a dozen European denizens of the Singapore brothels found themselves en-route to the New World, and not a thing to be done about it. The wailing, pleading, threats and bribes of these bravos, as well as the contemptuous retorts, and in one case a hefty kick up the backside from Charlie the Mate, reminded me of my own previous unexpected ocean voyages where I quickly learned to go along with the current. If it wasn't for my own woes and throbbing head, I might have enjoyed their predicament, especially one woebegone young fellow who claimed he was due to be wed in a few days and had only stopped off at the brothel by way of a last hurrah for old time's sake.

'What's this?' laughs Charlie to the crestfallen youngster, winking at nearby crew members. 'What will your new in-laws say? Well now, I'd reckon' that depends on their imaginations, haw haw.' The other sailors laughed at this, and I may have harrumphed a little myself. After all, he wasn't the first fiancé to come adrift on his stag night, nor the last. Serves the silly young bastard right.

For myself, once I realised the journey was a straight one to a relatively civilised country, I took stock and decided things weren't too bad. I'd been through San Francisco before, ten years ago, and the place was already booming. By now Frisco should be halfway to being a proper city. All I'd have to do was seek out the British Legation or Consul, if there was one, and present myself as Tommy, VC, and I'd be on my way home to England and beauty with a shilling from the poor box for tips. Penniless, I'd need it too. Meanwhile, if they hadn't yet got around to installing a British representative, the American government owed me a favour for loyal service a while back, when Allen Pinkerton's Yankee secret service hired me to ride shotgun on the sainted (or cursed, depending on which side of Mason and Dixon's line you came from) John Brown. He's the one whose body lies a' mouldering in the grave, by the way, not our Queen Victoria's Scottish sidekick. The mission was a failure, but that wasn't my fault, much. The U.S. government thanked me (unofficially) for my services and told Our Man in Washington, Lord Lyons, all about it. So I was none too worried about arriving penniless in Frisco. The Lord, Legation or Yankee government would provide. My only concern, prophetic as it turned out, was to disembark from the Venus gracefully, and not be booked for a return trip.

Tommy is an old hand at being a deck hand, so to speak. I adopted my standard shanghaied sailor's approach; stern and silent, volunteering no sailing knowledge whatsoever, that way avoiding the more dangerous duties monkeying aloft in the rigging, leaving me confined to swabbing, holystoning and general dogsbodying. And to set your mind at rest, I kept well away from the wenches, children not holding any carnal interest for me. Besides, the Captain kept them out of sight, deck exercise apart, for the whole journey. The deck exercising, I noted without surprise, differed not one whit from the dancing the traditional slavers, if I may call them that, forced on black slaves transported from Africa. Well, slaves are much the same whatever the colour, and what were these yellow girls to be, if not slaves?

The Venus made good time, as far as I could tell. Six weeks passed uneventfully enough and the weather got fresher, which made up for the food. I don't believe we saw another ship until the day we sighted the Bay of California, where the San Franciscan harbour, such as it was, awaited our delivery. The coast grew before us, and after carefully negotiating Mile Rock, for we arrived as dusk was gathering, we came into full view of the harbour. Ships of all shapes and sizes lay at anchor dotted around the bay, lanterns aglow, while skiffs darted nimbly to and fro between them, ferrying Pilots, passengers and shore-leave sailors to town and back. San Francisco had grown considerably in the last ten years, I noted. From the deck I could just make out several wide and brightly lit thoroughfares. These would be interspersed, if memory served, with dark, mazy alleys leading up from the waterfront to anonymous back-doubles choc-a-bloc with brothels, saloons and boarding houses. Just the place, I noted with approval, for a reluctant sailor to jump ship. All I needed was a yard start and Neptune could go whistle.

Before coming to anchor, Charlie called the crew to the stern and had us crowd round while he blasted out our instructions.

'Right. Listen up,' he roared, and I can see him in my mind's eye yet; lardy but carrying easy authority underneath what passed at sea for bonhomie. 'Ye will be on the Barbary Coast this night, wi' your pockets full of well-earned cash' (cheers from the boys), 'and ye won't find a better or quicker place to spend the lot (more cheers as Charlie unshipped a leering wink at our older and wiser ex-fiancé in case he or anyone else didn't get the gist). 'But, boys,' he lowered his voice to a boom; 'afore ye get paid ye have one more service to perform. That's to keep our cargo safe 'till our Captain hands it over to his agent. Ye'll notice every officer is carrying his side arms so ye will stand at the ready until the Captain says "Aye".' He smiled reassuringly, 'then its payday, me lads, and ho for the Barbary Coast.'

The crew cheered and hollered like shellbacks the world over when arriving at port and payday after a long voyage. My gang of Shanghai-ees, I noticed, didn't join in the general air of merriment. The news that the officers were packing pistols brought home to them just what they had got themselves into, but your loyal correspondent wasn't worried. Not much anyway. You see, as mentioned, I had been through San Francisco before, and knew the wiseacres hadn't nicknamed it the Barbary Coast because of its climate. Gold-financed mayhem abounded along the whole waterfront, up the hills to Little China and beyond. Debauchery, drunken and opium-fuelled violence and petty thievery were only the start of it; the whole town bulged with two-bit brothels where you pays your money, drinks your drink laced with Spanish Fly and wakes up in the back alley without your wallet.

And that wasn't the worst of it. Whenever a ship was spotted approaching San Francisco's Golden Gate, Whitehall boatmen - a kind of aquatic hansom cab service - would ferry gangs of runners around the bay armed with guns, knives, blackjacks, even soap to ruin the sailors' soup to persuade them to desert, and storm aboard the ships to steal cargo, crew and anything not nailed down. These runners worked for the local boarding houses, and would entice sailors by promising harlot heaven to get them to desert willingly, or cudgel them if they showed resistance. The boarding house masters, or crimps, kept the sailors stupefied with drink or drugs until they sold them to unscrupulous sea captains for $25 or thereabouts per body. Of course, the captains desperately needed crews as their own had likely been kidnapped when they first dropped anchor. Sailors who avoided kidnapping often deserted anyway, to try their luck at the gold diggings, so between kidnap and desertion the poor captains had the devil of a job finding an outgoing crew and would pay the crimps for whatever dregs they had, including sometimes their own former shipmates.

Well it had been like that ten years ago and I doubted the Mormons had taken over since - though some of them tried - and I mentally raised my cap to the Captain and mate for preparing for trouble with the runners. Not that I expected it.

Knowing me, you might wonder why I was so sanguine, leaning over the rail with my cheroot, idly marking time while the ship drew nearer to land, finally dropping anchor a little way off the shore. Well I jump at shadows, and being a windy so-and-so has kept me in one piece, more or less, for over ninety years, and I can tell you I saw no shadows here. We were an armed ship's crew for goodness sake; surely no crimp's runners would dare attack us? I'll own my mind was chiefly focussed on how I would wipe away a tear and bid the dear old vessel goodbye without attracting Charlie's suspicion - no great problem for a professional ship's absconder like myself - so I ruled attack by runners as altogether out of court. No, I dismissed Charlie's scaremongering as just his way of keeping the crew on their toes until the Captain handed over the girls to the agent and collected his commission. This seemed imminent as two dandy skiffs pulled alongside. They were fairly large for Whitehall boatmen, but I figured they'd need to be to transport our girls without relays. One thing I felt certain of, we were safe.

Which shows just how wrong you can be. I realised that things were amiss when I saw a boathook flung artlessly from one of the skiffs across our bows. Another immediately followed, and another, and before you could say blister me barnacles they were swarming over the deck, pistols in hand, some with knife clenched sideways in teeth, the finest bunch of pirates you could wish for. In seconds they had fanned out along the main deck, threatening our crew with their pistols but not firing - they could only sell live sailors, after all, or so I thought in my ignorance - while sober files, ugly as ogres, began clubbing the nearest deckhands and hurling them overboard to be collected by the runners in the skiffs below for handy transportation to whichever boarding house had hired them.

'Stand fast!' hollers Charlie, wasting his breath as our crew decided as one that below decks was the safest place to be. Our officers hadn't even fired a shot in self-defence as they scampered to illusory safety as a child may hide under the bedclothes. The ship echoed with the yells and screams of the crew and girls - oh yes, the runners had discovered our cargo, and mighty pleased they sounded about it too. Shameful thinks I, while casting around for a likely spot to disembark. For as yet more runners vaulted over the sides, hopelessly outnumbering the crew, it was clear that everyone, girls and all, would be prisoners and at their mercy of which they had none. This being the case, t'was time to depart.

Even when I am panicking I keep my powers of reason. To dive off the near side where the runners were hurling our crew was to invite a cosh on the head and a trip to the boarding house for resale. The only answer was to dive over the lee side and make for the coast a hundred yards or so further up. Surely the lads in the skiffs would be too busy coshing and lifting to notice one head bobbing shorewards in the dusk. And I was a strong swimmer, having swum the Mississippi in my time.

Not letting thought stay action, or whatever it was the Bard said, I launched myself over the rail, just noticing the third skiff from the corner of my eye as I hit the freezing water.

My mind works quickly in a crisis. As the water enveloped me - and the cold cut through me like a knife - I was already breast-stroking underneath the skiff. Let me once get to the other side and I'd switch to the crawl. God it was cold!

I broke surface gasping. One second, that's all I needed to restore myself, and I'd break all records for swimming as sheer blind panic sped me along. But it was no go. I couldn't last another thirty seconds in that icy sea; with a sickening feeling in my stomach, I knew that my only hope of survival lay in getting aboard the third skiff. Time enough to worry about anything else when I was warm and dry.

'Up ye come m'laddie', spoke my unlikely saviour as a couple of the runners hauled me over the side, floundering like a gaffed fish as I plunged into the bottom. I was their first customer but I wasn't alone for long as erstwhile crew members jumped or were hurled overboard. Some showed fight and received an efficient whack on the back of the head from a blackjack, the use of which the runners seemed mighty skilled. The sensible fellows, me included, lay lip-chattering, shivering and wheezing, prone in the heart of the skiff as it filled up with bodies, awaiting developments. These bodies included several of our girls, dry I noticed, having been dropped down carefully into the willing arms of the runners below. They were too frightened to do more than whimper, which made up for me. Sure enough, the skiff's Captain, a huge Mexican scoundrel sporting a bright red shirt, rippling muscles and no coat on a wintery night, made a signal and unseen hands above released the grappling irons. We were off, runners, ship's crew and tarts together, to whatever fate awaited us.

Frozen and winded though I was, I still had my wits about me, and saw that my chance to skip for the California hills would occur as we hit the waterfront. By now night had fallen, and amongst the chaos and confusion of disembarkation, there was sure to be an opportunity to run. Once into the back alleys, I would be safe from pursuit. All I'd then have to do was lie low someplace providence would provide for the night, then tool round to the British Legation or failing that, the local police station, and I would be halfway home. Ah, Tommy old lad, the optimism of youth. When I think of the times I thought I was safe home bar the shouting, only to find myself deeper in the mire than ever. And this time it wasn't even my fault.

Nobody was taking a blind bit of notice of me, quiet, humble and dripping as I was, and my hopes rose as I realised that the runners seemed to think the heavy work completed, and all that was left was to shepherd us sailors to their boarding house and repair to the nearest groggery to toast a job well done. Grabbing the yellow girls was an unexpected bonus for them, I imagine, and would fetch a rare price in the local amusement palaces. Well, I determined, this being the case, they wouldn't need me. Disembarkation, that's when I'll make my move.

And I succeeded, after a fashion. The skiff made short work of the journey back to shore and presently we scraped alongside a low, wide jetty. A few runners skipped ashore and secured the skiff, while others manhandled the girls onto the pier, warning us crewmen - those of us who remained conscious - to keep still and await our turn. Well this wasn't good enough for me. As we neared the shore I prepared for an instant bound. Oh joy - one of the runners was standing just in front of me on the jetty, waving his pistol at the girls to frighten them into obedience. Naturally they spoke no English, and being frightened noisily witless were a bigger handful than any tarry-jack sailors. All attention was on them as I made ready my leap for freedom.

Inhaling deeply I bounded out off the skiff and on to the jetty like Dick Dauntless, rabbit-punching the runner's neck with my left hand and snatching his piece with my right. By great good luck he packed a Colt Navy Revolver, one I was familiar with. Not standing on ceremony, I about-turned and raced full steam ahead along the jetty for dry land. Or rather, I intended to. For I had hardly made three paces when the red-shirted skipper leapt in front of me roaring like a bull in a butchers and smashed a straight jab to the kidneys, taking all the bounce and wind out of me and leaving me sinking to the ground, pistol in hand.

I just about had the sense to topple away from Red Shirt to avoid the inevitable booted broadside, and as I sprawled athwart I imagined as in a dream I could hear piercing whistles from the ether, and the jetty seemed to shudder as under a stampede. For a wonder I found myself left alone, again, curiously disinterested as I sought to regain my breath. As reason returned to its throne I saw why.

17

It was a police raid. The whistlers were the Frisco peelers announcing their arrival. By the time I got my breath back the jetty was a battle royal, for although the cops were out in force the other two skiffs must have landed alongside and the runners were in no mood to parley. Amid the hysterical screaming of our girls both sides grappled with knives, brass knuckles and blackjacks, for the waterfront police, like our Northwest frontier guards, knew that against a death-or-damnation foe you soldiered well or not at all. Fists, boots, and bludgeons were clashing all around me like Saturday night in a Glasgow pub. No place for peaceable Tommy, you'll agree, and as I stumbled, breathing heavily, to my feet, I reflected that I hadn't heard any gunfire yet.

Too soon. A shot rang out from the runners, then an answering shot from the police. Time to go, thinks I, rising, and immediately tripped over Red Shirt, who was grappling with one of the officers while busily bludgeoning him down, and measured my length on the jetty. Enraged, Red Shirt dropped the flatfoot and aimed his bludgeon at my head. I screamed and jerked out of the way as the bludgeon splintered the wooden jetty where my head had been. Rolling over, I was now laying face up, my right hand - clutching the pistol for dear life - under my body. Arching my back, I struggled to whip my pistol around and give the red shirted gaucho what he had been asking for all bloody day, but someone beat me to it. A shot rang out above me. Red Shirt jerked like a puppet, swayed backwards for a moment, righted himself and toppled forward towards me like a poleaxed redwood. Once again I screamed, and tried desperately to scramble upright, but this time his flailing arm caught mine, trigger finger and all, and squeezed off a shot - I swear - straight up in the air. #Note_2

Clambering frantically from under the bleeding Red Shirt I heard a scream almost in my ear. Someone cried 'Jack's been shot!' Jack, evidently one of the police raiding party, had had the bad luck to be standing downwind of a runner's bullet, and caught it in the vitals, by the sound of him, just as I accidentally fired my gun. The police surged forwards. Not to be outdone, the runners surged back into them, poor Tommy carried hither and thither in the mêlée between the two, until a cry went up from the runners that Red Shirt had taken a bullet. The mob parted, slightly, and there was Tommy clutching his winded stomach in one hand and a smoking pistol in t'other. Both groups looked at me and no prizes for guessing what they thought. Backing up quickly to the side of the jetty for space, I waved my pistol at police and runners alike.

'Stand back for your lives' roars I, red-faced with fear, for I needed elbow room like I needed my next breath. Luckily they obeyed, and in less time than it takes to think, I was off and away, halfway down the jetty before anyone knew what was what.

Whistles blew and the peelers tore after me, along with several runners and God knows who from the jetty, intent on avenging their Officer Jack and Red Shirt. Gasping for breath I hurtled off the jetty and on to comforting terra firma for the first time in nearly two months. A shot zinged past my ear to remind me I was still in mortal danger. Both groups of pursuers thought I had shot their boy, blast 'em, and I didn't intend to stick around to explain their error. Run now talk later, as the Pathans almost say.

I cannot impress enough on young chaps that when you are being chased, run, run, run and don't let anyone or anything get in your way. Time enough to reckon up the future when you are clear of pursuit. With this in mind I bounded into the first handy alleyway and tore Hell-for-leather, knocking aside trivial obstructions like townsfolk unable to jump clear fast enough. Left and right I hammered through the alleys and side streets, heedless of the noise behind me or the complaints from upturned citizens. Luckily I had landed on just about the only part of the Frisco coast that wasn't steep uphill. In short order I came across a well lit thoroughfare. Heaving, I peered back down the alley from which I'd just emerged. No sign of the hunters, though I could still hear whistles in the distance. A moment to get my breath back and I could seek to hide up somewhere until I could get my bearings. Conscious of my sodden clothes and bedraggled appearance, I edged carefully along the side of the thoroughfare, avoiding the more sober citizens' gaze and seeking a darker path that might lead me further from the sea front.

'There he is! This way boys!'

I don't know whose side the caller was on; cop or runner, and I didn't linger to find out. I was off again like a Leicestershire fox along the thoroughfare, seeking handy alleys and confound it; there were none to be had. Still, Tommy powered by fear and panic can outrun any pursuers, and I held my own easily until I came to a sharp turning. And, praise the Lord, the street was ill lit with a seedy saloon on the corner and three handy alleyways to put the pack off the scent. I was bolting for the far left one when a sharp, agonising pain jagged through my ribs. Stomach cramp or something, doubtless brought about by an icy ducking, fist in the stomach and recent vigorous exercise to say nothing of mental torment, after a six week cruise. Sailors aren't natural runners, you know. We're not built for it.

I couldn't run. But I could hide. I must have five seconds start on my pursuers, just enough time to duck into the saloon before they turned the corner and trust to luck. I had just time to note the name above the door; *The Cobweb Palace.*

It lived up to its name. Striding quickly into the interior, I was startled to find a mass of cobwebs smothering ceiling lamps and mirrors and all fixtures and fittings and even the fancy bottles above the bar. Despite my distracted state I had to do a double-take, and that's when I became aware that the clientele seemed to be screeching hysterically. It was something of a relief to discover that behind the cobwebs the far wall was piled up to the high ceiling with cages containing monkeys, parrots and smaller animals and birds, making a racket to startle Satan. Just what I needed to top a trying day, you'll agree. I thought I had stumbled through the looking glass. (I later discovered that the owner, one Abe Warner, bought the beasts from passing sailors and along with the spider webs which he happened to like, they were a great town attraction where low-life and swells mixed freely).

Not a haunt I'd frequent under normal circumstances, but a likely dive like this could harbour me splendidly from the storms outside. Cavernous, crowded and noisy, even in my dishevelled condition I drew little attention. I was just about done in and couldn't run another step. My stomach was beginning to worry me, hurting more than it should from a single punch. Let me mingle with the cobwebs and crowds for a few minutes to get my breath and composure back and I could take my leave when the coast was clear.

'Who in Hell are ye and what'd ye think ye're doing here dripping all over the carpet?'

Dressed in some kind of livery, I guessed my challenger was employed by the establishment, probably to keep vagabonds like me out. He wasn't friendly, and I could see I would have trouble persuading him my intentions were pure, so I decided on immediate action.

'What's that on your shoulder?' says I in my friendliest voice. As he looked instinctively, I turned and strode through the throng. Thank heavens it was jam packed, I could lose him in seconds, maybe hide in the privy at the back or somewhere until it was safe to go outside.

'You come back here right now, y'heah?'

Just my luck to come across a jack-in-office determined to do his duty by his employers and to Hell with the inconvenience he causes to honest folk. Unsure what to do, I played for time striding deeper into the crowd and up a few steps, hoping he would lose interest, not that I had much expectation of that.

Evidently the back of the Cobweb Palace was where the swells and high-rollers took their evening's entertainments, for the crowd thinned and I found myself facing a group of tables laden with wines and sweetmeats and populated by a well-dressed clientele a cut above the coastal packrats down in the crowded area. I was feeling dizzy and worn out, and all in a blur crashed my way through, falling at the table of a flamboyantly attired mature gentleman with authority written all over him. His young entourage stiffened in their seats and looked about ready to feed me to the monkeys but he stilled them with an easy wave of the hand, and, waving a chicken leg in the other, addressed me sharp.

'What are you about, Sir? Kindly take yourself off and leave decent folk to their business. Off with you at once Sir.'

Even in my distraught condition, I recognised him as a well-to-do Southerner, educated and better spoken than most, plantation owner likely as not. Not that it mattered, but something in his cool, calm manner gave me hope. And the Southerners often had a soft spot for the English having deluded themselves they were akin to British aristocracy. If I could convince him I was as respectable as he was, I felt I should be safe. Staggering to my feet and taking a deep breath to compose myself, I donned my best parade ground voice.

'Pardon me, Sir. Sorry to impose on you and your, err, associates in this unruly manner.' For the first time, I noticed the worthy's fellow imbibers, and a tougher bunch of likely lads you could not wish for. No scum of the levee neither, like the rabble chasing me, but the real deal, killing gentlemen. If I could get them to help me I felt I would be safe. But if not...

'Colonel Armstrong, Sir, at your service. British Army, late of India and China. I am afraid, Sir, that I find myself waylaid by footpads, and must appeal to your good self and your associates to help me.'

It sounded impressive, though I say so myself. Wasted on the lads around the table, alas. They hooted at me as my liveried doorman caught up and grabbed me by the scruff, but my Southerner sat bolt upright. Eyes widening, he motioned dismissively to the scruff-grabber, who released my collar with alacrity.

'Colonel Armstrong did you say? British Army?' He peered intently up at me through steely eyes. 'The VC hero?'

I could scarcely believe my ears. I'd received little Vicky's new Victoria Cross for my heroics in India in '58. How this gentleman could know about it was beyond me, but time enough for that later. Smartly I replied.

'That's me.'

'Armstrong VC? And a knight by all that's holy?'

I nodded modestly. By Jove this was an unexpected goose. The table was silent now, and my liveried friend had stepped back a pace, flummoxed at the turn of events. He wasn't the only one.

'What was your first regiment?'

'Why, the Eleventh Hussars.'

'Their nickname?'

'Ah... the cherrypickers.'

'And who was your commanding officer?'

'My Lord Cardigan.' And a first rate louse he was too, but let it pass. Beaming like I was the prodigal son home at last, my Southern beauty rose and clasped my hand in both of his and wrung it like the church bells. For the first time in two months I began to feel safe. This Southerner, whoever he was, was clearly a man of substance and influence, and for a wonder he seemed to know all about my glorious military career (the official version). Still befuddled, I failed to remember that when powerful men are pleased to see you, its time to make your excuses and leave. But I was tired, dishevelled and not at my best, or you wouldn't have seen me for dust.

My new friend's eyes widened and a great beaming smile creased his features.

'You are Armstrong indeed. Why Sir, delighted to make your acquaintance, I surely am. And you say you're waylaid by footpads?'

Now he was getting to the point. I made to reply in the affirmative, but before I could open my mouth, a sudden loud commotion behind me drew everyone's attention.

'Thar he is!'

My erstwhile pursuers had caught up with me. In an instant I found energy anew and bounded sideways around the Southerner's table. Too late. Last I remember was a dull thud to the back of my head and an explosion of stars in my mind's eye. How pretty they look, I remember thinking, as consciousness ebbed peacefully away.

Chapter Two

It is a rum do coming to after a knock on the head. If you drift back to life face down in your own congealed blood - or as happened to me once, tied to the muzzle of a cannon - then you tend to think that the worst is yet to come. If, on the other hand, you find you are in a comfortable bed with sheets and blankets, well, then all is as it should be, and you relax on the plumped up pillow while the throbbing dies down.

My awakening after this latest head-flogging began as one of the better ones, if not quite up there with the best, until I recalled just what had brought me to this position. I had indeed woken up in a good bed, and at first imagined I was back home in England, my wife due to appear at any moment to summon me to breakfast. This was just for a fleeting moment, of course, as recollection slowly surfaced and I began to take stock of my position and surroundings.

Craning my neck slightly, I found myself in a small but brightly clean room, barely more than a cupboard, with low sloping ceiling, whitewashed walls, and a rickety-looking chair as the only furniture. Winter sunshine beamed through the tiny slit windows illuminating fine dust floating aimlessly in its rays, and somewhere below me, for I was clearly in an attic of sorts, could be heard the gentle burble of many voices in amiable conversation.

Encouraged in my dreamy condition, for all appeared pleasant and with nothing to hinder my exit should I choose to leave, I considered my immediate future. The mother-luck that protects the wicked had come to my rescue once more. I may have had some confounded fortune in my time, but have always managed to slide out somehow before the curtain falls, as we villains so often do. It's my belief that the Good Lord is in no hurry to meet us, and lets us linger to a ruinous old age while the good die young. And you'll notice that our bishops and archbishops also live to a great age while you're about it.

Meanwhile, I was left to ponder which Good Samaritan had pulled me out from under this time. Well, no doubt I'd find out in due course. Barring unexpected hiccups, and I'd had more than my share of those in my time, I would simply amble downstairs, thank my benefactor should I encounter him, and put into motion my plan of enlisting legation or police to assist me on my way back to the aforementioned home and wife. Julie her name is, and after several years of absence, she had probably noticed I was off the household strength and might be missing me.

The police! As I awoke fully the memories of last night's events - if they were last night's events - rushed into my head like cold furies. The police were chasing me, aye, and boarding house runners-come-pirates were chasing me too. I now recalled the events on the jetty as clear as the Pope's soul, and I knew that whatever else I may do to reach England and salvation, enlisting the interests of the police was completely out of court. Why, if their comrade was as injured as he'd sounded, there might be a price on my head. And were the runners also still after me? But stay, I wasn't in a police cell, and the room was far too clean to be a runner's dive, so the rabble chasing me had clearly be given the right about one way or another. Someone had saved me, but who? And why? I was old and hard used enough by now to distrust the motives of any unexpected patron, and the bigger the favour bestowed, the greater the favour - and probably ghastly adventure - expected in return. Cynical, says you? Perhaps. I'm like that myself, and if I sometimes misjudge my fellow man - there are some genuine saints about, they tell me - well, I've been right a shot more often than t'otherwise. Assuredly, my best bet was to rise, find out what's what downstairs and go on from there. One wrong look or hint of trouble from anyone and I'd be out and away on the first convenient horse, sure as knife.

The above notions, you must understand, took place in an inkling. My course of action clear, I made to get out of the bed by rising suddenly. As I did, a sharp, agonising pain shot through my stomach and innards like forked lightning. I gasped and collapsed, breathing hard. The pain seemed to diffuse into a numbing nausea. I tried to rise once more, gingerly this time, only for the room to start dancing around me as if it were a ship's cabin during a tempest. I flopped back down again onto the sheets with sweet relief in my bones, but panic in my head. I'd had these symptoms before. Just when I needed to be at my fleeing best, beset by foes, my freezing immersion and scares had rendered me helpless. I had caught some kind of coastal fever.

I said I thought I had awoken in this welcoming bed the day after my jetty adventure dancing the quadrille with pirates and police with red shirt conducting the band until giant spiders entangled me helplessly in their web and monkeys screeched approval as they came at me with cudgels. Aye, it might have been so, but I confess I lost all track of time while the fever worked its course through my ill-used frame. I shan't catch fever again, I suspect, as my creaking body has already suffered every variety on God's green earth.

The quadrille described above was just one of the many dreams and hallucinations I experienced while drifting in and out of consciousness, and deuced unpleasant the lot of 'em. Amid the fantasies, I became aware of visitors. One regular bedside companion, a black matronly woman who seemed to be a nurse of some kind and who probably fed me though the recollection is unclear, and a dapper young man with a lot to say for himself, addressed to my nurse in a broad Southern accent, and by the way he gesticulated, obviously concerning my feverish self. I was too far under to recollect anything he said, or care, but I did notice he was a good-looking fellow in a slightly effeminate way; clean shaven, neatly manicured hair and smartly dressed, sporting a bow tie. A young man - he couldn't be much above twenty summers - he had the cocksureness of youth and I remember wondering if he would be good news for me, or t'other kind. Well I found out soon enough.

I didn't take note of his utterances at the time, but at last I began to regain my wits and strength, managing to crawl out of bed one morning and, standing precariously on the chair, peer out of the high windows down to the street four storeys below. My nurse arrived just then carrying my vittles, gruel of some kind for the convalescent, so I opened the batting along the lines of *where am I* and *who do I have to thank for my deliverance*. While picking up her bowl after dropping it with a squeal, she gave voice.

'Lansakes. You'se didn't orter be out of bed Suh. Not 'till you'se better.'

'But where am I?'

'In Frisco, Suh, in a gambling house.'

That didn't surprise me. Declining the gruel and requesting some more substantial fare, I asked for more details, like where in San Francisco and who was the youngster who kept visiting.

'Why Suh, we is in Grant Avenue, the finest gambling street in the State. And yore visitor is Mass' Harpending. He a mighty fine young gentleman, shore 'nough.'

'But what does he want with me?'

'I can't rightly say, Suh, he jus' looked in to see how you wuz.'

Well that figured. Dapper young men would hardly discuss their business with the staff, especially when black, but I wasn't in the political service for nothing. Folk usually say more than they intend, and if he had I meant to know what it was.

'Is that all? I seem to recall him doing most of the talking. Surely he must have said something? Anything at all?'

'No Suh.' She considered. 'Well, he did say he jess wanna know if'n you're with the Sout'. He say all Englishmen are.'

'The South?'

'Yes Suh. For de war wiv de Nort.' Everyone know it due 'bout any day now.'

Everyone but your correspondent. Amazing as it now seems, I let this bombshell fly over me.

'I err... I take it Mass' ...Harpending?'

'Yussah. Mass' Harpending.'

'Ah yes. I take it Mass' Harpending is for the South?' She chuckled.

'You bet. An' his friends too. Everyone in dis house is for sure. Dat goes double for me.' She swelled up as if mustering for parade.

In that case, thinks I diplomatically, I'm for the Sout' too. After all, it don't pay to antagonise your hosts, especially when you are adrift in a strange town with your pockets hanging out and the peelers and local villains on your tail. Not that I care twopence about slavery or any of the other piddling disputes that eventually led to four years of slaughter, not to say some slight inconvenience to myself, but I know which side my bread is buttered.

'Well,' says I, 'you and Mr. Harpending can rest assured, no one supports the South more than me.'

She beamed down on me like a bishop at the collection plate. 'Ah knew it, when ah saw youse a'sleeping with the ague, youse too darn handsome to be a Yankee lover. 'Scooze my language.'

'Excused. I mean, I don't like them any more than you do. I'll have no truck with them... ah Yankees, no truck at all.'

You may wonder why I was bothering to keep in with the political babblings of a nurse who would, if her beloved South had their way, be sent to backbreaking work in fields too hot for white folk, followed by an unmarked grave, yet she supported them and hated her would-be liberators. Mind you, nothing surprises me. But even in my convalesant condition, if there is one thing I was certain sure of, it was that anything I said to this nurse would find its way to the ear of Mr. Harpending. And if there was one thing I wanted him to know above all else, it was that I was on his side and all Yankees could burn in Hades and I would supply the matches. Then I caught up with her bombshell.

'You say that the North and South are about to go to war?'

'Dat's right Suh. Mebbe it already started back east. One thin' for sure, if'n it comes, when it comes, California is going for the South or Mass' Harpending an' a whole passel besides will know the reason why.'

This was my introduction to the War between the States; that horrific conflagration that threatened to set the world ablaze and damn near did, Britain included. But I was behind the times just then; to be sure, the world knew that North and South had been eyeing each other askance over the slavery issue for years, with the North allowing the South could keep slavery where it already existed, but insisting the new States opening westwards would be free, meaning rather than working the slaves to death they could work poor white folk to death instead. The South in its turn wanted a great slave empire from Mason and Dixon's line right the way down to Cape Horn if they could manage it, with Cuba thrown in for luck. Creating new slave States across to the Pacific coast was stage one of their expansionist fantasy, and that meant thumbing their noses at the North and keeping tight hold of the White House and Congress to allow them to do so. Neither side trusted the other an inch, but nobody apart from a few crazed fire-eaters actually thought it would come to bloodshed. Well, they were wrong.

This was all in the future for me, though I was enlightened considerably, and by much more than I wanted, that evening when who should arrive to ask after my health but the mysterious Mr. Harpending.

'The warrior awakes,' was this worthy's first words to me, smiling broadly and stretching out his hand, a warm welcome thank goodness. 'Don't get up, don't get up. Asbury Harpending at yore service. Dee-lighted to make yore acquaintance Colonel Armstrong. Ah surely am.' And he wrung my hand like a sponge.

Well he couldn't say fairer than that. My qualms about just what he may have wanted from me diminished considerably, and I deemed it politic to toady him a bit.

'Sir, let me thank you for all you have done for me. Lord knows where I would have been were it not for your timely intercession.' Truth to tell, I wasn't exactly sure who had done what to help me in my hour of need, remembering only being smashed over the head in a spidery saloon. But here I was, mending nicely and the gentleman standing over my sick-bed, looking at me as though I was the cavalry arriving in the nick of time - an uncomfortably accurate description as it turned out - was plainly a major player, if not the leading man himself.

'No need to thank me,' replies this beauty modestly. 'T'weren't my doing, exactly. I was jus' obeying orders like a good soldier. Fact is,' he pulled up the chair and made himself comfortable, 'the gennleman you have to thank is a lil' distance away, but he hopes to meet you at yore convenience. Jus' as soon as you are up an' ready.' Studying my prone body, like jolly Doctor Goodenough making a diagnosis, he added, 'which I hope will be in a day or two.' He frowned absently and I wondered had he farted, then returned to the agenda. 'Don' wanna rush you, Suh, but time is pressing.'

I was with him there. The sooner I could meet this benevolent gentleman and convince him to bail me out of his benighted country on the first available steamship, the better. But stay, why was time pressing for him?

'Why the hurry?'

For the first time Harpending lost his calm assurance. 'Don't you know? With Lincoln in the White House it can only be a matter of months, or weeks even, until the abolitionists,' he looked like he was going to spit, then thought better of it, 'fall treacherously upon the peace-lovin' South to try an' destroy us. That, Suh, is the hurry. An' when they do, we have jus' got to be ready for them, especially right here in Californy.'

I heard the words but my mind had frozen at *Lincoln in the White House.* So he had defied all logic and

31

common sense to become the sixteenth - and almost the last as things turned out - president of the United States. Honest Abe Lincoln of Kentucky and Illinois and blessed memory. I had met him a dozen or so years earlier when he helped me out of a trifling scrap. A clever man, resourceful, far seeing and able to read his fellow man with unnerving clarity, leavened with a singular sense of humour. For example he spotted me as a wrong'un from the off, but didn't expose me to the proper authorities as he found my plight amusing, and besides he seemed to take a liking to me as folk often do. I liked him too, against my better judgement, for *qui male agit odit lucem* (the evil doer hates the light), as another old friend of mine used to say.

That's not to the point; for all that Lincoln was an impressive character, he couldn't possibly convince folk he was presidential material. One look at him would settle matters. Not even the American electorate with their universal suffrage - women and blacks excepted - would be so witless as to vote for a country bumpkin who, with his undersized clothes and his oversize top hat, resembled an undertaker left out in the rain. I'd known he was standing, to be sure, but I'd have laid bankrupt's odds that the pro-slavery Democrats would flay him alive and stroll back into power, safeguarding slavery and stagnation in the South and generally keeping the lid on Northern abolitionists and their industrial trailblazers.

Where I would have lost my money is that I underestimated the ability of the Democrat Party to snatch defeat from the jaws of victory by failing to settle on a single candidate. Unable to agree a united policy, they had selected two, if you please, one from the North and one from the South. This of course split their vote, leaving the new anti-slavery Republican Party with Lincoln at the helm a clear run right up Pennsylvania Avenue, as a blind donkey could have foreseen. Suicidal strategy from the Democrats, but not a whit worse than the behaviour of our own politicians back home. Why, we hadn't had a proper majority government since they repealed the Corn Laws in 1846. No wonder we despise politicians; they effect to run our lives but can't even win an election with two-thirds of the voters on their side.

'So Lincoln made it to the White House then?'

'Damn right he did.' He gave me a keen look. 'Why? You a supporter of his?' He wasn't so affable now and I coughed into my sleeve to hide my reaction to his question. Rhetorical, I'm sure, but it wouldn't do to let this firebrand know how Lincoln had befriended me in the past. Not that it would make me vote for him, but the least said about my previous American adventures the better. For the first time I began to wonder if the seemingly rational youngster stirring agitatedly in his seat at the mention of Lincoln was perhaps another one of the army of fanatics it has been my misfortune to encounter all too frequently during my saunter through this vale of tears.

Suitably chastised, I put away my incredulousness and made excuses. But I wasn't going to crawl - yet. I needed to know where all this was going, and how best to escape it. Find out the lay of the land, as it were.

'Lincoln can eat crow for me, and like it. I was just surprised to learn there were so many fools in the country to elect him, that's all.'

He softened as I hoped he would, and I pressed home my advantage.

'Sorry to sound ignorant old fellow. I've been away. I only just arrived from China where I was serving with the British Army when I was waylaid by criminals and rescued by your splendid friend. I am afraid I am quite out of touch.' Reminding him of my military antecedents, you'll notice, so he would know he was dealing with someone who merited respect.

'He's not my friend, though I reckon' to admire him powerfully. You kin judge for yourself soon enough.' He leaned towards me. 'But say,' he brightened, 'if'n you only just arrived from China, then you won't know the news. About Lincoln and our succession and suchlike.'

I informed him that the last news I had heard from America - from a Yankee abolitionist naval officer in a Singapore brothel as it happened, but I didn't care to tell

33

him that - was that the election had been due in November and Lincoln was the Republican candidate. I didn't add that I could not see what difference Lincoln's presidency would make to the slave question. My naval pal from the brothel had told me that with the secessionist temperature rising, Lincoln was all for a quiet life and had maintained that he wouldn't touch slavery with a bargepole. So in the unlikely event of a Republican victory, all the Democrats had to do was sweat out Lincoln's reign and unite themselves behind a single candidate for the subsequent election. Win that - and they would - and they could keep their slavery and their eighteenth century ways until kingdom come.

Aloud I opined that a single candidate would surely have won for the Democrats, proving that most Americans North and South were happy to live with slavery. Knowing this, a cowardly hoosier like Lincoln wouldn't dare suppress it, they'd run him out of town on a rail (I'm always ready with a stretcher or two to keep in with folk I need).

He listened impassively, snorted, and proceeded to bring me up to date.

'Democrats should have stuck by Breckinridge, our true Southern Democrat, then we'd a' given them Black Republicans the whipping they deserved. Those Northern dough-face Democrats' - again he looked ready to spit - 'sold us down the river with their traitor Douglas selling out Kansas to the 'bolitionists and then opposing our true Southern man. That's why we done got ourselves Lincoln and that's why we got ourselves a war.'

He was nearly off on a long-practised rant, but I asked how come, and he simmered down and continued my education.

'Here's the way of it. Once Lincoln got hisself elected, we of the South finally woke up to Yankee scheming. Lincoln says he'll allow us to keep our peculiar institution where we already have it, blast his impudent eyes, but nobody's fooled. He'll stop us spreading our ways west, so's the rest of America will be Free States, and why,

34

in a few years we'll be so outnumbered and surrounded they'll abolish slavery over our heads and us too weak to resist.' He checked himself again and got down to cases.

'Well we ain't licked yet, nor will we be by any Yankee schemes. Soon as the results were in, near 'nough, South Carolina told them what they could do with their abolitionist flag and struck out on her own self. She wuz the first, but now we are growing fast. 'Miss', Florida, Alabama and Georgia have joined us, with more joining ever faster. We have declared ourselves the Confederate States of America, a new nation under God, and the Yankees kin slide.'

The light of enthusiasm exulted in his eyes as he contemplated the break-up of his homeland, like an Irishman on Cromwell's birthday. 'Texas, Louisiana, Virginny, Tennessee, Kansas, Arkansas, Kentucky, North Carolina will show themselves true, to be sure. Maybe even Maryland.'

I was stunned. I knew, as did all the world, that the United States was two separate countries, North and South, with two vastly different ways of life, maybe even living in two different centuries, but I'd always thought that leaving the warmth of Uncle Sam and striking out on their own was a pipedream of a few fire-eaters, not to be entertained in civilised company. Like giving Home Rule to the paddies. But if against all common sense the South had cut itself adrift of civilisation, why should this mean war?

'Because Lincoln and his conniving cohorts want to destroy our ways and our freedom. With their consarnit rules and laws and gov'mint interfering in common folk's lives, taxing folk as they like, they can't abide a new country on their borders where the flag of liberty still shines with the spirit of our founding fathers. No Suh. So we'll fight... and we'll whip 'em.'

Well, this was very interesting, no doubt, and I'd look forward to dazzling them in my club when I got home, giving the origins of the war straight from the shoulder, but I couldn't see what it had to do with me (fool that I was). I nearly said so, for I'd heard this kind of patriotic moonshine many times, and no good ever came of it so far as I could see. No good ever came out of it to me, leastways; though similar European maniacs had nearly got me skinned a few times. So I clucked sympathetically, and hinted that I was tired.

'Thank you Sir, for bringing me up to date with the Black Republicans' shenanigans and the South's principled response. I always suspected that Lincoln was a scoundrel, and your timely words have confirmed my suspicions. When I get back to England you may rest easy I shall let them know what a fine bunch of fellows you Southerners are, and confusion to the North. All true Britons will hurrah you on, and cheer at your valiant defence of freedom.' Fearful gammon, I know, but I needed his good will so why not lay in on with a trowel? 'Meanwhile, please drop in any time you wish, and I hope to meet the gentleman who saved me from footpads and... and suchlike.'

He beamed at me.

'Why that's mighty good to know. You mean you will do what you can to help our great cause?'

Like an ass I replied, 'Pon my soul, anything, anything at all. You can rely on me from Hell to Huddersfield.'

To my surprise and consternation he sniffed with emotion, piped his eye and looked at me nobly.

'I am much moved, Suh. You are everything the General said you would be an' that's a fact. May I shake yore hand once more?'

And stab me, he rose and sprung his fin almost into my prone chest, clasping my hand in his and staring me straight in the eye.

'Thank you Suh, thank you indeed.' He released my aching paw, stood erect and bowed. 'You are tired Suh, and I fear I may have exhausted you. Forgive me please for mebbe allowing my emotions to overcome me, but freedom for the South is my passion and events are moving fast. I will return tomorrow and if you are able, bring you to meet the man who saved you when you appealed to him for help in *The Cobweb Palace*.'

'Oh absolutely,' I replied all eagerness. 'I can never repay the favour he did me, a stranger, that night. I am fully in his debt and if there is anything I can do...'

'Don' fret you'self', Colonel Armstrong. Don' fret. There sure is something you can do, count on it. Till tomorrow then.'

And with a flourish he was gone. I noticed he fancied himself a bit of a dandy. Maybe his love for helping his Confederacy included hopes of being proclaimed a hero of the South. Well being a hero attracts the women, thinks I, stroking my martial whiskers, and what else is being a soldier good for?

But notwithstanding friend Harpending's probable lust for glory, his last remark left me perplexed, or fretting, as he would say. What was this something I could do? Of course, I had always suspected that my true knight in shining armour was the mature swell in *The Spider's Bollocks*, or whatever that saloon called itself; he had been mighty impressed when I told him who I was, and seemed to know all about me (the official version I mean, had he known my true character doubtless I'd now be feeding the fishes in San Francisco Bay). My benefactor styled himself the General. Was he a real one? More likely it was a *nom de guerre*. Bad news for me if it was, for such deception invokes images of plots, intrigue and villainy. I should know; I've been snared in more plots than you can shake a stick at and nearly all of them involved folk sailing under false colours. And this General knew me only by my military reputation, which was all about blood and gore. If Harpending's suggestion that I could do something for the General meant more than regaling him with tales of my derring-do, then I might have to make alternative travel arrangements. One thing of which I was certain, at the first sign of the offer of a commission in his non-existent army, I'd be off faster than our chaps when bushwhacked by the Americans in the Battle of New Orleans. Fought, incidentally, three days after we signed the peace treaty.

37

Looking back, I can see that I was still not quite right in the head. Had my coward's antennae been working properly I should have realised immediately that anyone calling himself the General, who had rescued me from the runners - a powerful element in Frisco and not casually crossed - and kept me out of the arms of the police, didn't do it to enrol me as a member of his sewing circle. And with Harpending's war on the horizon...?

As I say, had I had my wits about me I'd have squeezed through one of the narrow windows, scaled down the four stories (the General would be sure to have guards posted downstairs to stop me sneaking out by the front door) and fled to the hills before I was roped into leading an attack on New York, or assassinating Lincoln or similar lunacy.

As it was, I convinced myself that most likely the General just wanted to bathe in the reflected glory of a Victoria Cross winner and sound out my military opinions on the chances of the South in the unlikely event (so I thought) that it would come to war. I'd tell him too, whatever he wanted to hear. On that happy complacent note I dismissed Harpending's wild talk from my mind and settled back into a dreamy sleep.

Chapter Three

'Colonel Armstrong? Col' Armstrong! You 'wake Suh?'

Well I hadn't been, but his gentle yet urgent shaking roused me soon enough and I found myself staring up into the candlelit silhouette of my self-appointed guardian angel, Asbury Harpending.

'What the devil...?' I almost screamed, jerking myself upright, for his manner and timing were enough to panic Wellington, let alone a windy beggar like me.

'Tis okay,' replies he *sotto voce*. 'Didn't mean to anxious you none. I've come to collect you.'

'Mmnn?'

'You're going to meet the General.'

'The deuce I am. What time is it?'

'Midnight. I got a carriage awaiting. The General wants to see you... now.'

He stepped back from the bed and produced a valise.

'Get these duds on and let's go. Quicker we go less chance we get spotted. I'll wait outside. Hurry man.'

He'd bought some clothes for me - well-fitting and fine quality - to replace my weatherworn seaman's rags, but that's where his Southern hospitality ended. Forgetting his earlier concern for my condition and taking it for granted that I was fit for travel, he whispered through the door that Englishmen shore took a long time to dress and he hoped I wouldn't douse myself in pomade 'cuz it was a closed coach we wuz travelling in. I could hardly refuse, damn him, so shaking with cold and fright, I clambered into my new outfit, shoes and coat too. I splashed my face from the water bowl, and took some deep breaths to straighten up outside and inside, so he wouldn't notice my funks. Why was he all afire not to be spotted? There was nothing for it but to play along and see where the fates were leading me. I'm a philosophical man; when forces beyond your ken are sounding the reveille you must present arms front, show a bold face - and steal a glance for a handy back exit.

By the time I was properly awake I found myself ensconced in a closed growler rattling through the winding hills of Frisco 'till I thought I'd throw up my first solid meal in weeks. On what I guess was the outskirts of town we turned into a middling long crunching gravel drive leading to a discreet mansion, shining through the gloom as if to protest innocence. I knew the feeling.

The General did himself proud. His mansion, assuming that it was his, was set on its own, well apart from the stables and other dwellings, with entrances - and exits for quick flight - in several directions. The speed and secrecy under which Harpending delivered me set my nerves a' jangle, and it was a pensive VC hero who crossed the threshold where Harpending presented his card to the soft-shoed Chinese butler. A short wait while I screwed my eyes against the bright light and wondered what this furtive tryst portended - nothing good I was sure of that - and presently we were escorted along a lushly carpeted lit corridor and into a high-ceilinged spacious room.

It was decked out part comfy, part office, with dark panelling, fireplace and warm lamps aglow, a huge table stage centre sporting ink, pens, papers, maps, glasses, bottles, tobacco and spittoons. Around it sat about a dozen keen-eyed men. A spattering of older blowhards behind beards and watch-chains but most of them young and well set up, all eyes towards me whilst Harpending nodded to them familiarly. Oho, thinks I, if this doesn't smell of conspiracy, Victoria is a virgin. I recognised the General seated at the top of the table - where else - and he rose and beckoned me over.

'Colonel Armstrong Sir, we meet again, pleasure Sir, pleasure to meet such a heroic and valiant man.' Sticking out his craggy, ring-laden hand, he added, 'An' God's blessings 'pon us all, in the very nick of time.' He smiled grimly, like a crocodile before grace, while I, torn between his kind words of welcome and wondering what the devil he wanted with me, tried to look stern and noble.

'Why thank'ee Sir. The pleasure's all mine, I'm sure. And let me at once take this opportunity to tell you how much I appreciate all you have done for me, a stranger in your land. Why, without you I'd be in Queer Street, err... that is to say, I don't know what I'd ha' done without you.' Awful filibuster, you'll agree, but the whole situation was beyond me and I had a fretful feeling that as soon as I shut up I would hear something I'd happily miss. I was right, too.

'Weren't nothing, Colonel, nothing at all. The least I could do for a man of your heroism and capabilities.'

There he was, going on about my bloody heroism again. I didn't like this above half.

'But where are my manners? Mister Harpending, get our friend a drink while I introduce him to the boys.'

Harpending jumped while the General took me around the table. Every man-jack of them rose and shook my hand as though it was the door handle to Ali Baba's cave. I swear I was waiting for someone to shout 'Open Sesame', and expect jewels to come tumbling out of my backside. As it was, they budged down a seat and allowed me to take my place, drink in hand, next to the General.

'Your health, Sir, and your future.'

Both subjects close to my heart, as the General would find out should he put either of them at risk. The table drank heartily, and, ceremonies over, hushed down to business.

'Now Sir,' states the General, 'Mr. Harpending here says that you're heart and soul with the South in this coming conflagration that's due to break out any day now due to them Yankee abolitionist meddlers poking their infernal noses into our affairs and trying to ruin us all.' Every eye was on me as he got to the nub. 'Is that so?'

I'm not slow on the uptake, and it didn't take my extensive knowledge of deeper than damnation plots, reluctantly acquired you may be sure, to know that it had better be so and with a tiger, if I knew what was good for me.

'Oh absolutely,' agrees I, all pep and mustard. 'I have nothing but contempt for those interfering Yankees with their abolitionist claptrap, you may rest assured. Why, all England knows that the cotton fields of the South are what makes the world go round, and if Lincoln and his government in Washington have an ounce of sense they will leave the South be and tend to their own business instead.'

Well it sounded OK. Now maybe the General would drink my health again and buy me a first class ticket on the next homebound sloop to spread the good word. Fat chance.

The General nodded, and looked around the table at his companions. 'Well gentlemen, what do you say?'

One older man, all jowls and grey gravitas, growled at me suspiciously.

'Suh. The General heah tells us you are just about the greatest soldier the British Army evah had and pra'cally saved India single handed. Now we don' doubt yore a brave man, why your Vick-toria Cross jes 'bout proves that. What we around this table wanna know is, how come you so fired up to help us?'

Well I wasn't of course, but I could hardly tell them that. The whole table awaited my answer so I trotted out the sort of moonshine I thought they wanted to hear.

'Ah, it's like this you see. We British have always had a soft spot for the underdog, don't ye know, and we hate to see big government interfering in folks' lives and telling them what to do. Why, you in the South are our cousins. Your quality gentleman run the show for the benefit of everybody and everyone knows their place. The only difference between you in the South and us in England is that we keep our Negroes - most of 'em - working overseas whereas you let them live on your plantations and whatnot. Ours think themselves free and yours don't, but when all is said and done they all work for the white man.'

This last bit is true, by the way. We made much ado about abolishing slavery; old Wilberforce beating his breasts and crying infamy at the way we forced the blacks to tote dat barge and lift dat bale, so we freed them and now they tote and lift for a pittance; about the same as it

42

cost us to keep 'em as slaves but now they have to pay us rent. The liberals are happy and nobody grows fat on the difference.

They sat looking blank and my spirits drooped. What did they want me to say? Inspiration made me recall a plantation owner I once had the doubtful privilege to work for giving me his views over late-night drinks. 'And besides,' I added, hoping to hit the target this time, 'slavery is the natural condition of the black. Why, without us they would still be in the jungle, savages bowing down to wood and stone.' I threw in religion, knowing just how God-fearing these slaveholders are. 'We have brought the Negroes to honest labour and to the Good Lord who keeps everyone in their allotted station. He gave Southerners a climate too hot for them to labour in, then in His mercy provided a race He designed for the job. It is in God's plan to have blacks work the fields and learn Christianity from their betters in order to save their savage souls.'

'That's true; says so in the Bible,' agrees one of the older men, but the others kept mum. What else did my slave-owning boss tell me? Ah yes, to be sure. I took a pull of my drink, wheezed slightly and continued.

'But it's not just about slavery, Gentleman.' I sat bolt upright, upped the volume and hit them with my last shot. 'It is about a free peoples' right to make their own laws in their own States and not have some Yankee mercenary telling them what to do. Says so in the Constitution.'

I struck home. Nods from the older ones, damn rights and you shore said a mouthful Colonel and dat's the trut' from the younger. I sat back and awaited developments with relief and foreboding mixed. Now that I had satisfied this coven of my Southern *bona fides*, where was it to take me?

I didn't have to wait long to find out.

'Well, gentlemen,' says the General. 'Does that satisfy ye?'

The table nodded or swore agreement, according to taste, and the General turned to me.

'Colonel Armstrong, I have followed your career since the Crimea an' right up to the Indian Mutiny, when you show'd the Indian Negroes who was master. Many's the time I wished we had more young men like you to defend the South against our enemies.'

Harpending growled. 'That's not to say we don' have heaps of t' right sort, no Suh. We got the finest young men any nation evah had an' that's a fact.'

'True enough,' agrees the General, 'But...' he again scanned the eager-faced young men - whom I was liking less and less - and continued. 'But one thing we lack, and that's professional soldiers of Colonel Armstrong's calibre; men with rich battle experience who have planned campaigns and who have charged into the jaws of death and come through laughing; men who have faced the odds and finding them overwhelming, conquered them; men who stand their ground against all that the foe can fling.'

This was ladling it on thick, but it impressed the table, my good self excepted. He looked me in the eye - most disconcerting - and wound up with the words I had been dreading. 'In short Sir, we need you.'

As the blow fell, I saw my worst fears realised. The General had read all the newspaper nonsense about my supposed heroics and fallen for every lying word. Not for the first time I wondered if he truly was a General. Probably, as it takes a peculiar type of military genius to believe every brave tale told of soldiers. They want to believe the men they lead resemble Greek heroes of the Odysseus and Achilles vintage and not the whoremongering lead swingers many of us really were. Well, I was, at any rate. I would see suicidal bravery in due course, both sides, but that was in the future. Naturally the Holy Joes who enjoy seeing the wicked get their comeuppance will rejoice in finding me once again with my nipples caught in the vice. I take all the undeserved plaudits, they will say, so I can't whimper too loudly if sometimes folk take me at my public estimate and enlist me in their cockeyed schemes. Well, looking back today from my brandy and fireside chair, I can see their point, but at the time all I could think was, what does this madman want from me and how do I weasel out?

'Colonel Armstrong,' the General barked, 'as I knew you would all along, you have satisfied our group here that you are with us and with the South.'

'Same thing,' says one of the table.

'And with their permission, I will now tell you how you can help us in our struggle.'

Oh Jesu, thinks I, here it comes.

'I have chosen to invite you to join our group and lead in an affair of great moment, an enterprise on which the future of the South might depend. Our actions,' he waved in his fellow conspirators while I tried to stop the glass chattering against my teeth, 'in the coming weeks may well decide the outcome of this battle for liberty which is all but before us. Now, ere I tell you more, I must hear one thing from your own lips. Are you prepared to risk life, limb and liberty in our great cause?'

Well you know the answer to that, but I ask you; what would you have said? For it was plain as a pikestaff what would happen if I politely declined. I was in too deep now. These smartly dressed gentlemen now gazing at me with pleading rapture as though their entire war depended on me, were as dangerous a bunch of desperadoes as I had encountered in a long life spent entangled with zealous villains, and I could imagine their reaction to an honest reply; a conspiracy scorned as it were.

I must stress to young men who come after me, when you've no choice but to say 'aye' to some suicidal adventure, show no reservations but agree pronto and with enthusiasm. That way they'll believe you are as cracked as them and let you alone, making it easier to slip your cable when chance allows. This being the case, I answered with an eagerness that satisfied everybody and earned a cheer and toast of approval.

'Oh course, of course,' I yelled, swept along by the tide of the General's oration. 'Thank you General, thank you beyond goodness for this chance to strike another blow for freedom! I had hoped beyond hope that you would

45

deem me worthy of your great cause and you...' I piped away a manly tear, '...and you have made my dreams come true.'

Now you or I would know that, as the Bard says, I doth protest too much, and eye me askance henceforth. What you have to consider, though, is that these men were fanatics; ardently devoted to their great cause and unable to contemplate anyone who wasn't, Yankees aside of course. Consequently they roared their cheers, drank my health and promised damnation to the Washington government. To hear them you would think we had won the war already. Which brought me to the sticking point - what exactly was this affair of great moment?

But first I had to swear the oath. The General produced a document from a sheaf of papers, damned indiscreet if you ask me, and handed it to me to read aloud standing up. The table rose to chant alongside, right arms raised as we did back at Rugby when we needed to use the privy, clearly knowing the words by heart. It was long and rambling, promising as Southern gentlemen not to breathe a word of their lunacy to the wives of their bosoms, and revenge to the traitors and suchlike, which made my heart miss a beat, and as we wrapped it up the General looked towards me and added, to the best of my memory, as follows:

'Do you, Colonel Armstrong, in the presence of Almighty God, swear that what I may this night say to or show you shall be kept secret and sacred, and that you will not by hint, action or word reveal the same to any living being, so help me God?'

There was only one answer to that. I agreed forcefully. And before said Holy Joes assail me for swearing an oath with treachery in my heart, for I of course had no intention of holding to it, let me point out that a good lawyer has since told me that oaths extracted under duress cannot be held against one, so there. They must have had doubts themselves, for as I discovered later, they repeated the oath at every meeting as if to reassure themselves that they were as mad as each other. Finally the

General retrieved the document from me, marched ceremoniously across to the fire and consigned it to ashes.

Formalities over, we helped ourselves to another drink, in one case sorely needed, and after another toast to the South and calamity to the North, or words to that effect, the General finally unveiled his scheme for dropping poor Tommy into the mulligatawny.

'Tell me Colonel,' he began, 'are you acquainted with an organisation calling itself The Knights of the Golden Circle?'

Had I not been so distressed by my predicament I might have laughed. The Americans set great store by kicking all monarchies out of their troubled continent, and brag of their universal suffrage and all men born equal and the rest of their democratic claptrap, but give them a cause to fight for and there they'll be, reintroducing nobility, King Arthur's round table and forays up misty mountains to extinguish fearsome dragons and rescue golden-haired damsels soon as belch.

Aloud I replied that they were new to me, and explained that I had been abroad until recently and was not, perhaps, as up on self-aggrandising organisations (though I phrased it differently) as I should be. He shook his head sadly at my ignorance, doubtless thinking *hiatus maxime deflendus* (a want greatly to be deplored), and pressed on.

'The Knights of the Golden Circle were born out of the philosophies of Senator John C. Calhoun, and the Southern Rights Clubs, which advocate the re-establishment of the African slave-trade. They were also inspired by a clandestine group called the Order of the Lone Star, which helped win freedom for Texas from the Mexicans. In fact,' he added proudly, 'reinvigorated in Kentucky, the Knights go back as far as the Sons of Liberty, who helped defeat you British in the American Revolutionary war.' #Note 3

'The fu'st American revolutionary woah,' hollers a young hothead. 'We's now in the second one, an we'll whup the foe this time too.' Hoots of agreement as the General called the meeting to order.

'Quite so. Now, the aim of the Knights is to create an independent, slave-holding empire with its capital at Havana, Cuba. This Greater Confederacy will consist of the Southern States of the United States, Mexico, the Gulf of Mexico, the Caribbean, and Central America. This empire will provide the world with cotton, sugar, tobacco, rice, coffee, indigo, and produce from our mines, ensuring prosperity, freedom and security for all. These industries will, of course, utilise slave labour as ordained in the Bible, and the institution of slavery will be guaranteed by our Constitution in perpetuity.' He paused, doubtless contemplating his Arthurian vision of a feudal Shangri-La, with darkies cheerfully whistling Doodah while they slaved, and gallant Southern gentlemen escorting their good ladies under parasols from carriage to church, tea and hoedown, according to the time of day.

'So you are all Knights of the... ah... Golden Circle?' Frightful though his revelations were, it was as much as I could do to keep a straight face. The Southern States were going to cut loose from the North and conquer just about all of Central America backed by an economy based on cotton and baccy with barely enough industry to deck their folks out with shoes. It seems unbelievable now, but didn't many die for this belief?

'No Sir,' he continued guardedly, 'I'm not saying we all here are members of the Knights, though some of us may be. No Sir I am not saying that at all.'

Then what are you telling me about them for? I wondered.

'We are,' he glanced around the table, 'shall we say... sympathisers. And we, in sympathy with the aforementioned organization's aims and objectives, have an objective of our own, which is to carry California out of the Union and into our new Confederate States of America.' He swelled up with pride and self-importance. 'We are The Committee of Thirty.'

But there's only about a dozen of you, was my immediate thought, followed by the realisation that, barking mad though these Knights of the Golden Shower obviously were, the General here could match them moonbeam for cucumber with his Committee of Thirty nonsense, whatever it was. Hoping that the Committee might turn out to be the accounts or catering department of the Golden Knights, I looked at the General for enlightenment.

'This is where we stand. The Knights are raising men for the oncoming struggle, chiefly in Texas, their stronghold. They'll control Texas in our Southern Congress when we are done with the Yankees, and look to expand into Central America and so forth. Alas, we in California are not so well placed. We don' have a militia ready to march -' you don't even have thirty, thinks I '- but we don't need one just yet, and when we do..., why, the numbers will be there.'

'You bet,' cries a young blood. 'They'll come a running jes' as soon as we raise the banner.'

'An' that's a fact,' agrees another.

'Every one of our Committee,' continues the General, 'has pledged to raise one hundred men for our cause. We have many already. This State, especially the Southern half, abounds with veterans of the Mexican war, disillusioned gold-diggers, former filibusters, ex-Indian fighters, all raring to go to war to keep the Yankees out and allow us run our own affairs ourselves. Those not so high-minded will engage in any undertaking that pays well. And we do, Colonel.' He guffawed. 'Why, we got all the gold in California!'

The table roared at this, while I digested its import. The General was hinting he would raise a mercenary army and use California's gold to pay for it. Well, it might work, though I wouldn't trust mercenaries against regulars, but then the regulars would be busy on the east coast, fighting the Rebels there, always supposing, and I still found it deuced unlikely, that this war actually got going.

'We are collecting bands already, dispersed all over the Frisco bay, apparently engaged in peaceful activities such as wood chopping, fishing and the like, but in reality waiting for the word from me. Each member of the Committee keeps his own counsel. Only I know the location of the various detachments. We have money a'plenty and God and right on our side. Now, Colonel Armstrong, many of our Committee are not present today; on account most of them are prominent citizens with faces familiar to all, an' tis better if they are not seen to-ing and fro-ing here too often. But rest assured, we are recruiting good men, mainly from the South of the State' he grinned, 'ready against the day they are needed.'

Well he'd satisfied me he could count to thirty. But what, I wondered, would they be needed for and more important, where did I come in?

'With Texas electing for the South, our new nation runs nearly from ocean to ocean. Spurred on by the Knights, the Texans will march west into New Mexico, Nevada, Colorado and Utah. At the same time, we here will rise up and deliver California for the South. So while Texas is marching west, we'll march east and lo! Our new Confederacy will span from Atlantic to Pacific shores.'

'Amen,' cries an older hand.

Well, this was all very fine, doubtless, and if he could get California to join the South and catch the western territories in a pincer movement with the Texans, then maybe his dream would come true. Meanwhile, the General was looking at me expectantly so I decided to react the way a true Southern fanatic should.

'Why that's marvellous news I'm sure. And let me be the first to wish you God's speed in your magnificent crusade. This'll show them in Washington and that's a fact.' And those Nevada Indians, sands and cactus plants won't know what hit 'em. Fighting for Nevada? Stab me. Then like a fool I asked the obvious question.

'But California's for the North isn't it? This isn't a slave State at all.'

There was a hush and the Committee shrank as though I'd passed port to the right. Harpending took a pull of his whiskey and replied.

'That's true Colonel; this heah State was hornswaggled into prohibiting slavery when they settled it's borders. Fact is, California by rights orter be two States, Norf Californy free' he wrinkled his nose like he'd found a bad smell, 'and Southern Californy slave. But,' he snorted, 'them Yankees swiped the lot by political bottom-dealing, and that's where they made their big mistake... 'cuz we're gonna swipe it back.'

A dark foreboding stole over me. I could see the General commissioning me into his army of three thousand - if his Committee lived up to its promise which I very much doubted - and striding forth into the empty wilds of the American west - Indians aside - looking for folk to shoot. Well I'd swim in blood first. Hold on though, the blood I'd be swimming in was mine. What a pickle, but all I could do was hold my peace and await events.

'I expect you are wondering just how we can win over the State,' continues my host. 'Have no fear, we got it all planned out.'

I thought he might.

'Here's how it is. Upwards of thirty percent of the population of California come from the South. Many of the foreign immigrants, Irish and German mainly, are either neutral or tend towards us. They detest being ruled from far-off Washington. We have more than enough support to take the State, provided we can show them a lead.' He took a pull of his glass while I wondered how they'd take rule from far-off Cuba. 'The United States' Federals have little more than a token presence here. Now that California is no longer under threat from European powers...' here he shot me a pained look, as though I personally framed Britain's earlier plan to steal California from under America's nose. I should explain that when California was owned by Mexico we British had tried to buy it off them in settlement of debts due, but with it now a U.S. State, just about, we'd lost interest. It has occurred to me since that had the

Mexicans found the gold before the Yanks won the territory, Britain, aye, with France and Spain hanging on to our coat-tails, would have grabbed California devil a doubt. A British-owned California flaunting its skirts at Washington whilst mining their gold would have enraged the Americans like a cat in a kennel, uniting North and South against us and probably sparing them their civil war. But they'd never thank us for it. Ah well, Britain seldom gets credit for anything these days, and besides, the Mexicans would never have found gold in California unless it lay on the ground in ingots with "gold" emblazoned in three different languages on the sides. A Mexican in his shirt sleeves swinging a pickaxe? Sooner find a teetotal Irishman. But I digress.

'...They are down to not more than three hundred fighting troops all told.'

He paused and stared at me intently. I can still see that moment; warm glow from the lamps and the crackling fire, richly upholstered walls and décor, solid oaken table fit to grace any directors' meeting with smartly dressed gentleman around it and the whole shebang looking as respectable as the Board of Trade. It's always the same; the more genteel the company, the deeper the plot, and this was as damned a coterie as Lucifer's cabinet. Notwithstanding, all eyes were on me and with mounting horror I saw all; this maniac wants me to lead an attack on the U.S. army.

'About two hundred Federal troops guard Fort Point, fewer than a hundred at Alcatraz with a handful at Mare Island and at the arsenal at Benicia which holds thirty thousand arms. We intend, Colonel Armstrong, to take these bases and also seize the guns of the San Franciscan Militia. Once we have the guns we will organise an army of Southern sympathisers more than capable of dealing with any local resistance.'

By God we've been here before, thinks I fearfully. Not yet two years ago, John Brown launched his crazed scheme to rob the arsenal at Harper's Ferry, arm the slaves and destroy slavery. And here I was today, getting the lowdown on an even greater lunacy, this time to rob the California arsenals and *preserve* slavery. But fearful though I was, I saw at once the difference. Brown's obsession with starting a slave revolution in Virginia (and being hailed the greatest champion since the Good Lord himself, the old humbug) blinded him to the absurdity of his whole wild idea. Brown never stood a chance. This General, I realised with a sickening feeling in my stomach, suffered none of Brown's utopian delusions. He knew what he was about. If his figures were correct, and I had no reason to doubt them, why, the thing should be a breeze. Surprise the under-strength, ill-prepared Federals, lift the weapons and distribute them to thousands of willing fools, and the State was theirs for the plucking. So, rot him, why was he dragging *me* into it?

'Once we have control, we will declare California for the Confederacy, and march east as the Texans march west under their Golden Knights.' He paused, wondered if he should add anything, then decided it was time for Tommy to earn his corn. 'Well Sir, what say you?'

I realised I was expected to lend my mighty military knowledge to evaluate this incredible plot. Well as I say, provided the General's information was accurate, his plot was sound, though insane. All that counted, of course, was that I could keep myself well out of it.

'General,' says I, much moved. 'This is magnificent. By all that's holy, I declare this is the greatest thing I have ever heard. You are clearly a warrior of the first order. Why, Napoleon himself would stand in awe of the brilliance, yet simplicity of it all.' Might as well butter up the old bastard, it never does any harm and will encourage him to believe me when I delicately council caution.

'It must succeed gloriously,' I continued, 'so long as your figures are up to date. Your number of Southern sympathisers, size of the arsenals, and types of arms with powder and ball, and bullets available. And cannon. Of course you will need campaigning equipment; horses, wagons, tents, food supplies, cooking utensils, axes, maps, medical equipment, oh, the thousand and one things a successful invading force needs. Then I am certain you will succeed in your righteous venture. You'll need to know the readiness or otherwise of the Federal troops, their lines of communication and their ability to whistle up reinforcements before you have your men trained and ready to combat a disciplined army... why, with all these things in place the whole operation should run like clockwork.'

You'll realise what I was about. I had to feign support for this outlandish military coup - aye and treason too - whilst simultaneously giving a hundred reasons why they should delay. For delay, if I had anything to say about it, was what we were going to do. Given sufficient delay I could find a way to jump on a homebound ship and leave the General and his followers to whatever fate had in store for them. For now, all I could do was plant the seed that raiding the arsenals and declaring for the South was the easy part. Holding the State with an untrained mob and invading the huge territories to the east, by the gods, was a labour to daunt a drunken Hercules.

I thought my tactful reminder of military reality would lower their spirits to the floor, so you can imagine where mine were when I cast around to see how the plotters were taking it, only to find they were beaming like fireflies round a picnic. The General, I promise, looked quite maudlin and snorted to keep his eyes dry. Raising his head, he addressed the table.

'You see gentleman? I know some of you have had doubts about my wisdom in recruiting Colonel Armstrong to our great cause,' from the corner of my eye I caught Harpending give a start at this, 'but now you see why we need him.' He turned to me and once again held out his great craggy paw for me to latch on to. 'Colonel Armstrong, the Lord has truly sent you to us in our hour of need. For though I, our Committee, can start this thing in motion and gain control of the State, still we need the wisdom of a seasoned campaigner to ensure we hold what we gain. As you correctly point out, we need to train our men, secure forage, horses, tents and all the rest for a successful drive to unite the Confederacy coast to coast. We have the plans, we have the men and guns, or soon will. What we have lacked up till now is the military intelligence, expertise and leadership under my command, and the Lord be praised, now we have you.'

So help me, that's what he said. Makes you wonder how these people manage to keep out of the loony bins. He released my hand and pronounced sentence. 'In fine, Colonel, we need you. Welcome, I say, to the Confederate Army of California.'

By George this was desperate. With bowels dissolving I tried to feign delight while tripping him up.

'You honour me Sir, all of you. Your plan is sound, and given time to train the men, muster equipment and... and all the other resources vital for success, we can look ahead to a magnificent victory for the South. And you flatter me with your regard for my military intelligence.' This last bit was true enough, at any rate. I sipped my drink for dramatic effect, and then eyed them all slowly. Establishing my credentials, you see. 'With your permission, I will give you my immediate thoughts on your, or rather, our... campaign. Above all, we must not allow patriotism and honest zeal to make us go off at half-cock.' Or at any cock at all, if I had my way. 'We need to know before we plan the training and so on, just how the Washington government will react to what they, I fear, will regard as treason and firing on the flag. And how quickly. We don't want their navy blockading us and bombarding Frisco with cannon, landing disciplined troops while Federal reinforcements march on us from the Mexican or Canadian borders, for example. Meanwhile, how is our manufacturing? We will need a supply of ball, powder and bullets, and in time more guns, not to say all manner of equipment. Can we make them? Can we buy them? Have we ships to run any blockade the Yankees will put up? We need intelligence sorely, as you General, rightly insist.'

Well that should have shut them up, you'd think. To discover the whereabouts of the American navy, scattered about the world, would of itself take years without

Washington's help. With me in command, we wouldn't have been ready to lift a finger in rebellion until doomsday.

Not this shower though. All eyes turned to the General.

'Thank you Colonel, every word you say justifies my faith in you. But with all due respect, you have only just heard of our plan. We have been working on it for quite some time and can allay your fears about Yankee retaliation and suchlike.'

I'll bet he can, rot him.

'In January this year Washington blessed us with a new commander of the Department of the Pacific. By the grace of God, this man, picked, as I say, by Washington, is a man of the South, Kentucky-born and an adopted son of Texas where he has resided these many years. He is General Albert Sidney Johnston, and we can I'm sure, rely on him to support us in every way. He has, of course, access to all the files and information required by a man in his elevated position, which includes the ability to hand over all U.S. naval ships stationed in the Pacific to the Confederacy.' He grinned like Guy Fawkes on November fourth. 'So you need have no fears on that score. We have all the intelligence we need, and then some.'

There comes a time when you have to stop fighting. This smug blowhard had it all down pat, the great craggy revolutionary. There was nothing for it now but to join in the self-congratulations with gusto before anyone noticed I was not as wholeheartedly ready to throw myself off the hurtling train as the rest of them.

'You have convinced me, General,' says I. 'Not that I had any doubts, but as you know, it is the job of military intelligence to be aware of all factors.' And jump at shadows, which is why I am such a damn fine intelligence officer myself, but no matter. 'So let me propose a toast, gentlemen, to an Englishman's small contribution to the creation of a brave, free and strong new nation; the Confederate States of America.'

They roared, and heaped great praises on me and the country that bore me, with welcome aboard, congratulations Sir, and you English is all right, yes Suh! I thought I had got them all fooled but there was one who wasn't. Harpending was looking at me slantendicular. Of course, he had known me longer than the others. Stay, perhaps I raved when fever stricken and he was in the room. God knows what I might have blabbed, nothing heroic I'm sure. He was one, I suspected, who would keep a close eye on me and report any backsliding. Well I'd have to watch him too. At any rate, once I was out of here, probably back at the dear old brothel, gambling house my eye, I'd sniff the wind, find a ship out of town, and beg, borrow or steal the fare. Then the general pipes up.

'Colonel Armstrong, you have made me a very happy man; a very happy man indeed. And rest assured, we will take care of you. Forget that den of iniquity Mr. Harpending was obliged to hide you in while you got back your strength. You won't need reminding that the police and some powerful criminals are still after you...'

Damnation, in the excitement I'd all but forgotten them. And how much of the truth did he know? He must have caught my guilty look for he added...

'Never fret, Colonel, we know you killed someone on the jetty, doubtless in self-defence so we'll say no more about it. Meanwhile, Mr. Harpending has kindly placed a room in his apartment at your disposal. Don't worry about the unlawful elements or criminal prosecution, when we take the State we'll reform the corrupt police and smash the criminal gangs. Meanwhile, Mr. Harpending will be at your side at all times. We don't want you getting waylaid again, do we?'

Do we not? This was a facer. Did Harpending suspect I was not the hero everyone thought I was? Or as true a supporter as I pretended? Why had he offered to look after me? Well one thing I knew; if Harpending or any of them suspected old Tom of treachery, or caught a glimpse of my yellow liver, he could deliver me to the police or gangs and goodnight sweet prince. Nothing to do about it, of course, so I must smile ingratiatingly at my guardian angel, thank the General and the table once more, and reach for the bottle.

Chapter Four

Despite the amount of drink I took on board, for we punished the bottle mercilessly when business was concluded, I slept fitfully that night. Harpending took me back to his apartments. He'd taken the top floor of a stately building on the edge of the better part of town situated a few blocks up from Montgomery Street, and after a brief desultory chat and goodnight, decanted me into a well-upholstered bedroom.

Alone at last, I wasted no time - well not much - cursing my predicament and the beastly luck that had brought me here. A once-over through the window at the sheer drop to the street scuppered any thought of instant escape that way. Harpending had locked the doors from the inside, protection against burglars, he said, so I was trapped for the night at least. This being the case, I undressed and took stock.

Here was I, erstwhile hero of the British Empire, now irregular military advisor to the Committee of Thirty, a desperate group of renegades who claimed three thousand followers and who were Hell bent on attacking their own country. Very good. Mad though it was, their scheme had a realistic chance of success. Handled right, they could waylay and rout the unsuspecting Federal troops, clear the arsenals and arm their deluded followers, then set about claiming California for the South. What Washington would do about it I didn't care to dwell on, but whoever else was listed among the ringleaders, they wouldn't find old Tom. Here's a thought; could I warn the U.S. army? If word of treason got out, they would rouse the State militia, alert Washington and seal the arsenals as tight as a Scotsman's purse. The General would have to drop it like a hot rivet, but he'd seek out the betrayer and the least suspicion... aye well.

On the plus side, I was nearly recovered from my fever, and given a half yard start could outrun any pursuit. I had a little leeway, I knew, before the General unleashed his great plan. He'd declared that we couldn't in honour fire on the Stars and Stripes until the war began, as it was still possible the South's secession from the Union would pass peacefully, and he didn't want to be the man who precipitated a war. No war meant no raid, and they'd surely set me on my way with a thank'ee for services bravely volunteered, but happily not required. This was my best hope. Meanwhile, I was convinced Harpending had his doubts about me. He was uncommunicative in the carriage home and I would catch him deep in thought and stealing sly glances sideways, as though weighing me up. The General had appointed him my keeper, supposedly to prevent me from blundering about the town and falling foul of the gangs or the police, but it was also a convenient way for Harpending to keep me on side. With him on poltroon alert he would watch me all the closer.

What to do? I could see two ways out for me. Peaceful secession or give my watchdog the slip; after all, the raid wouldn't take place for some weeks, hopefully, and he must drop his guard sometime. Running would be suicidal without money, of course, so my immediate task was to get some. I daren't touch Harpending for a loan, he would smell a British Tommy rat on the instant. Could I rob him? No, he was a lithe young blade - and armed with a derringer in his sleeve; I'd caught a glimpse when he removed his jacket before retiring - and unless I killed him and successfully concealed the body, he and his blasted Committee would be on my tail the instant I decamped. I'd never find an outgoing ship before the alarm was raised, leaving me skulking around the levees pursued by half the population of Frisco, what with one thing and another. Dare I jump a well-to-do citizen in the street? Again I'd have the peelers, Committee and Uncle Tom Cobley and all, view-hallooing like the Leicestershire hunt. 'Sides, I didn't have the stomach to be a murderer or footpad, so robbery was out of court. On reflection, my best chance to obtain the blunt was if Harpending left money lying around his apartment. A long shot, he struck me as the type who carried his cash about his person at all times, as many Americans do.

Stay, whatever Harpending's suspicions, the General thought me the answer to a plotter's prayer. I was his chief military advisor; surely I'd need expenses to carry out my work? On this note I wracked my brains for an excuse to lighten his war chest. A reconnaissance of our targets? Aye, that was it. No advisor worth his salt would plan simultaneous raids without spying out the land first. I'd need a free hand to study all our objectives in whatever way I deemed best. Plus sustenance, money to hire a fresh carriage every day, several new outfits to prevent recognition, a pistol and ammunition...

But no. Even if the General approved - and knowing him he'd have all the reconnaissance details already prepared and order me to remain under wraps for safety - Harpending would ride shotgun on me, clutching the purse strings. I cursed under my breath and set my thoughts back to my first tack.

The General would only set his plan in motion after shots were exchanged between the North and South and the carnage began. But would they oblige? The two sides loathed each other, of course, had done for years, but they hailed from the same stock, spoke the same language after a fashion, worshipped the same God and rammed their appalling Constitution down the throats of any foreigner who crossed their paths. Then again, they were akin to the British, Constitution apart, but that didn't stop them taking pot-shots at our flag whenever they got the chance. And I'd already encountered plenty of mad buggers on both sides, John Brown's pet lambs (as he called his murderous gang) for one and the blasted Committee for t'other, not to mention the Golden Knights, rot their visors.

Torn between hope and fear, I tried to assess the odds. My meeting with the Committee had brought me up to snuff with the current political position. It was late January '61, and Lincoln was president-elect waiting to enter the White House. Lincoln's election had incensed the South and caused the more hot-headed Southern States to secede from the Union in a fit of pique. According to the General, Lincoln claimed he wouldn't fire on his fellow

Americans and appealed for them to return to sanity and the fold.

(I later discovered that once in office, my old pal William Seward, Lincoln's Secretary of State, spent every waking hour stirring up trouble with any European power he could find, Britain for preference, in the wild hope that America would forget its quarrel and reunite against the external enemy. He damn near made one threatening bluff too many and enveloped his country in a real shooting match with us, but wily Lord Lyons, our Man in Washington, wouldn't rise to the bait. Everyone expected Seward to be president rather than Lincoln. Had he been, the South probably wouldn't have seceded but he would likely have invaded Canada and brought the British Empire down on his pointy head, but I'll have more to say about Britain's role in the war and my hellish mission to Canada for Lord Lyons later in my memoirs).

Anyhow, return to the fold pleads president-elect Lincoln. Nothing doing yell the hot-heads in return, we got ourselves a new country with our own Constitution an' all, so go suck a lemon. The South began confiscating all U.S. government assets in their States and dared the North to do something about it. With Lincoln waiting in the wings when the States began seceding, Buchanan, the outgoing president, sat on his hands like Pontius Pilate when there was no washbasin handy, leaving the new man to deal with the mess. This inaction produced months of government paralysis and created America's greatest crisis since the revolutionary war.

So this was where we stood in late January 1861. Lincoln was due to take the reins in March and by then pressure would be mounting for him to do something quickly before the U.S. government bonds and the stock market collapsed under him and the rest of the world split its sides laughing at the North's spinelessness. The cauldron was bubbling merrily, but would it boil over?

Sleep claimed me at this point, for the next thing I recall was a black servant bringing breakfast. I'd slept late, so after food and a wash and brush-up I wandered through the corridor to the living area. Harpending was there, of course, but to my surprise he was not alone.

'Morning Colonel. Jes 'bout,' greeted Harpending cheerfully. He waved me to a chair and continued, 'You know Mr. Randolph here? You'll remember him from last evening.'

The man rose and extended his hand, nervously I thought. 'Edmond Randolph at your service Sir.'

'And at yours,' I replied untruthfully. As a matter of fact I hadn't recognised him from last evening, or early morning rather, and in the brightness of the day nothing less akin to a bold revolutionary you ever did see. More like a banker's clerk.

'Randolph heah is the smartest brain in the San Francisco bar,' adds Harpending. That explains it then, thinks I. So we have a lawyer on our team. Well if the raid comes unglued, at least we'll get cheap advocacy in court. But my chief anxiety was that Harpending was not going to guard me on his own. This Randolph creature looked like a squirt of the kind I used to enjoy knocking around back at my dear old alma mater, but squirt or no, this made my chances of decamping a whole lot trickier. My spirits sank another notch as Harpending continued my education.

'Randolph is a big man in this town. Knows all kinds of folk, from the great to the small, ain't thet so Edmund?'

'I guess so.'

'Yessir, all the mos' powerful folk in the State, you met 'em. Why, yore on greeting terms with General Johnston hisself.'

'...I have that honour.'

'You shore have.' He eyed Randolph keenly. 'See here Edmund, yore a lawyer, with a lawyer's sharp nose for what a man is thinking. So now, mebbe you wanna tell me, and the Colonel heah, what kind of a man General Johnston truly is?'

Now, you must understand that I was listening intently to this discussion in the hope that it could provide me with a way out of my predicament. Aye, and watching carefully too. What struck me on the instant was the stark fact that Harpending was the lion and this Randolph a mere lamb in his presence. Harpending wanted to discuss General Johnston, so Johnston topped the agenda. He was, I recalled, the new commander of the Department of the Pacific, in other words the man in charge of the joint, and evidently a supporter of the South. Now, would whatever Randolph had to say be of any use to me?

I must have looked pokerfaced, for Harpending hushed Randolph's stuttering reply and addressed me direct.

'You see Suh, the General's plan is sound, we all agree that. But yore a military intelligence man an' you'll know if'n one word gets out then our hopes and ambitions are dashed. We must guard against loose lips, d'ye see?'

Was this a hint? Lord, if Harpending seriously doubted my trustworthiness I was in deeper than ever.

'Now we know General Johnston is a Southern man, an' as you'd 'spect, he's a man of honour and loyalty. He graduated from West Point back in twenty-six an' fought in the Black Hawk war back in Illinois in thirty-two, then enlisted against the Mexicans, an' worked hisself up to Commander-in-chief. He was secretary of war for the Texies, suppressed the Mormon rebellion in Utah and was rewarded by gitting his post heah.' He grinned openly, and I realised just how boyish he was; he looked like a teenager despite climbing twenty-three. Suspicions or not he was cheerful today. Clearly Harpending was a man of moods.

'I done my homework, you see,' he beamed at us, 'now this here's the lay of the land.' While Randolph sat sheepishly, arms folded and legs crossed, Harpending held the floor.

'Like I say, we know General Johnston is a man of honour an' loyalty. Question is, what would he do if he learnt of our little scheme?'

'How do you mean?' ventures Randolph suspiciously.

'I mean, what if someone upped and tol' him of our plan to take the State? Would he join with us? He's a Southern man but he has taken the United States oath an'

64

is right now a Federal soldier. Would he jump to us when he heard we wuz taking Californy for the South?' He leaned forward eyeing Randolph carefully, settling my momentary qualms. Call it guilty conscience, but I thought he meant me. 'If'n he did, if'n he came out for us an' ordered his men to surrender the arsenals, why, we cud take Californy without risk nor bloodshed.'

And if'n he didn't, thinks I with spirits soaring, he would quash the plan in an instant. By gum here was a heaven-sent reprieve. All ears, I turned to the splendid Randolph, the most unlikely saviour since Moses. Come on Randolph old fellow, tell us that Johnston would leap at the chance to throw in his lot with the South. Damned dubious he would, of course. West Point generals don't lightly betray their loyalty oath and surrender their command to the first bunch of plotters who whisper 'psst' in their ear. But it didn't matter whether he did or no. If he stood down his troops and handed across his arms, the Committee wouldn't need me to plan their raids, and if he gave them the right about, the jig was up and the raid blown to Hell and beyond. Either way, by George, I was the off the hook!

Randolph, bless him, leapt at this, eyes agog, and eagerly delivered his verdict.

'I am sure,' he announced firmly, 'that General Johnston will be true to the South. He is heart and soul with us, and will not allow any oath given to that forsaken nest of Yankee vipers stand between the South and freedom.'

He was a red-hot secessionist, this one, behind his diffidence and nerves, itching to set his country alight in the name of liberty, States Rights and keeping the Negroes in their place.

'That yore firm opinion?' Harpending seemed disappointed, unlike me. Tell Johnston you fools, I wanted to holler. Go to him now and inform him that three thousand maniacs are about to declare war on the U.S. See what he does.

'...Well, I presume so.' Randolph simmered down, his natural diffidence back to the fore. He looked nervous, as if reluctant to be probed by Harpending's sharp questions. God knows what he was like in court.

'So whut are you suggesting...? Go on, out with it.'

'He is a venerable soldier and true Southern gentleman. He knows where his true duty lies. If he heard a whisper... well, I'm convinced he would come across and, as you say, we could take the State without risk and without bloodshed.' His eyes lit up pleadingly, a supplicant begging a favour from his superior.

Harpending rubbed his chin in scorn. 'You seem mighty convinced o' this, Randolph. Mighty convinced indeed.' He paused, and I guessed he was enjoying himself, then delivered the blow. 'Well I'm not. No one doubts the drift of General Johnston's inclinations. He is with us, as you say, heart and soul. But he is the U.S. chief in these heah parts and until Texas secedes he will stay loyal to his oath. We dare not risk discovery by informing him of our intentions.'

Randolph's face fell like a puppy refused a sweet.

Ah ha, thinks I, what have we here? I can read the signs. Devil a doubt this put-upon weakling saw himself swaggering back to the General and his confounded Committee proclaiming they needn't sweat themselves over their raid. "Fear not boys," he would brag. "I, Edmund Randolph the First have won your war for you. Using my initiative I bearded General Johnston in his lair and persuaded him to give us the keys to every arsenal in the State with the navy thrown in for luck. He was reluctant at first, boys, you may be sure, but I persuaded him where his true duty lay. No need to thank me, just show a little respect from now on and stop kicking my backside for sport, hey?"

Well Harpending had poured sawdust on his axle, no error. My respect, if not admiration, for this baby-faced revolutionary increased considerably. Clearly he had sniffed the wind and smelt Randolph seeking to use his acquaintance with General Johnston for personal glory, and set out to squash him flat. His sharp questions had unveiled Randolph's dreams of bragging his way to fame and fortune as the man who saved California for the glorious South. Not that I cared about that, but he had done for me too, preventing Johnston getting wind of the plot. Unless... Could I take a hand? After all, Randolph was convinced that a word from him to Johnston would ensure success. He was sullen now, studying his fingernails like a rejected suitor. A miserable creature and a lawyer. Could I get him alone? As (in all modesty) countless women can testify, I have great personal charm. Five minutes and I could convince him that Harpending knew he was right, but had put him off the scent in order to grab the personal glory himself. He mustn't be cowed by Harpending's out-of-hand dismissal of his views. Go to Johnston, I'd suggest - subtly of course, trust me for that - and he'd come across like the true Southerner he was. And then... who'd have the statue in the town square? Aye, all I need to do is convince Randolph that he needn't value the opinion of a jackdandy like Harpending and he would be off to town to glory-hunt Johnston before you could say guilty, m'lud. Five minutes alone was all I'd need. Now, how to go about it?

'So we'll forgit any dangerous talk of alerting General Johnson, hey?' Satisfied that Randolph was suitably cowed, Harpending was willing to let him down gently and get on to the next part of his agenda.

'Your pardon Colonel, you have work to do an' so have we. Don't fret, we kin do both at one an' the same time.' He reached for the bell and summoned his servant. 'Fetch us a carriage, boy, and be swift about it.' The servant departed and Harpending gave us our instructions.

'See Colonel, while we are making our plans, life and bizney goes on. You bet. Edmund here is, like I say, a first class lawyer, with his card in all the finest houses in Frisco. He an' I have some real estate to discuss. Meanwhile, you need to sound out our objectives 'thout any of the interesting gennlemen who so want yore company, nor any Yankees neither, seein' you 'bout the town. So we'll be taking a good long ride around, you

67

familiarising yorsel' with the lie of the land while Edmund and I talk business. I'd be obliged if you will wear yore coat an' hat so's not to draw attention. Apologies for the uninteresting nature of our discussions, Colonel. Talking real estate won' hold the attention of a man who settled the Indian mutiny, never mind our own plans right here, but like war, bizney don' wait.'

In no time we were trundling up and down the streets and avenues of Frisco, Tommy peering discreetly out through the window, wearing his serious face to suggest he was concentrating on troop movements and good spots for ambush, while listening intently to Harpending and Randolph discussing Californian real estate. I marvelled at how someone barely off his mother's tit could gas airily about buying up blocks of houses, whole streets and even gold mines, with a confidence of one thrice his age. And how could he afford it? Well, I didn't know at the time, but I've since read his crime sheets, and if there was any confidence trick sprung in the nineteenth century he hadn't sprung, it can only be because he was busy filling his wallet elsewhere. He made his first pile down in Mexico, dishonestly you may be sure, which was now funding his speculation in Californian property. He became penniless until he discovered a gold mine by sheer chance, so he said, cleaned up buying land and property dirt cheap after a Californian earthquake, when he convinced folk the whole State would soon fall into the sea, and was later one of the brains behind the Great Diamond Hoax of 1872, though he claimed to be a victim. Quite a man after my own heart, really, but his dedication to the Southern cause was genuine enough. He even contributed one hundred thousand dollars of his ill-gotten Mexican swag to help fund the General's plan. He wouldn't thank me for saying so, but for a Southerner he had a fine Yankee nose for enterprise, mixing patriotism with business for the benefit of both. I discovered this at first hand when he sought a privateer's licence from Confederate President Jefferson Davis in order to plunder U.S. merchant shipping in the Pacific, but I'll come to that later in my tale.

We drove north to what is now called Fisherman's Wharf to enable me to gaze two miles out to sea at Alcatraz Island. This was a fort on a rock surrounded by hazardous currents through freezing waters, guns facing out to sea to protect the city from pirates and thieving foreigners. Barely a hundred soldiers manned the island, the General said, but with such natural protection that was all they needed. And the Committee expected me to take it? I'd want a regiment and half the fleet before I'd willingly contemplate such a stroke, but whatever happened, you wouldn't catch Tommy shivering at the head of a flotilla of darkened skiffs one fine moonless night, heading the invasion. I'd sooner wrestle with a Welsh Dragoon.

After strolling with my minders along the coast, pretending to weigh up the odds, we turned west and made the journey along the coast to Fort Point. Another edifice designed to protect the good citizens, and with two hundred troops this time. At least it wasn't halfway into the ocean like Alcatraz, but as I gazed at its forbidding walls I wondered once again what in God's name I was doing here. But I've learned the hard way that it is no good shaking your fist at Lady Luck, you must simply look her in the eye, shuffle the cards, and cheat.

We took the ferry across the water, then another growler up to Mare Island, which is in fact a peninsular, and the easiest objective by far. Not that that was any consolation to me, looking keen with spine melting just to contemplate the whole insane conspiracy. But I had one more objective to stare pointlessly at before we could return. To Suisun Bay and the arsenal at Benicia where I was astonished to see camels strolling about the place; belonging, I'm told, to the U.S. Camel Corp. I gave it my usual martial examination for Harpending's benefit, and we about-turned back to town. A fine reconnaissance, thinks I, provided I was working for a tourist guide.

Conversation in the carriage was damned dull too. Harpending surprised me by having a talent for financial details quite rare in a man of action, and seemed to enjoy disputing minutiae. He and Randolph hurled building regulations, bylaws and compound interest rates at each other till I almost fell asleep. I was despairing of catching Randolph alone when, stopping in Market Street alongside the new rail line, Harpending hailed the driver to stop the coach, then made to jump down alone.

'Shan't be long,' he waved cheerfully, 'got a bit o' bizney to conduct. You two stay put in the carriage an' I'll return presently.'

This was my chance. Fully awake now, I turned to Randolph and opened the batting.

'Impressive man, Asbury Harpending, and that's a fact.'

'He certainly is,' agrees Randolph.

'Yes, most impressive. Couldn't help overhearing your conversation, not that I understood much of it. Noticed he has a fine head for figures.'

'I should know,' he agreed again, without much enthusiasm I thought.

'And he's a man of his hands too. Why, I'll bet he could plan our... err... upcoming takeover, if I may put it like that, as well as me... nearly. Yes Sir, our comrade is a man of many talents.'

I hoped Randolph would take the bait and retort that he wasn't such a good judge of character, and was throwing away a golden opportunity by not letting Johnston into our circle. But he didn't, the measly little bean counter, so I had to press further.

'Funny thing about men of many talents,' I mused, 'my old grandfather told me on his knee that each and every one of us has a blind spot. The Good Lord ensures that we all have reason to be humble, and what price salvation for the man with no faults?'

He looked at me with a quizzical expression, as well he might. 'What do you mean?'

'Well...' I sucked my breath in, contemplatively, then let him have both barrels.

'We agree he has many talents, and is a fine gentleman. But... is he a good judge of character?'

The idiot still didn't get it. 'I don't follow you.'

'I mean, can he judge a man he has never met, better than an intelligent man who has?'

At last the penny dropped.

'By the gods he cannot. How can he possibly?' He sat up straight, fire in his eyes and looking for the first time as though he had a spine.

Got him. In the nick of time, too, for Harpending arrived back at the carriage just then, looking pleased with himself as usual.

'Ok, bizney done. Now, let's drop you off, Edmund, and the Colonel and I will be going home. I'm famished.'

He was too self-absorbed to notice Randolph eyeing him like a snail in the lettuce. Right, thinks I, I've given it my best shot and landed it in the bull. Now, will Randolph go home and crawl into a self-pitying bottle, or march around to General Johnston's house and invite him to join in the greatest betrayal since Brutus? I gave him a knowing, supporting look as he exited the carriage and briskly bade us good evening while avoiding Harpending's eye. I had planted the seed. Time would tell if it would bring forth fruit.

Chapter Five

'Gentlemen,' began the General, calling the meeting to order. 'The time for action is nigh. Word has it that Texas is about to secede any day soon. That will make us six, with others to surely follow.' Standing upright, he raised his voice and I wondered were his britches too tight, and hollered. 'The time is upon us to ensure California joins the new free nation of independent States.'

I joined in the answering yells like a good secessionist, and wondered for the thousandth time how was I going to sidle out before the storm broke?

Nearly a week had passed since my coach trip along the California coast, and I had heard nothing more concerning General Johnston. I daren't ask, of course, and Harpending didn't mention him. He always kept a gentleman-ruffian or two about the place, with various high hats and businessmen - folk in the know, he called them - coming in and out of his apartment like a revolving door, so I was never lonely. I was beginning to despair of the oaf Randolph queering the pitch by blabbing to General Johnston, and was casting around for some other exit.

This was my third or fourth attendance at the Committee of Thirty's meetings, and damned monotonous they were too. Or would have been had I not been in such a frightful bait that I should soon be called upon to lead the attack on Uncle Sam. I could see the headlines in the *Times* already. *British officer leads assault on friendly Power*. That would raise an eyebrow or two at Horse Guards. The excitable Yankee press, knowing how England would love to get its hands on all that Californian gold, would doubtless claim I was there as a spy, cashing in on the Union's troubles with the blessings of perfidious Albion. Why, if Prime Minister Palmerston didn't look sharp, Britain might find itself at war. Coward's reasoning? Perhaps, but fearing the worst has stood me in good stead thus far, and I've had more reasons to thank it than t'otherwise.

After standing to chant their preposterous oath, members took it in turns to badmouth the U.S. government, abolition of slavery and Yankees in general, each trying to outdo the others in proclaiming their devotion to the Southern cause. They all repeated the same claptrap about States Rights and freedom for all - except the Negroes of course - and generally behaved like new recruits at a revivalist rally. Randolph, incidentally, had failed to appear at the meetings since our charabanc trip.

This meeting was different. The General gathered us around the fireplace and informed us that he was disappointed to learn that several members had failed to reach their quota of one hundred followers. This was essential if we were to have sufficient numbers for our crusade. Bravo thinks I, three cheers for the wise folk of California and let's call the whole thing off.

No such luck of course. The General responded to the bad news with a fireside speech to rally the slackers.

'Gentlemen, some of you tell me that there is lethargy stalking this land. You report that many good Southern boys say while they support California coming out for the South, they don't see how that will affect the course of the war, which will surely be decided back east. They want to go back east then, and enlist in our forces there.' Shaking his head sadly, he delivered judgement. 'Laudable, certainly, and just what I would expect of true Southerners, but in this case, misguided.' He reached down to an armchair and produced a sheet of paper.

'I have some points here that you might care to report to those good fellows. Points to show just what effect we will have on this coming war when California secedes.'

More whoops at the word *secedes*. I was beginning to learn that America was spoiling for a fight with itself. Had all the slaves in the country given notice and retired to Africa on the *Mayflower*, they would have picked a fight over the first thing that came to mind. Lincoln's dress sense, perhaps, or who owned the Mississippi. They were a young country, and maybe the war was something they just had to get out of their system.

'Gold, gentlemen, gold. Why, with California declaring for the South, and the city of San Francisco and its impregnable fortifications in Confederate hands, the stream of gold on which the Union cause depends to buys ships, arms and all the essentials of war will be cut off at the neck, as a stream of water is shut off by turning a faucet. And with the gold in our possession we'll buy those same ships and supplies for the Confederacy. Our first step will be to open and maintain a route through untamed Arizona into Texas, and thence onwards down the Mississippi to Orleans or wherever the Confederacy shall so deem it most advantageous. We'll transport by sea too, our gold will purchase warships to protect our merchantmen and impound or sink theirs. And our gold is not confined to California; folk think the mines of Nevada are played out, but my sources inform me that the surface has been barely scratched. Once California is ours, gentlemen, we can carry Nevada out of the Union alongside. This wealth will ensure us ultimate victory, and lay the foundations for a Confederacy stretching from shore to distant shore, and from Mason and Dixon's line down to, one day, the furthest reaches of our continent.' He sniffed sentimentally at this glorious prospect and raised his voice to finish on a flourish. 'This, gentlemen, is what we are fighting for.' He thumped the mantelpiece for emphasis. 'This is what you must tell our supporters when they express doubts of California's importance to the Confederacy. And knowing our vital work here, in this State, all true Southerners will join us and together we will march to honour and victory.'

The Committee exploded into raptures, but as the General cast his paper into the fire, I stole a glance at Harpending to see how he was taking it. As I suspected, he cheered for form's sake, but his thoughts were elsewhere, and it did not take much imagination to see where they were. There was no doubting his devotion to the Southern cause, but if he could he see his way to helping the South and making a dollar on the side, well, why not? With

Nevada seemingly awash with gold for the picking to add to the Californian treasure, there was wealth and to spare, so why not take a slice? I could see patriotism and self-interest having a lively tussle, and declaring honours even.

Not that it mattered to me. They could have taken the entire goldfields and dropped them in the sea for all I cared. I had money enough at home, mainly from loot I'd rescued during the Indian mutiny, so all I sought was a fast ship home away from this madness.

Meanwhile, the noble crusaders simmered down and returned to the table for more blackguarding of Lincoln and the Northern vipers over drinks. The General quietly quizzed me about my Indian and Crimea heroics, which I answered pretty offhand as a modest hero should, and then got down to cases.

'Tell me Colonel, my comrades here will move heaven and earth to raise the numbers for our coming mission, but...' he gazed wistfully around the table then leaned towards me confidentially, '...should they fail to raise the full complement, can we still succeed with reduced numbers? Say half the number we are aiming for?'

By all that's holy, a way out! The honest answer was they could, provided they held the element of surprise, but I was hardly going to tell him that. Nor could I say his crazy scheme would doom many men to the eternal fires, myself possibly included, and he'd be better advised resigning his commission and going in for gold mining, or enlist in a minstrel troupe. But I could counsel delay. Not directly of course. Right now delay was my best friend, for with events moving so quickly, who knew what tomorrow might bring. Texas was on the brink of secession, it seemed, and with more States likely to join the Confederacy almost daily, Washington might wake up to reality and recognise the new country. This shot was never on the board with Lincoln in the White House, but I didn't know that then. Meanwhile, with the Committee blundering up and down the State hollering *come one come all, and join us in a surprise attack on the U.S. arsenals*, it could only be a matter of time before somebody noticed. Donning my most martial expression, I replied carefully.

'Well Sir, your Committee here are the finest group of comrades it has been my pleasure to encounter, and if you proposed a march on Washington itself, every man-jack here would follow you.' Oiling the wheels, you see. 'And I don't doubt the courage and valour of the volunteers you have raised so far. My judgement then, Sir, since you ask it, is that even with merely half the numbers you sought, we have every chance of success and victory.'

He beamed like a candle on its birthday.

'So you believe we can still achieve our aims even with half our expected number?'

'Indeed Sir, with the Good Lord on our side, anything is possible.' I looked him in the eye. 'Of course, it is of the topmost importance that we secure *all* our objectives, not just most of them. Can we capture all our objectives with half the men? Mostly untrained and with civilians officering them against regular Federal troops? It is a tough call, but given luck and a fair wind, I believe we have a fighting chance.' I frowned as though considering the odds. 'Of course, should lack of numbers leave even one arsenal remaining in Federal hands or one company of Federal soldiers still under arms, they will rally the militia and arm their Northern supporters, and before you know it we'll have a bloody civil war right here in the streets and across the State. Many good men will perish and the winners will take the spoils. Thirty percent of the people are for the South you say? So, neutrals aside, seventy percent for the North? Aye well...' I used a phrase I had heard frequently since landing in this nightmare. 'One Southerner is worth ten Yankees.' I nodded grimly. 'It will be a deuced serious business, one slip and... but as I say, with God on our side, how can we lose?'

The General seemed to think God might need a little help, as I'd hoped he would. Clasping his hands together as if in prayer, he thanked me courteously for my advice.

'I am obliged to ye, Colonel. This is, as you rightly say, a deuced serious business. Now if you will excuse me...?'

I left the meeting in Harpending's carriage well pleased with my military advice. The General would surely see that it was no-go without the full three thousand, and the Committee living up to its boast of recruiting one hundred men each before raising the curtain. On this happy note I retired, hope rising that my military expertise and even worse, heroism, might not after all be required. But there was more good news to come.

'Colonel Armstrong?' begging yore pardon Suh, but Mister Harpending sends his compl'ments and requests yore presence at yore earliest convenience.'

This was worrying. Under Harpending's roof I was accustomed to take my breakfast in bed. Wondering what was up, and fearing that my advice to the General had backfired spectacularly, I hastened to the drawing room. Harpending was sitting bolt upright in his chair, white-knuckle clenched fists, his face an expression of cold fury.

'What's the matter?' says I, for his manner was all at odds with his normal superior attitude. Clearly something had rattled him, and I hoped against hope it wasn't anything to do with me. It wasn't, well not directly anyhow.

'Randolph. That's the matter. You heah what he's upped and done?'

Well I hadn't, of course. With my heart in my mouth, I asked him.

'The blasted imbecile has gone an' approached Johnston an' tol' him of our plans. Every damn detail; our organisation, aims, means, everything but the date an' that's just 'cause he don't damn well know it. Seems he tried to recruit Johnston to our cause by impressing him how serious we wuz.'

Looking suitably shocked, I asked him Johnston's response.

'Response? Why he hooted Randolph out of town. A General take stock of a no-account lawyer a'calling on him in his own home on Rincon Hill an' demanding he join a rebellion? Randolph must ha' been drunk even to consider it. Why d'ye think I warned him off? Randolph called on one of our Committee late last night and he was ravin' like a man possessed. He won't tell us 'xactly what General Johnston said by way o' reply, but whatever it wuz, it's done driven him stark crazy. He's cursing Johnston like he's the devil hisself. Seems it's turned his brain.'

This was magnificent. So good old Randolph hadn't let me down after all. He heeded my wise words and confronted General Johnston in his own home, if you please. This was the raid holed beneath the waterline, devil a doubt. My task now was to be as shocked and disappointed as the rest of them and bide my time until they tired of feeding a British military advisor with no military to advise, and sent me on my merry way. I began by damming Randolph for a fool and asking for further details. And by gum, didn't I get them just?

'Seems he confronted Johnston a few days back. Since then he's been flying about the town indulging in all kinds of loose, unbridled talk. This morning he told several of our Committee that he had met with Johnston and he was sure our cause was lost. He been cursing General Johnston as a traitor to the South and wants us to string him up.'

I couldn't believe my luck. In all modesty, I am a persuasive man, but even I, turning on all my Tommy charms, could hardly have expected such a result. And this was only the half of it. On Harpending's urging we drove up to consult the General, clandestine evening meetings thrown to the winds in the sensation. He cursed all the way, much to my amusement, and in due course we presented ourselves at plotters' headquarters. There I discovered that my helpful words of advice to Randolph had outrun even my wildest hopes.

'His mind has turned. He's unbalanced, that's what he is, and he was once elected a member of the lower Legislature too.' The General bristled. 'The fool has ruined everything. If there's anyone in California who is not aware of our mission he must be a deaf mute.'

I struggled to contain my glee whilst appearing as appalled as the others.

'Why can't we stop him?' cries Harpending. 'Where is he now?'

'Now? Nobody knows..., but the shave is he is holed up in the hills.' He switched off his fury and became icy calm. 'Care to ask what else he's done?'

Jesu there was more? With an effort I remained solemn.

'He boasts he has written a letter to President Lincoln warning him of a vast conspiracy to carry California out of the Union and questioning the trustworthiness of General Johnston, who he describes as a backstabbing renegade.'

Harpending swore at the ceiling and called on the heavens to rain down destruction on his lawyer and erstwhile co-conspirator, while I marvelled at human folly. So Randolph, an inflamed Southern patriot, had convinced himself against all rhyme and reason that fellow Southerner Johnston would forget his oath and join in the conspiracy. When he refused, why, Randolph cracked up. The General agreed.

'Nothing but downright lunacy could have inspired such a betrayal of our cause. He's sent his letter by Pony Express so it should reach Lincoln by just about the day of his inauguration.'

This laid my last qualm to rest. An unhinged Randolph hiding in the hills plucking white dormice out of teapots and inviting the Hatter to tea would not be able to reveal that I was the inspiration for his betrayal, nor be believed if he tried. I was safe!

Harpending sank into an armchair.

'So now, General, what we gonna do?'

'What can we do? General Johnston will have secured the arsenals and alerted the militia by now. The only thing we can do is bide our time and establish our alibis in case of nosy questions. I am sure,' he continued, 'we can rely on our mutual discretion to ensure we meet no Federal unpleasantness.'

Could I blackmail them? No, I dismissed the thought as suicidal as soon as it appeared. Anyway, with the plot the worst kept secret in town, I was as good as homeward bound. But this was all too feeble for the bold Harpending.

'Say General, we cannot give up just like that. Texas will secede any time now. What say we send a delegation to General Johnston an' plead our case? Sure he gave Randolph the bum's rush, but a properly constituted delegation...?'

In fact they didn't approach Johnston formally, but delegated three men to visit him on an ad hoc basis to sound him out. By Jove that was one delegation I wanted no part of. *Good evening General Johnston, my name is Armstrong. Yes, the Armstrong from England, VC and so forth. I was wondering if you can see your way clear to surrendering your arms to me and my friends so we can take over the State and steal your gold.*

The General actually wanted me to be one of the three musketeers. He seemed to believe my army reputation and experience would add weight to the plotters' credentials. Disconcerting, to be sure, but I found a deuced clever way out.

'Well General, I would dearly love to add my small contribution, but...' I rubbed my chin doubtfully, '...would an American general surrender his arms to a British officer?'

'No by God he wouldn't!'

And that was that.

Using the General's influence to set up the tryst, the chosen three, including Harpending naturally, called on General Johnston at his Bush Hill headquarters by way of a social visit, and tried to extract some kind of discreet cooperation for our enterprise. They got nowhere, naturally, and in due course a crestfallen Harpending recounted the tale to an emergency meeting of the Committee.

'He bade us courteously to be seated,' says Harpending. '"Before we go further," he said, in a matter-of-fact, off-hand way, "there is something I want to mention. I have heard foolish talk about an attempt to seize the strongholds of the government under my charge. Knowing this, I have prepared for emergencies, and will defend the property of the United States with every resource at my command, and with the last drop of blood in my body. Tell that to all our Southern friends." He said much else, but nothing to the point, an' in good time we took our leave.'

No surprises there. Now that the raid was off, for surely they could not proceed, I allowed myself to relax. With something of an academic interest I listened over a glass as the Committee spent a useful hour or two bewailing their luck and calling the wrath of God down on all Northerners and fellow travellers. Eventually, as I knew they would, they turned to finding the scapegoat.

'We must discover Randolph's whereabouts an' make him account for hisself.'

The meeting closed with general agreement that Randolph was going to get what's coming to him, and in no time I was in the carriage home to my soft bed, congratulating myself on a job well done. All that remained was to commiserate with the Committee over their hard luck, assure them it was a brave attempt and there'd be a warm spot in my heart for them all, then accept a ticket on the first sloop home. I should have known better. #Note_4

'Texas has seceded.'

Harpending welcomed me with the news the following morning, causing me again to miss breakfast. His eyes were alight with joy and destiny, all thought of Randolph apparently forgotten.

'You see what this means?' cries he.

I saw that it bit yet another chunk out of Uncle Sam's backside, but ass that I was, with the conspiracy blown, I didn't see it affecting me.

'General Johnston is an adopted son of Texas. With Texas out of the Union, his loyalties must go South, and with them maybe the arsenals.'

So he was back on that tack again? Didn't Southerners ever give up? My heart leapt to my mouth until I realised that if Johnston came over to the Committee, which I doubted, he'd hand over the arsenals peaceably so my participation would not be required.

In the event, General Johnston stayed true to his U.S. oath to the last. When Texas joined the rebellion he soon resigned his post, but not before giving proper warning to Washington and keeping order until his replacement arrived. He gave no help whatsoever to our happy band, and told Californians that if their sympathies lay with the South, why, they should go back east and join the Confederate army, so there. In due course he joined the Confederate army himself, and was accounted their best general until Robert Lee took command. A true gentleman, he fell at Shiloh, giving his life bravely for his cause. I, on the other hand, a true poltroon, am still here, full of vim and vigour, creaking bones apart. You can guess which I prefer.

Two long months passed. You'll hardly credit it, but the Committee did not disband or even give up its mad, publicly-known ambition to grab California for the South. The meetings stagnated, however, and lost their froth and zip, and it was all the General could do to keep up full attendance. Edmund Randolph went to ground, sensible chap, though rumours surfaced saying he was touring small villages and hamlets blasting out volcanic speeches damning the North and calling for everyone to rally to the Confederates.

The cauldron was coming to the boil, but life in California carried on as normal. I dropped hints, as far as I dared, that they had no further use for me and I should depart, but to no avail. I eventually approached the General alone and told him I should like to follow General Johnston's advice and enlist for the South. Give me a ticket east, thinks I, and you won't see me again this side of the Rapture. The General clapped me on the back, declared I must have Dixie blood in me, and bid me bide my time. He was loath to abandon his great plan and would not countenance the loss of his military advisor. What he meant, damn him, was that my leaving would signal the end of his dream, so he sought to delay it.

Then one night I got what I had been waiting for. The Committee members trouped into the room as usual, to see a careworn General bid us welcome. After standing for the oath, he addressed us from his favourite fireside position.

'It is plain,' says he, 'that the Committee is no longer of one mind. The time has now come for a definite decision, one way or another.' He paused to collect himself.

'I propose to take a secret ballot that will decide whether or not our organisation shall continue... or disband.' Cries of *no*, and *shame*, but plenty of silent mouths too. Disband you fools, I was screaming inside. Tell this jumped-up buffoon you are tired of his power-mad ambitions and go home to your firesides. They would, too. I was sure of it.

He had it all prepared. He had written the word *yes* on thirty slips of paper, and *no* on another thirty. Don't know what he did about Randolph's slip, probably wrote *moonbeams from cucumbers* on it. Jumbling up the slips, he placed them alongside a hat in a recess of the large room. Each member had to step into the recess and drop a slip in the hat. Yes for continuation, no for disbandment. I had no vote, being staff. When all had voted, the General took the hat, opened the ballots and tallied them; then threw everything in the fire.

'I have to announce,' says he in a calm, unemotional voice, 'that a majority have voted "No". I therefore direct that all our forces be dispersed and declare this Committee adjourned without delay.' He glanced away and I swear he piped his eye. 'Good night, gentlemen.'

We filed out in silence. One by one the members departed in their carriages, and I am happy to say that

Harpending and the General aside, I never saw them again.

Several days passed and I wondered when I might broach the subject of my departure. One morning I awoke early after sleeping the sleep of the just. With the Committee disbanded, I intended to take a moment or two sympathising with Harpending and his lost cause, then plead a desire to go back to England and promote the Confederacy there. All I needed was the fare plus incidentals. After a leisurely breakfast in bed I had a relaxing bath then, feeling like a million dollars, as the Yankees say, ambled into the drawing room.

'The General wants to see you Colonel, now.'

My heart leapt back into my mouth and this time stayed there. With this crew it was one bloody thing after another. In due course we fetched up at the General's house and I asked him what the devil he wanted this time, or words to that effect.

'Colonel Armstrong,' says the General, 'I know you are heart and soul with the South. Now, with Yankee impudence growing by the day, the war draws ever nearer. I am aware that when the cannon roars, you will follow' - that's all you know, thinks I - 'and you may wish to leave us and enlist with the Confederate army of Virginia or one of the other States. Your presence will be more than welcome in any of our armies. However, there is one major blow you can strike for us, a signal service you can render. Now...' he hesitated, and I wondered if he wanted me to marry his sister or go searching for another goldmine. '...are you aware of the Fort Fillmore, in Mesilla? I want you to bear a message from me to certain U.S. officers there. Ones of Southern birth who will certainly rally to our cause.' He winked at me knowingly, like a ruptured owl. 'I think you will find this a mission after your own heart.'

Why do they always pick on me? Left alone, I am a peaceable soul, asking no more than bed, preferably filled, board and beer. Yet all my life I seem to encounter madmen who think diving into blood and gore is my meat

84

and drink. I couldn't refuse. Without their support I'd be destitute, and I'd learned enough of San Francisco to know that anyone wandering homelessly was fair game for the police, who were still chasing me over their punctured fellow. Harpending had made enquiries and the red-shirted dago they thought I'd shot had turned out to be a powerful gang leader, and even months later I was sure his mates hadn't forgotten. With innards quaking, I nodded sternly and waited for the blow to fall.

'I shall need a little time to assess who you may safely contact, and must give careful consideration to the wording of the letter. You need have no fear, I shall also arrange an escort for you so you are in no danger of going astray.'

Trust him to think of that, the calculating bastard. Not that I had much hope of sloping off without money. Once they dispatched me east from California, I'd be into the badlands, full of frantic Indians, wolves and God-knows-what. My liver froze at the thought.

'You'll need money. Besides, you have earned a reward for your sterling advice to our Committee and myself, sadly never utilised.' He produced his wallet and counted out five hundred dollars. My heart soared. At last! This would buy my ticket out of Frisco no error. I'd catch the first ship going, to New York or Baltimore, or anywhere far from here, and once afloat I could snap my fingers at the Frisco police, cutthroat gangs, the General, Harpending, the maniac Randolph and the whole boiling lot of them. With the great raid now finally dropped, Harpending had loosened his grip on me, leaving me alone at times while he made a dollar. I daren't run as I hadn't the wherewithal. Until now.

'Thank'ee General, much obliged. And thank you for entrusting me with this mission to ah... Fort Fillmore? To serve the South. You'll let me know when I'm required, as I trust?' I wanted to find out how much time I had in case there wasn't a ship leaving handy, like.

'My boy.' He wrung my hand like I was Saint George off to fight the dragon. Harpending looked on approvingly.

'Don't worry about a thing. I need a little time to learn which officers at Fort Fillmore, and the other forts in the area, will join with us. Then I'll send for you.'

Hope you don't send for me by telegram, thinks I. San Francisco to London will cost you a pretty packet.

A Chinese servant knocked and entered, handing the General a note. He unfolded it and perused the contents.

'It's begun,' he almost whispered.

'What's begun?' asks Harpending.

He passed Harpending the note.

'Our troops have fired on Fort Sumter. The Yankees in the fort returned fire. The talking is over; we are at war.'

Chapter Six

Her name was *Syren*. A medium clipper, designed mainly for transporting cargo, but to an absconding military advisor, as welcoming as a luxury yacht. She was bound for New York via Boston, with a cargo of grain, and, praise the Lord, she was leaving this very day.

From the instant the General announced that America had opted for insanity, I knew it was time to go. A country at war with itself was no place for old Tom, and with money jingling in my pocket and my watchdog half asleep there was nothing to keep me. Travelling home I nodded absently at Harpending's ravings about how the South would give the Yankee despots the licking of a lifetime and ruin the day, whilst formulating my plans. I'd wait until Harpending was looking t'other way and sneak down to the waterfront to seek out departing ships. I'd need to find one quickly, for with the nation at war God knows what effect it would have on shipping, let alone much how it might raise passage fares.

Slightly to my surprise, I slept that night like an Italian sentry, and awoke refreshed, ready for action. For the first time since landing on this troubled shore, I had money in my pocket and knew what I had to do.

As I say, Harpending had left me alone on several occasions since the General called off the raid. I had some time before the General would summon me to my briefing, and in that time I was sure to find a departing ship.

Harpending was supping coffee and poring over the *California Times* in the drawing room when I bade him good morning.

'Busy day today, Colonel, got lots to attend to.'

This sounded hopeful, so I changed the subject.

'I hope to be rather busy soon myself.' I gave a martial snort. 'Now that the Yankees have finally screwed up their courage to start the shooting match, how long d'ye think the General will keep me kicking my heels here?'

He gave a laugh. 'You itching to spill Yankee blood? Well don' you fret none, Colonel, the General is making his plans. When he's done he'll send fer you soon enuff.'

'The sooner the better,' I snarled.

'Well not today Suh. Now you take it easy a spell. Me, I gotta go see a man about some bizney. Wit' this war finally gitting underway, I need to settle my affairs a'fore setting about them Yankees.'

Intrigued, I asked him how he proposed to do his bit for the cause. Enlist back east, perhaps?

'Nope. I'm not a one fer soldiering in line up to the enemy camp with a knapsack on my back. Don' think I'd be much use at it. River smuggling now, that's my ticket. Or mebbe buy a sea-going vessel an' sink me a few Yankee merchant ships.'

Still half an eye to profit, I noted. It was all one to me, but if Harpending survived this shooting match I could see him winding up the biggest land owner this side of the Mississippi. Good luck to him. With ill grace I submitted to frowsting in Harpending's apartment until the General summoned me. Over coffee I perused the *Times* and the *Alto*, ostensibly keeping up with events, but actually checking for news of departing ships. My heart gave a lurch when amongst the titbits I saw an announcement that the good ship *Syren* was departing today for the east coast. Quickly skipping the page, I flicked unseeingly through the rest of the paper, preying that Harpending wouldn't notice my excitement.

Presently he finished his coffee and summoned his servant.

'Well Colonel, lots to do. Don' know what time I'll return. Guess I'll be a while, so don' concern yoursel'. You wan' any more noozpapers jes ring and ask. Take care now.'

And with that he was gone.

Shaking like a fan dancer, I gave him ten minutes to get clear, then went to my room and collected my coat and hat. I didn't dare remove my shaving kit or any of the spare clothes and effects I'd collected since my sojourn here, in case my first attempt as disembarking was unsuccessful. Should I fail to get aboard the *Syren* I would have to return, and it would look deuced odd had I taken my entire wardrobe out with me to sample the air.

I was obliged to order the servant to let me out as Harpending always kept his doors locked against thieves. An educated man, for a black, he attempted to protest, so I told him I was bored rigid with being cooped up all the time and was taking a day out to test the mood of the people now that war was upon us. I told him it was my duty as an intelligence officer to know as much about morale as possible. The servant still argued but I silenced him with a military glower and within minutes I had descended the stairs and hopped into the street. I was free!

Slipping around the corner, I hailed a growler and in short order arrived at the waterfront. Discreet enquiry led me to the offices where I asked tentatively after the *Syren*. Oh ecstasy! It was leaving this evening and had space for paying passengers! I handed over the cash, a good deal more than I'd hoped, and made my way back up into the town. All I had to do now was lay low until I could embark, and ho! for the eastern coast, then home and safety. I wasn't clear yet, I must kill the hours to embarkation without falling foul of any pursuer. Keeping to the broad avenues, I entered one of the better class of restaurant and secreted myself in a dark corner with my back to the wall, well away from the windows.

Returning home for the afternoon was out of the question; I might not be able to get out again. I lingered as long as I dared over the meal, fearing any moment that Harpending, or some member of his blasted Committee of Thirty (disbanded) would mosey in for lunch. They didn't of course, but my nerves went to pieces every time the swing doors flew open. Taking my leave, I briefly considered whiling an hour away at one of the many deadfalls - that's brothel come dancehall come groggery to you - which abounded along Pacific Street westwards to Kearney, for I hadn't had a taste of mutton since my ill-starred visit to the knocking shop in Singapore. Recalling my fate that time, I chose discretion as the better part of valour and strode on. I spent an instructive few hours investigating the new stores that were sprouting like weeds along the south side of Pacific near Sansome Street. One that caught my eye boasted an elaborate tailed overcoat, with brass buttons and a huge straggly fur coat, with a cardboard sign pinned to it proclaiming *Bought & Sold Solomon Levy*. It was a downmarket dive, and seeing a well-heeled gentleman like me paying attention, the seedy looking storekeeper approached, and with a flourish, handed me a card which I have in front of me now. It proclaimed the following;

> *My name is Solomon Levy,*
> *And I keep a clothing store*
> *Away up on Pacific Street -*
> *A hundred and fifty-four.*
> *If you want to buy an overcoat,*
> *A pair of pants or vest,*
> *Step up to Solomon Levy,*
> *And he'll sell you all the best.*

All perfectly true, no doubt, and a fine example of Yankee salesmanship, but I passed, as his merchandise was better suited to a tramp who's down on his luck.

The air was electric; a great energy enthused the streets as the townsfolk digested the colossal news just in. Well its not every day your country goes to war on itself. I passed a street-corner orator proclaiming "Liberty and Union now and forever, one and inseparable" What price the General's dream of a Confederate California, thinks I, as he drummed up support. He stared straight at me and seemed to expect something, so I looked him in the eye and hollered "The Union, the whole Union and nothing but the Union". He grinned and stroked his chin, and I moved on.   The citizens' preoccupation gave me comfort as nobody paid the slightest heed to the big, bluff gentleman with buttoned up coat and hat strolling among them.

Up into the respectable part of town, I chanced upon a matinee theatre, and spent the rest of the afternoon safely ensconced in a seat in the corner. Can't remember the performance, but afternoon theatre is almost always dreadful wherever you go, and I had other things on my mind just then. #Note_5

At last enough time had passed for me to attempt to get aboard the *Syren*. My nerves, which had eased when playing the tourist about town, grew tight as fiddle strings as I made my way back down to the waterfront. This was the time the low-life and dockside scum began to make their appearance, and I dreaded chancing on police or gang members who might recognise me, or even falling foul of a random footpad, numbers of which infested the area, as they infest most docksides anywhere.

Lady Luck was with me, however, and I reported to the waterfront office, where I was directed to a pier and in no time my guts heaved with relief as I found myself hauled onto the eastbound clipper. I had made it!

There was no cabin available, but after an anxious hour spent sitting on my cot, one of a row tucked tidily astern, noises above alerted me to our imminent departure. Sure enough, we cast off and began moving slowly forward, and my heart sang.

Sold again boys, I gloated. Harpending would have returned home by now, cursing my absence, but with the servant explaining my reasons I doubted he'd yet guess I'd abandoned the South to let it fight its own battles. By the time he got wise I would be long over the horizon and far away.

It wasn't quite dark yet, so for safety's sake I decided to remain below decks for the time being. Besides, now that I could relax, a tide of weariness stole over me like a warm blanket. I'd had a trying day to cap several damned trying months, and I felt I could sleep all the way to Boston. Ignoring my fellow passengers on the adjoining bunks, I stretched out on my cot, yawned, and fell blissfully into a peaceful, dreamless sleep.

What caused the War Between the States? To this day, Americans cannot even agree on whether it was a civil war or one between two nations, let alone the rights and wrongs. Both sides blame t'other, and if you give your views in the wrong bar, or stateroom, or church even, you'll likely as not get a fist in your face.

But from the safety of my brandy and armchair I am fearless, and if you are to understand the rest of my tale it is as well you know the facts behind it. So if you will bear with Professor Tommy the noted historian for a few moments, this is how it happened.

The South is hot, its climate ideal for growing cotton, rice, tobacco and sugar. Especially cotton. It developed into an agricultural, feudal society, organised almost on military lines. The slaves were the troopers, the poor whites the sergeants, keeping the slaves in line and driving them in fields too hot for white folk. The junior officers constituted the tiny middle class; architects, tailors, doctors, small farmers and the like, while the generals were the big plantation owners, whose word was law. It was a settled society, deeply religious with the rich man in his castle and the poor man at his gate, where all was arranged satisfactorily as ordained by God and the Bible, world without end amen. The height of ambition for a poor Southerner was to own more than twenty slaves and so rise up the ranks. They didn't need manufacturing as the world was crying out for their cotton, and stuffed with foreign currency they could buy from Europe everything they wanted. Thus slavery was the South's bedrock, without which everything would crumble.

The North, with its more equable climate, developed along Dickensian lines; factories sprouting like radishes, towns and cities, roads and railroads, schools and all the general infrastructure essential to a modern country. It was changeable and dynamic, fuelled by immigration of ambitious folk determined to make new lives for themselves. Slavery had no place here; the poor whites opposed it as they could not compete with slave labour which would undercut their own efforts and drive them destitute. Manufacturers had no time for uneducated slaves, who made useless factory hands, and moreover, if the workers were unpaid, who would buy their produce?

The government introduced trade tariffs on European imports to protect their fledgling industries against foreign competition, which infuriated the Southern plantation owners who now had to pay more for their imported European pianos, carpets and chandeliers. Meanwhile the growing cities threw up their usual quota of affluent liberals who denounced slavery as morally wrong and produced countless tracts and newspapers campaigning against it. The Northern churches, seeing which way the wind was blowing, joined in the campaign to free the Black Man.

So the North wanted a dynamic meritocracy where anyone could get rich through hard work, ingenuity or lucky breaks. The South wanted a feudal empire where everyone knew their place and stayed there. The stage was set; America could not chase two opposing destinies indefinitely. Sooner or later these visions of their country's future would clash.

The American Constitution apportions seats in the House of Representatives according to States' population. The more people, the more seats, and North and South both wished to control it for their own ends. Question was, do we count the blacks? In the 1780s the total black and white population of the South outnumbered the North so the South claimed dominance. Ah, says the North, you call slaves property so how can they be people? Counting whites only, the North outnumbers the South and we control the House. Get out, roars the South. You say blacks are human, even if we don't, hardly, so you've got to count 'em.

They argued each way for a while, then did some figuring and finally settled on an ingenious compromise. A black, they decided, was counted as two thirds of a white. Hey presto! This evened out the numbers splendidly and they shared the seats betwixt them.

Mad, says you, but with two halves of a nation pulling in opposite directions over what kind of country they wished to be, those who wanted to keep America united had to tie logic in knots to keep the country from splitting asunder.

When immigration let rip in the nineteenth century the population of the North overtook the South, blacks and all, so they had to rely on the Senate, where every State has two senators each regardless of population. This meant the South could block any anti-slavery legislation coming from the Northern dominated House of Representatives. Fine, so long as the number of slave States equalled or surpassed the free ones. Snag was, America was opening up the west, and when territories such as Kansas applied to become States, would they be slave or free? At first the compromisers batted the ball into the long grass by only admitting new States two at a time, one free one slave. Maine-Missouri, Arkansas-Michigan, Texas-Iowa and so forth. This kept the balance, you see, but they were balancing on a razor blade. The wobbles began when the next two territories up for statehood, Kansas and Nebraska, were both North of Mason and Dixon's line, and so in the free half of the country. To get round this, the compromisers passed the Kansas-Nebraska act, which said that from now on the population of any new State could vote on whether to allow slavery or not. Well this blew the two-States-at-a-time system out of the water. Both sides kicked up a stink and when the dust had cleared all eyes turned to Kansas. Whoever won the vote there would dominate the slavery question from now on. The question being, should America be a slave or free labour nation? With the stakes so high, Kansas earned the sobriquet Bleeding Kansas, as Northern abolitionists sponsored settlers to move in and cast their votes against slavery, while Southern border ruffians raided the State, stuffing ballot boxes and intimidating abolitionists. They completely destroyed the town of Laurence, for example, and rode roughshod over the territory. Not that the Northerners took this lying down. New Englanders armed anti-slavery vigilante groups who matched outrage for outrage. My old friend John Brown, for example, oversaw the slaughter of five unarmed slaveholders at

Pottawatomie Creek. The Northern authorities winked at this atrocity, enraging the South still further and driving the two sides wider apart.

States Rights? Aye well, the Northern Republicans wanted Washington to have the power to overrule States which disagreed with them. The Southern Democrats supported each State deciding matters in its own interests. They resented Northern interference in their affairs, be it slavery or anything else. The tariff on imported goods being a case in point.

Slavery's champion in Washington was the Democrat Party. Strongest in the South, they needed some support in the North to win national elections. They drew their Southern support from just about everyone, and their Northern support from frontiersmen and small farmers who wanted America to expand west and take slavery with it. The chief opposition party had been the Whigs, imported from the old country. They supported industrialisation and modernisation, strong central government and collecting taxes to build up the nation's infrastructure. They garnered their support overwhelmingly from prosperous farmers, manufacturers, industrialists, poor whites - everyone had the vote, remember - and city dwellers. But they needed Southern votes too, and with feelings running high the Whigs were torn between rapid modernisation and the old ways of the South. They couldn't support both, so they splintered.

The political North was in turmoil, with new parties arising overnight and disappearing just as quickly, but you can look up the fortunes of the Whigs, Free-Soilers, Know-Nothings (so-called 'cos if you asked them about slavery they would answer they knew nothing) and the rest of them in the books. While you're at it, you might check the Fugitive Slave Law (slaves who escape to free soil must be returned to their owners), the Dred Scott decision (can a black man sue for his freedom? No, said the judge), Californian Compromise (a baffling hotchpotch of five interrelated Bills which makes the Schleswig-Holstein question look simple) and devil knows what else. What matters is the Northern politicians eventually congealed into the new Republican Party, who won their first election in 1860 headed by, of course, Abraham Lincoln. They won with forty percent of the popular vote against a split opponent (bravely handled, the South!), then the fun began.

Your pardon for the lecture, but its as well to know the background, and see that though the South was fighting for independence and the North to save the Union, both sides were fighting to preserve their way of life. This may be one reason why they fought so savagely and brought about such slaughter. Me? I would have let the slaves earn their freedom by, say, twenty years working for their masters. This would have led to multitudes of middle-aged free blacks competing with poor whites and demonstrating the folly of slave driving when you can increase profits by hiring them as wage slaves instead. Perhaps I should have run for president. Ah well...

Thump! I flew off the cot nearly cracking my head open as an ear-splitting thwack resounded through my ears accompanied by violent spasms shaking the ship to its foundations. Sprawling uncomprehendingly in pain and shock, I lay helpless as the ship lurched terrifyingly to one side and screams and whistles punctured the air like lost souls falling into Hell.

Clutching my bleeding head, heart palpitating in confusion and fright, I scrambled to my knees vainly trying to comprehend what was happening as another crumpling thud threw me back across the floor, colliding with God knows what and bruising me black and blue.

This second thump brought me to my senses. There was only one explanation; the ship had struck a reef.

The next few moments are unclear, but eventually I managed to stagger up on deck, shaking with fear and apprehension, to find out what in blazes was happening.

Above the cries of my fellow passengers the crew were wrestling with the ropes, yelling for pumps and scampering hither and thither, whistles adding to the general panic, and nothing useful being done so far as I could see. Behind us the lights of San Francisco were twinkling brightly and I realised we were only about a mile away from shore, and I cannot have slept more than an hour. There must have been a great gash in the hull as we were taking in water at an alarming rate. Coming to my senses, I cast around for a lifeboat, and finding one aft, presented myself alongside ready to join in lowering it, and myself, to safety. If anyone was going to drown or freeze to death in the water, it wasn't going to be British Tommy.

In the event, lifeboats were not needed. The *Syren*, after much effort from the crew, eventually limped back into San Francisco harbour. She had been passing the entrance to San Francisco's Golden Gate when she struck Mile Rock twice. Holed below the water line, she managed to beach onto mudflats with four feet of water awash in the hold.

Where did this leave poor Tommy? Along with crew and passengers I stumbled up the mudflats onto the shore proper. A goodish crowd had assembled to gawp at the stricken ship and I realised at once that this was no place for me. Time had passed and I'd recovered my wits to some extent, and with a sinking heart I knew that I would have to return to Harpending's apartment and make up some tale to explain my bruised and bloodied appearance. No difficulty for someone of my talents, but as I hastened to escape the waterfront I again decried the jinx that held me in the United States just when they had decided to start a civil war. I could have wept at how close I had been to escape, and cursed the dilatory ship's Pilot who couldn't avoid a bloody great rock sticking out of the sea, a rock so well known it had its own name. There was nothing for it, of course, but to compose myself as best as possible, stop a cab, if one would pick me up in my dishevelled state, and make my way back to Harpending's apartment.

'What in Hell happened to you?'

This was Harpending's welcome after I rolled up at his home and was ushered into the drawing room by his servant, who at least seemed pleased to see me. I guessed Harpending had given him a tough time for letting me out, not that it mattered. Meanwhile, I had worked out my story in the taxicab.

'Apologies for my appearance, old fellow. I was out on a bit of a reconnaissance, as it were, when I bumped into a few of those gang members who are so eager to renew acquaintance.'

I said this with a good deal more confidence than I felt. Nevertheless, I pressed my story home. The gist was, as you will have gathered, that on my travels throughout the town I had been waylaid, hence my blooded head and general appearance, and had to duck and dive my way home.

I certainly looked the part and it sounded convincing, put across with a twirl of my whiskers to suggest I had given the crimps more than they bargained for and you should see the other fellow, and to my relief he fell for it. Not that I blamed him, I'd have fallen for it myself.

While his servant dressed my cracked bonce, which was none too bad once cleaned up, Harpending gave me a ticking off, pointing out that I was too valuable to risk coming a cropper nosing around the town when I was earmarked for greater things. The General needed me, and so did the South, so no more gallivanting about on my own in future. From now on my job was to wait patiently until the bugle blew and I could march onwards for the greater glory of the Confederacy and blast the abolitionists to Hell and beyond.

I didn't mind. I'd got off lightly, considering I could easily have been drowned or marked out as a deserter from the greater glory of the Confederacy. Devil knows what he and the General would have done had they suspected the truth. I'd had a narrow escape on the ship and my luck had been stretched as long as a bookie's memory, now all I wanted was a bath and bed. Time enough to consider my plight in the morning.

I had blown my one chance of escape. From now on Harpending or some of his goons stuck to me like barnacles. It was as much as I could do to visit the privy without one of them coming along to hold my hand. And I had spent nearly all my money to pay for passage on the *Syren*. I daren't try to claim it back, as the ship was the second most talked about subject after the war, and should Harpending, who seemed to have fingers in every pie, get wind... I told him my cash had gone astray wrestling with the gang in the hope he'd get the General to stump up another instalment, but nary a penny was forthcoming, the tight-fisted swine.

I spent the next few weeks in a stupor. Confined to Harpending's apartment, I had nothing to do but take early evening escorted walks for exercise, read the newspapers, eat, drink and play cards with my minders. Harpending was out and about much of the time, leaving me in the care of various hard-hats who were pleasant enough, but under orders not to let me out of their sight.

News of the war was sporadic, with rumours of significant manoeuvrings by the Great and the Good, commanders who would destroy the enemy - North or South according to taste - at a stroke, but nothing concrete. Fact is, now that the shooting war had finally started, neither side knew exactly how to go about it.

California declared for the North, as expected. The General's machinations came to nothing in the end, and I gritted my teeth at the thought of what a waste of my time and nerves his confounded Committee had turned out to be. They'd have been better employed taking up crochet.

'Good news Colonel, the General wants to see you tonight.'

About as good as a dose of the clap, thinks I, butterflies awakening in the pit of my stomach, but I put on my ardent Rebel face and tried to sound as enthusiastic as he.

'Not before time,' growls I. 'I was beginning to think he had forgotten me.'

'Oh, nevah that, Colonel. The General don' fergit nothing. Jes you be ready tonight, is all. I got an inkling yore mission may just turn the tide heah in California. The General he ain't given up on this State jus' yet.'

This was a worrying thought. I knew Harpending and the General were all for stealing the Californian gold for the South but I'd fondly imagined they had given up on their loony idea of grabbing the State. If all Confederates were as stubborn as the General, Uncle Sam might have bitten off more than he could chew.

Harpending escorted me to the General's house and, putting on a bold front to hide my shakes, I strode in to his presence.

'Good evening Colonel,' says he clasping hands warmly. 'Well,' he grinned like a dentist, 'Mister Harpending here tells me you are chaffing at the bit to be off to the war.'

'And not before time, if you'll pardon me for saying so Sir,' replies I, seriously. 'This war has been going nearly three months and I have not even said boo to a Yankee yet.'

He laughed, as I'd intended he should.

'Don't you worry Colonel, soon enough you will be doing far more than saying boo. Far more indeed.'

He marched me to the table and unveiled a map.

'Here is the area surrounding Fort Fillmore in the Territory of New Mexico.'

We peered over it, while I wondered how I could use this knowledge to my advantage.

'As you can see, Fort Fillmore is just one of several forts in the area. Fort Stanton,' he pointed a craggy finger across the paper, 'Fort Craig, Fort Thorn, Fort Webster and others. These are all United States forts, presently, but...' he lowered his voice theatrically, 'there are many good Southern boys in blue uniforms, just waiting for the word to come over to us. And here,' he produced a sealed envelope from out of his side pocket, 'is the word.'

Oh Lord, thinks I. He wants me to be the postman, like Sir Roland Hill, delivering his treasonous note to half a dozen forts in the wilds of the desert, dodging Indians left, right and centre. For this was the badlands with a vengeance. The thought of scurrying about this treacherous back of beyond knocking on the doors of forts and asking the officers and men to change sides and start shooting Yankees was almost enough to make me puke. With gaseous intestines, I listened as he continued his plan to drop Tommy head first into the stew.

'I have here a list of officers we can trust. Memorise the names and we will burn it. You will reveal yourself secretly to them and produce my letter of authority. It is a call to action. Once primed, they will rally the Southern boys and take over the forts. With the element of surprise it will be a simple task. Once we have the forts, we will take the territory for the South, next stop California...'

I had to admire his tenacity. He wanted California for the South and by the gods he would keep striving for it against all reason. The old fool.

'Some of the officers are at Fort Fillmore, some in the other forts in the territory. They move around the forts as need dictates. I have an escort who will deliver you safely to Fort Fillmore, and leave it to your discretion as to how you proceed from there.'

'But how can I just show up at Fort Fillmore? I can hardly say I was simply passing by on a walking holiday, can I?'

Harpending laughed and the General smiled at the Tommy *bon mot*.

'Have no fears, Colonel. All sorts of folk turn up at these forts seeking assistance. You will present yourself to U.S. Major Lynde, the new commander, as the Californian representative of the London *Times*, commissioned by your superior, Mr. William Howard Russell, to report on how the war is progressing in the far west. Mr. Russell, you may truthfully inform him, is currently reporting for the *Times* in the east. So you will be accepted without demur.'

He had it all worked out, damn him. But I was intrigued to learn that my old friend Billy Russell was about. I had known him well in the Crimea and India, and he was a good scout, was Billy. If I ever got back east I made a mental note to look him up. I could cadge my fare home from him. On that note a thought occurred to me.

'Will I be alone? I mean to say, will anyone at the forts know of my true purpose?'

'Oh no, Colonel, you will be quite alone until you reveal your true self to the officers on your list. None know your reasons for arriving at the forts and none will save those names there.'

I exploded in a coughing fit to hide my true emotions. I saw the way out! It was so simple I could have laughed. With no-one watching me, all I need do is humour this buffoon and allow his men to escort me to Fort Fillmore as planned. Once there I would present myself as a *Times* journalist, and write a story or two about camp life for form's sake. Meanwhile I'd burn the General's precious letter and to Hell with his mission. And as soon as a large enough party was travelling back east, I would accompany them. Saved at the eleventh hour! I'd had some devilish luck, but as I always say, you only need to win on the last throw of the dice. I was almost home already.

The General went over the plan in detail, explaining just how we were to take the forts when I'd alerted our side and showed them the General's letter. He gave me the lie of the land, potted guide to the Southern officers' likely attitudes, and everything I need know in order to carry out the perfect military coup. I barely heard him, struggling to contain my excitement that I was at last on my way home, spirited on my way by this fool of a General, had he but known. Luckily, my strained expression looked like firm resolve, and in taking my leave with Harpending, the General, wracked with emotion, wrung my hand for the last time and said I was a champion of the Confederacy. He added;

'Just as General Washington founded America in the great revolutionary war of independence against England, so you have helped found the Confederacy. You are as great a general as Washington himself.'

We made our farewells, and as Harpending whistled for the carriage I recalled the great revolutionary war. If there was one general I resembled, it was Benedict Arnold.

Chapter Seven

Fort Fillmore was a small garrison near Mesilla, in what is now New Mexico but was then part of the territory of Arizona. Not far from the Rio Grande, it was built to protect settlers and traders trekking between Texas and California. Migrants were forever coming under attack from Indians and Mexican bandits, so the U.S. government built a chain of forts in the Arizona wilderness to encourage westward expansion.

It was nothing to look at, a low, spread-out group of buildings made to look tiny in front of a high range of hills, surrounded by rolling sand dunes and mesquite bushes, but as I waved goodbye to my escort and spurred my horse onward, it looked as pretty as a palace. Once ensconced safely behind its walls, all I need do was await the next armed group travelling east - soldiers returning for supplies, for preference - and I'd be as good as back in Leicestershire.

I had the General's sealed letter of authority, calling for the Southern officers to mutiny sewn carefully into my coat lining. I had no intention of showing it to anyone, of course, and agonised about whether or not to destroy it. Should any officer loyal to Uncle Sam discover it on my person it would be a hanging matter, no error. On the other hand, it was safe enough where it was, and might come in handy should I encounter any Confederate forces between here and safety. So with reservations I left it intact.

I also had a letter of introduction to Major Lynde, Seventh Infantry, Fort Fillmore's commanding officer, which the General insisted would ensure I was treated as a privileged guest and given the freedom of the fort. This would enable me to approach the Southern officers. Not that I would go anywhere near them with seditious talk, but he didn't know that.

Cantering through the gates, I was halted by a sergeant who demanded to know my business. I told him I had come from California with a letter for his commanding officer, and he bade me wait. Presently the officer of the day appeared, and after repeating my request brought me to Major Lynde's spartan quarters, desk with papers neatly stacked, rough wooden furniture and floors of low fired clay brick.

'Who are you, Sir, and what do you want with me?'

He stared me up and down disapprovingly. Well, I had been days in the saddle and didn't look of my best. His manner suggested I had better crawl back under the stone I had come from pronto. He was a busy man and didn't I know there was a war on? A man arriving alone at his precious fort, he suggested, should show proper respect by enlisting in the Union forces. He had no time to spare for day-trippers, so good day to you Sir.

I wasn't concerned, the General had warned me that every type of ne'er do well fetched up at the far-flung outposts constantly, so I was ready for him.

Proffering my letter of introduction, I introduced myself as George Jeffreys of the London *Times*, number two to the great Billy Russell himself. The General had provided me with the letter purporting to be from Russell, asking to whom it might concern if they would be so kind as to cooperate with the bearer and let him file his newspaper reports for the benefit of the Great Readership of the *Times*, God, Queen and Empire, in that order. Major Lynde scanned the letter carefully, whistled and returned it to me. The General had done me proud; the letter would have convinced Doubting Thomas himself. He fell for it immediately, supported, I humbly add, by my own demeanour, which was a considerable cut above the normal riff-raff who knocked on his doors seeking succour. I confess I may have hinted that with a little cooperation from him, I would promote his sterling endeavour and proclaim him to the world as *The Man Who Saved the West*.

'The London *Times* you say? Working alongside Mr. Russell of the Crimea? Why, this is famous! Capital, Mr. Jeffreys, capital. Welcome to Fort Fillmore. It is indeed a great honour to entertain a gentleman of the press. The press, did I say? Far more than that. The London *Times* itself, by far the greatest newspaper in the world, Her Majesty's own. Care for a drink?'

Returning my letter, he pumped my hand enthusiastically and called for refreshments, as I marvelled at the vanity of humanity. With his country newly at war you'd think he would have more urgent things to do than entertain a gentleman of the press, yet here he was rolling out the red carpet for me and letting his duty go hang. It's the same the world over, give a nonentity a sniff of fame and he'll move heaven and earth to secure your good opinion.

'So tell me, Mr. Jeffreys, what exactly are you hoping to report on here?'

I was ready for this.

'Well Major, my superior, Mr. Russell, thought it would be instructive for our readers to learn how the U.S. army is dealing with the deplorable insurrection of several Southern States. He is, as I am sure you are aware, travelling about the eastern portion of your great country, reporting on conditions there, and we agreed it would add to the world's understanding of the emergency for me to report in a similar manner on the state of play in the west. It is just a flying visit, you understand,' I didn't want the fool to think I was there for the duration, 'and with your permission, I will observe how you and your men are coping here. At your convenience I will beg to impose on you to allow me to join your next party travelling east in order to file my copy and write on conditions elsewhere.' Waxing confidentially I lowered my voice. 'I cannot name names, obviously, but I am assured by important people in California that you are just the man to make the Rebels rue the day they fired on the Stars and Stripes.' I gave him my winning Tommy smile, winked, and he was mine.

'Well Mr. Jeffreys,' says he, chest puffed, 'modesty forbids, but let me assure you if any Rebels poke their treacherous noses into my territory, I'll shoot them off. You can rely on me for that.'

He prosed on for quite some time about how he had no truck with Rebels and knew just how Washington should treat the traitors when they had brought them to heel, implying that what Lincoln needed was some top-notch boots and saddles soldier accustomed to authority - a western Major, say - to set them straight. I gathered from this that he had political ambitions, and saw this war as a heaven-sent opportunity to stake his claim on the first rung of the political ladder. Of course, having a man from the *Times* in his corner couldn't hurt, and he was as flattering as an encyclopaedia salesman. At last he remembered I had human needs, and arranged for me to park my esteemed rump in a guestroom of sorts, while he arranged dinner and a bath.

That evening, having rested and eaten my fill, I reflected on how well things had turned out. I could simply follow this puffball about the fort, write a few lines to the effect that with Lynde running the show, the North may sleep sound in their beds, and in a week or two depart homeward bound with the Major's blessings and a squadron of troopers for escort. (Incidentally, much later I told Billy Russell about my self-appointment as his western war correspondent. He roared and hoped I wouldn't ask him for salary). That's what would have transpired, no doubt, had it not been for the unwarranted arrival of another in the long list of maniacs of my acquaintance; John R. Baylor, Lieutenant Colonel, Army of the Confederate States of America.

Mind you, all was well for the first few days. I trotted after Major Lynde, met his officers, who held their commander in no great regard I noticed, and inspected the troops, horses and general day-to-day activities in the fort.

The garrison had been recently reinforced due to the Southern insurrection. It consisted of several hundred men and officers. Some five of the officers had their wives and children with them, always an unwise state of affairs for when bullets begin flying they will look to their loved ones before their duty. It's only natural, ain't it? None of my business of course, as I was already angling to be out with the first mounted column east, and I duly played up to their children to impress the parents and create a good impression. Each evening I read out my reports to Major Lynde, and you may be sure they were as complimentary as could be, but he wasn't altogether happy with them.

'Admirable accounts, Mr. Jeffreys, but I fear they read like a garrison at peace. With all due respect, I cannot see them galvanising your readership when compared to the great doings back east.'

Won't galvanise your career either, but I looked stern and agreed, aye, t'would be fine if I could report you challenging Rebel troops and dispersing them, but alas, you cannot fight an enemy who doesn't show up.

'True enough, Mr. Jeffreys, but keep your hopes high. Our patrols are out everywhere and if they so much as smell a Rebel, I'll let you accompany us as we teach them to respect our flag. And how.'

Little chance of that, it seemed. Why, I would have wagered there were no organised Rebel forces within five hundred miles. Lucky I didn't place the bet; I would have lost.

The two men arrived at the post in the early hours of the morning. They were pickets for the Confederate army of Texas, they said, discharged U.S. army veterans who remembered their duty to Uncle Sam at the last moment and came over to the North's side. They had urgent news of enemies nearby. Major Lynde couldn't believe his luck. What a chance to show Washington how he dealt with Rebels, and me, a senior correspondent for the *Times* (well... I may have promoted myself a tad) here to tell the world.

Camped less than a mile away were up to four hundred Confederate soldiers - so much for Lynde's patrols smelling Rebels - planning to ambush the fort in a surprise attack at first light.

This woke up the fort to be sure. Lynde sent for two companies of the Seventh Infantry stationed at San

Thomas nearby to reinforce us, while we were kept on full alert till daybreak. In their hurry to comply, the Seventh had left several troopers behind. These laggards eventually limped to the fort to tell us the Rebels had captured them and learnt our troop numbers and dispositions, and carried away or destroyed much Union property. Glad I'm not in this army, thinks I.

The noise of troops mustering, wagons shuffling, horses stomping and jingling, topped by the long roll of the drums signifying imminent attack, alerted the Rebels to the fact that their presence was discovered, and by first light they were nowhere to be seen.

Let's hope they have fled back to Texas, I remember praying, for the last thing I wanted was to be saddled beside a sorrow-seeking Major charging through the desert sands seeking a fight against an unknown enemy. For neither side had any experience fighting organised white troops and who knew how the Rebels or Federals would shape up? If there was one person who had no wish to find out, you can be sure who it was.

No such luck. Reports soon came in that the Rebels had occupied Mesilla, the nearby town, and had been welcomed by the Southern sympathisers there. This sent my little Napoleon into a rage. We would destroy the Rebel force, he fumed, and then deal with the traitors of Mesilla.

So with enemies at the gates, our numbers and disposition revealed and the local civilians backing the Rebels, what was the first thing our commander should do? Why, call a press conference.

'This is your chance, Mr. Jeffreys,' cries he. 'I am about to launch an attack on these traitorous secessionists and you will be there, at my side, reporting on just how we deal with traitors in these parts. I trust you have plenty of sharp pencils?'

Lord save me. He thought he was going on a Sunday picnic, and there was nothing I could do but follow closely behind him and hope I didn't stop a stray bullet. I cursed the General for inventing my role as *Times* Correspondent. Why couldn't I have travelled as a patent medicine man, flogging hair restorer to the Indians?

We set off late afternoon. He took a good-sized force, six companies of the Seventh Infantry, some mounted, a howitzer battery and two companies of rifles. Properly handled they should take care of anything short of a veteran regiment. We left behind one company of infantry, the sick parade and the fort's band to garrison the post. Let's hope the Rebels don't send a couple of old women to attack the fort while we are out, thinks I, or we will have no home to return to.

We called a halt about two miles short of Mesilla. I say we, but you may be sure I took no role in anything that occurred. My job was to ride safely behind the Major, making notes.

He sent his adjutant Lieutenant Brooks and the fort's surgeon, of all people, under a white flag, to demand the surrender of all Rebels "to the proper constituted authority of the United States".

Well, he should have known *that* wouldn't work. You don't march all the way from Texas to pull up your stumps before the batsman has bowled the first ball. Sure enough, they were met by a pair of Confederate officers who curtly told them that if they wanted the town they must come and take it. They reported back and despite the heat, I shivered. This was it; we were going to take the town. I consoled myself that I was a neutral observer and hoped the Major would have the sense to realise that the senior officer was far too important to risk his carcass anywhere near the firing, and so, for the matter of that, was his newspaper chronicler.

I needn't have fretted. Major Lynde gave the command to advance, mounted troops to the front followed by infantry, under howitzer artillery cover. He kept well to the rear himself, with a knot of senior officers and Tommy safely planted behind him. The howitzer battery fired two shells at long range but they fell well short, landing on a nearby hilltop and killing some of the townsfolk who had gathered to watch the fireworks. This wouldn't do, so he ordered the battery to advance behind the troops, giving covering fire over their heads. Unfortunately, my Napoleon had not considered the heavy sand that lay between us and the grassland in front of the town. This in a desert. In no time our howitzers were hopelessly mired and out of the battle. The crashing of the howitzers had set my bowels a'gallop in the old style, recalling nightmares of shot and shell from Russia, India and Lord knows where else. I steadied my horse ready for a sharp about turn if the Rebels returned fire.

Nearing the town, the Union troopers formed front to charge. Suddenly, from a cornfield and solitary house to our right came a heavy pop-popping of musketry. They shot several of our riders straight out of their saddles, which was good shooting, damn 'em. To my amazement the rest of our troopers immediately about faced and retreated in disorder through our own advancing infantry, causing cries of panic and confusion. Once the riders were through them, the infantry went to ground, sensible chaps, and stayed there. It was stalemate, with our fellows unable - or unwilling, if you ask me - to advance without artillery support, and the Rebels showing no sign of wishing to come out and fight in the open. I gave thanks we were out of musket range, and the Rebels apparently possessed no heavy guns, so Lynde, his chief officers and your loyal correspondent were safe enough. As darkness fell it was plain that we were achieving nothing, our men lying out in the long grass being shot at from the outlying fields and houses to no purpose, and a dispirited Lynde gave the welcome order to call the attack off. We had lost about four men killed, I believe, and twenty wounded.

It was a different Major Lynde who led his demoralised troops back to the safety of the fort. On the way to battle he had been full of buck and bluster, promising slaughter of the traitors and a swift victory for the forces of liberty. His demeanour now was of a drunken braggart in a pub who had offered to fight every man there only to find they obliged. T'weren't his fault though, he whined, his officers had let him down. He'd ordered the attack, you see, and it had dissolved the instant the Rebels showed fight. Well he couldn't be to blame, could he, so it followed the fault must lie with his subordinates.

I was at the hastily arranged staff meeting the following morning and mighty informative it was too.

'You let me down,' he fumed, rounding on the nearest officer, a Captain Gibbs, as I recall. 'I ordered an attack on the town and your cavalry fled and your men hid in the grass at the first show of resistance.'

'We were expecting artillery support, Major. You cannot expect our men to charge defended positions in broad daylight without cover.'

Bristling red at this refusal by his subordinate to accept blame, Lynde swung round to his adjutant.

'Lieutenant Brooks, you heard me give the order. You were with me and saw how the men quaked under fire. Did you see Captain Gibbs rally them, as he was bound to do?'

Lieutenant Brooks clearly had no wish to take sides in a spat between his two superior officers.

'Well Sir, in the heat of battle it is difficult to say...'

'What battle?' roars our brave commander. 'We didn't fight, our men lay prone, taking in the scenery whilst our cavalry fled and our officers stood by and did nothing. Captain McNally, what say you?'

'Well Sir, as Captain Gibbs points out, our men could not advance wi'out artillery support.'

The Major picked up this ball and ran with it.

'And why was there no artillery support Sir? Tell me that.'

'Our artillery was ordered forward right into a sand dune, Major. So they couldn't give support. You must have seen what was happening from your vantage point at the back.'

I hadn't thought Major Lynde capable of going redder in the face than he had been thus far, but he managed it. As the full import of Captain McNally's remark, suggesting both tactical incompetence for advancing his artillery through a sand dune, and implied

112

cowardice for remaining behind the attack in safety - between you and me, the right and proper thing to do - struck home, he ripened like a sunburnt Comanche.

'Get out. Get out the lot of you. We will have more to say about this later. In the meantime you can see about fortifying our defences against any Rebel attack, if that is not beyond your capabilities. Dismissed.'

I'd seen it before, of course. All inquests after military cock-ups are pretty much the same. The commander maintains his plans were perfect so it was the implementation that went awry. The next in command sees a court martial looming and so bites back as far as he dares, blaming the overall strategy, while the junior officers shuffle their feet and try to avoid the eye of the chief.

The officers exited, doubtless badmouthing their red-faced commander and establishing alibis, and Lynde took a great breath, exhaled, then remembered I was in the room.

'Your pardon, Mr. Jeffreys. I am sorry you had to witness such a shambles, but what am I to do?' He flopped down on his chair and bade me take a seat. Here it comes, thinks I, a long, winding justification of his behaviour in the recent farce. He won't want me reporting the truth, that's for certain.

'You see what I am up against? My own officers do not support me. I am surrounded by open and secret enemies, sympathisers of the South some of them, I'm sure. I cannot trust a one. Since I first arrived at this benighted post I have been unable to obtain reliable information on enemy troop movements or numbers. My officers flout my orders, and my men show no fight in the face of the enemy.' He buried his face in his hands, then looked up at me and whimpered. 'The Rebels, seeing our disarray, are sure to attack us in force. I cannot hold this fort against sustained assault. Mr. Jeffreys, what am I to do?' By God, he was asking me!

'If I understand you right, Major, are you suggesting the Rebels can take this fort?' It sounded unlikely. We didn't know their strength for certain, but we had a garrison still, and heavy guns, and we could surely defend our position easily. Why, only yesterday he was demanding the Rebels surrender to *him*. I marvelled at how a minor setback had completely unmanned this pompous jellyfish and worried at what this might mean to my hopes of an easy ride home. Surely we were safe enough behind our walls?

Perhaps embarrassed at breaking down in front of the *Times* correspondent, he scrambled back into his dignity.

'With all due respect, you are not a military man, and do not know what I am up against. Not only treachery in the ranks. I have had a report that the enemy will tomorrow receive a battery of artillery. Our fort is indefensible against cannon, surrounded as it is by hills affording a clear shot into our very heart. Once they mount guns on the hills above us we are helpless. Meanwhile our nearest supply of water is one and a half miles away.'

Then why by the gods did his government build the bloody fort here? Stomach churning, I sought a way out. Could he not intercept the artillery before it reached the Rebels?

'I cannot take a strong force to intercept the artillery train before it reaches Mesilla for fear the Rebels will sally forth and attack the fort in our absence.' He stiffened, and summoned up the dregs of his courage. 'We can only stay here and await our doom, and hope to die like soldiers.'

Speak for yourself, thinks I. This was appalling. During the staff discussion, if you can call it that, I had taken a slightly detached view of the Major's problems. He'd had a setback, certainly, but I thought I could lie snug behind the walls of the fort with adequate rations and a comfortable bed until the Rebels became bored with the entertainment the local town could provide and meandered off and away, maybe back down the Rio Grande, or on to California to try their luck at the gaming tables there.

Truth to tell, up until now, I had not taken this rebellion seriously. I had assumed that either the truant States would calm down after their tantrum and grovel back into the Union, or Washington would say good riddance and let them find damnation in their own way. What I had not bargained for was a real shooting war with besieged forts, funk-filled commanders and poor Tommy stuck in the middle, hiding under the horse trough.

Well, if we couldn't fight we could always surrender. I suggested this, tactfully, to avoid unnecessary death and ensure treatment for our wounded and suchlike, but he wouldn't hear of it.

'I will not lower the Stars and Stripes to a pack of traitors. We must fight, to the death if necessary.'

'Can you send for further reinforcements?'

He calmed down, shook his head sadly, and replied.

'My dear Mr. Jeffreys, San Thomas held the only reinforcements in the territory. We are the garrison to which *other* forts look for reinforcements. There can be no help forthcoming. Here we must fight and, if our Saviour so ordains it, here we must die.'

There was no moving him, so I excused myself, saying I must write up events - his version - for the *Times* and therefore posterity. Perhaps the victorious Rebels would see the *Times* received it. I had one last shot.

'Fear not, Major,' I paused as I was going through the door. 'I will explain that you fought to the death for the flag, and if in so doing you sacrificed the wounded, the mothers and their young children, well that's a price you deemed worth paying.'

I left him gaping. You will see what I was getting at. This Major Lynde was the world's own born fool. Vain as a peacock, he had ambitions far above commanding a fort at the back of beyond, but he had sense enough to know that should he survive the Confederate attack, the newspapers, and therefore the public, would take a dim view of him sacrificing the wounded, women and children for a ragbag of wooden huts in the desert. Traitors or no, the Confederates were civilised white folk. Before they fired a shot, they would allow the Major to evacuate the non-combatants. Including, of course, any neutral newspaper correspondent who happened to be about the place.

I retired to my room, wondering what our gallant Major would do. Outside I could hear the sounds of urgent preparation as the troops strengthened their fortifications in expectation of attack. Why they hadn't thought to strengthen them the day the war began was a mystery to me, but one I was familiar with from my own army. Should I light out? I had a good horse, supplied by the General, and I could fill my saddlebags with fodder and water, ready to depart at the first whiff of danger, though devil knows where I could go. As a non-combatant the Rebels would have no reason to hold me. But flight wouldn't be necessary, surely? The more I pondered, the more I thought it unlikely it would come to a siege. Either the Confederates would move on and let us alone, or they would mount their artillery on the hills as Lynde feared, and demand surrender. For all his braggadocio, I was certain the Major wouldn't fight. His talk of dying round the flag was so much moonshine, designed to impress me so I'd give him a good write-up. I know a fellow poltroon when I meet one, he just didn't have my style. He'd surrender at the first sight of a Rebel gun, claiming concern for the non-combatants, which was why I'd dropped my heavy hint. Hold on though, would his officers overrule him? Despite the Major's whining about disloyalty and treason, they'd looked disgusted at his botched attack, and some of them seemed likely lads who knew what they were about. If they took over they might make a real fight of it, cannon and all. But no, they had their wives and children with them. They wouldn't risk their loved ones, so I'd be safe too. Unless... would the Rebels allow surrender? Surely they would, Southerners were civilised people. Dammit, I'd eaten with them.

As you can see, give me leisure to worry and I can drive myself crazy with conflicting theories. There was nothing I could do, really, except take a sleep and a meal, ensure my horse and saddlebags were ready for quick flight, and hope for the best. In the end, of course, all my imaginings were wrong.

'Evacuate the fort? Are you serious Major?'

I don't know by what tortuous train of logic he arrived at such a decision, but late evening, with nary a Rebel in sight, Lynde summoned his officers and his tame journalist to a portentous meeting. He had decided to evacuate the fort.

'I am deadly serious, Captain. I understand the Rebels have received reinforcements of one hundred men from Fort Bliss. Added to traitors from Mesilla, their force stands at over seven hundred men plus artillery. We can muster about three hundred fighting troops. I am convinced that if we remain in the fort we must be compelled to surrender, not to save ourselves but for the sake of the women and children. I do not trust the Rebels with their safekeeping. Our only hope of saving the command from capture is to reach some other military post. Therefore we shall evacuate the fort, and destroy such property as we cannot take with us. We will leave the fort at one o'clock tomorrow morning and make our way to Fort Stanton, the most practicable point to reach. I have no personal knowledge of the road, but it has been reported to me that one day's march will take us to Saint Augustine Springs, twenty miles away, where there is an abundance of water sufficient for all the command. The total distance to Fort Stanton is about one hundred and ten miles.'

You can imagine what I thought of this. We were to sneak out into the freezing desert night, trundle twenty miles with women, children and dozens of wounded to the first water stop while the hot desert sun arose, being shot at all the way by cock-a-hoop Rebels. The thing was madness.

Major Lynde stood firmly behind his desk, silently daring his officers to object. He didn't have long to wait.

'You say, Major, that the enemy have seven hundred men to our three hundred. But we also have a fort. Three hundred men can easily hold Fort Fillmore against three thousand Rebels.'

'Not when they rain cannon down on us from the hills, Captain McNally. Now does anyone have anything useful to say?'

They didn't, of course. Major Lynde had already decided to evacuate the fort, and as commander he could not be gainsaid. The order went out to load up our wagons, buggies and ambulances with military and personal supplies and materials, and destroy everything that we could not carry with us. This last instruction caused mayhem. Soldiers began setting alight to buildings and stores with people still in them, causing much ribaldry as the inmates raced out through the flames cursing those who started the fires. The black smoke from the burning buildings drifted high up into the skies, alerting the Confederates in nearby Mesilla that something was up. Meanwhile, unbeknown to the officers (and me, luckily for what was left of my peace of mind), when burning the camp hospital, some soldiers took advantage of the confusion to steal large amounts of a particular medical supply, which they shared liberally around the camp. When we were finally assembled, ready to depart for a long march through the desert, about half the men had their water bottles secretly filled with medicinal whiskey.

At one o'clock in the morning, the entire garrison, including the wives and children, many wounded and sick soldiers, and your loyal correspondent, evacuated Fort Fillmore, travelling along the road to Fort Stanton, more than one hundred and fifty miles (not 110, as the Major thought) to the northeast. Captain Gibbs, with three companies of horse, manned the rearguard, some way behind the main column to protect us from Confederate ambush.

I cursed all brothels, swearing I would never cross the threshold of a one again, steadied my horse and cradled my gun for comfort. Wrapped up against the freezing desert night, I rode at the head of the column with Lynde and the senior officers, always the safest place.

The worst of it was, with Fort Stanton and safety so many miles off, I couldn't even plead a pressing newspaper deadline or an urgent dental appointment, and spur my horse up and away, leaving them to look after themselves. I had learnt from the officers in the fort that Washington did not take the war in the far west seriously, and were recalling U.S. regiments east to shore up their armies there. With Uncle Sam looking the other way, this left the road clear for Indians and Mexican bandits to let their natural greed and blood lust come to the fore, and they stalked the land in huge numbers, raiding and pillaging to their hearts' content. I daren't risk travelling alone, and must cling fast to Major Lynde and trust that whoever else was picked off by pursuing Confederate soldiers, it wouldn't be me.

We got off to a good start. To my surprise the Rebels did not contest our leaving, and the column made solid progress throughout the cold starry night. It was not until daybreak that our troubles began. As the mercury rose, and the sun shone high in the sky, our soldiers began to flag under the dry, desert heat. Little attempt was made to maintain discipline and soldiers began to drop their arms and equipment, and soon there was a long trail of debris stretching into the distance behind us. About six miles short of San Augustine Springs, we came across a sharp hill leading up to a pass in the Organ Mountains. This was too much for many of our troopers as they began to suffer the effects of intense heat and thirst with many men falling out and unable to continue.

Eventually Major Lynde called a halt. We could advance no further without water, he decided, so he gathered a mounted force to set off for the Springs in order to return with water supplies. This was one detail I wanted to avoid, so I cantered casually back to the wagons to help the invalids in the ambulances. The Major and his party departed on their errand, so I found a shady spot behind a wagon and watered my horse from my own supplies and had a much needed gurgle myself.

Up until now all had been quiet in the rear, but suddenly we heard sporadic firing perhaps a couple of miles back, and my heart began to beat the polka. Serves me right, says you, for not helping collect water supplies, but I hadn't asked to be here. Twern't my war. It looked as though we might come under attack from Confederates any time soon. Should I stay? The firing was nearer now. Our rearguard was crumbling, by the sound of it, and we were leaderless and disorganised. I led my horse to the back of our column to see what kind of show we could put up should we be attacked. I soon found out. There were no officers in sight, debris and discarded guns everywhere, no order whatsoever, and I noticed something strange about our troops' behaviour. Many of them were raving, or lying on the sandy ground in a stupor, and I saw one who had opened a vein and was drinking his own blood. A sickening suspicion leapt to my mind. I picked up a discarded water bottle. One sniff and all became clear. They were drunk.

Time to go. In a funk, I galloped back up to the front of the column, just as our great leader returned, without water and without most of the riders he had set out with. It seems he was suffering from the heat and could ride no further. He had sent the rest on and returned with a small escort. Before I could say or do anything, and by God I had no idea what I could say or do, a lieutenant appeared from the column and reported that large numbers of our infantry had become totally overcome by sunstroke. Well I could have told him that. Suddenly a galloper pulls up, all dash and daring, from Captain Gibbs, reporting that eight companies of Rebel riders, supported by artillery and a large force of infantry, were approaching our rear guard.

'We must rally our men,' cries the lieutenant, 'lest they tear us apart.'

Lynde, curse him, was ready to make a fight of it.

'Sound the Call to Arms,' he roared, and the bugler belted out the discordant notes. Officers and men scurried in all directions and when order was restored we found that we could only muster at most one hundred men in any fit state to fight. Captain Gibbs himself now thundered alongside, his cavalrymen raising dust waist high, with the news that our rear guard had been driven on to the main column and the Rebels had captured three of our four remaining howitzers.

This shocked me out of my paralysis. To fight was certain death. I couldn't flee alone into the desert, so there was only one thing to do. The thing we should have done back at Fort Fillmore and saved ourselves this stroll in the sunshine. I rapidly dismounted and barged through the milling throng surrounding our leader and confronted him face-to-face.

'Surrender Major,' thank providence I found the right words. 'Save the women and children.'

He goggled at my sudden appearance, but shook his head determinedly.

'Honour demands we fight. I won't entrust our womenfolk to a pack of Rebels. I will stand and fight as a soldier.'

'And go down as the man who condemned the womenfolk, children and, aye, our wounded, to certain death?' I leaned forward, shouting in his ear above the clamour of men, horses and screaming children, barely visible in the rising dust-cloud as men circled the wagons in a pathetic attempt at a defence. 'Listen Major,' I bellowed, 'if we fight to the death history will blame you for losing the garrison. Let us live to fight another day and I will see the world knows the truth; that you acted properly at all times and any failings here were due to traitors in your ranks.'

That did it. Death and shame, or life and credit. It would take a Wellington to refuse, and had our hero been a Wellington we should not have been in this position to start with.

By now we could see the Confederates forming on the plateau a quarter of a mile in our rear. Straightening his back, Lynde strode over to the knot of officers directing the wagons.

'Lieutenant Brooks, ride out to the Rebels and ask them what terms they require for our surrender. Captain

McNally, burn the regimental colours.'

The other officers protested violently at this. The fools wanted to fight on to certain destruction, but Lieutenant Brooks knew his duty, sound chap. Without hesitation he mounted his horse and made for the Rebel position.

Thank the Lord, with his officers circling him and arguing that honour demanded they must fight, Major Lynde stuck to his guns for the first time since I'd had the misfortune to cross his path. Short and sweet, he put sense before futile heroics, and surrendered.

As the victorious Confederates moved in on the column and disarmed its defenders - treating us with decency and respect by the way, giving us water and suchlike - I knew one thing now that I hadn't known back in California.

The Confederates could fight.

Chapter eight

You will recognise the position British Tommy now found himself in. Here was I, in the hands of an enemy, helpless but with a possible way out. The letter in the lining of my coat, the General's missive to the Southern officers, might be the ace to set me free, and back on my way to home and beauty. But dare I play it? This was my dilemma as the victorious Rebels herded the defeated Yankees into line, offering assistance where needed, while their commander decided what to do with them. What, I wondered, would become of us, and more to the point, what would become of British Tommy?

I didn't have long to find out. Word came down the line that the prisoners were to be disarmed and relieved of their equipment (including, claimed the Yanks, $17,000 in Federal drafts. The Rebels said they only took $9,500, so someone must have had sticky fingers), marched to a place called Las Cruces a few miles away and there given parole. They would issue us with just fifty of their oldest muskets to protect ourselves against the Indians, and compel us to tramp northeast across the desert to Santa Fé, then on to Fort Union or Fort Wise in Colorado, a distance of more than three hundred miles.

The mere thought of trudging through hundreds of miles of badlands without proper protection, to say nothing of food and water, set my bowels a'gallop once more. I'd experience of such flights, and I knew that they would be lucky if one in ten got through alive. Too long odds for me. There was nothing for it. Girding my goolies, I wandered away casually from the Union officers and made my way towards the wagons where a couple of Confederate guards were casually watching us while taking a smoke.

'Whut kin we do fer you, Sir?' asks one politely. Well, I was in civilian togs and they were unsure of my standing.

'Your pardon, gentlemen,' says I in my best military manner. 'I need to speak urgently to your commanding officer on a matter of great import.'

'Great what? And who are ye?'

'I am a British citizen. I am not a member of this Yankee outfit. And I respectfully request an interview with your commanding officer.'

'The Colonel's busy,' laughs one. 'But we'll go fetch us an officer. See if'n he'll do.'

The upshot was that they produced a young Captain, who learning that I was English and a civilian, conducted me away from the other prisoners behind one of the wagons.

'Now, Sir, what do you wish to see our commander for?'

'I have a letter for him.'

'You do? Let's see it.'

I gave him my coat, which I had retrieved from my saddle before the Confederates confiscated our Yankee horses. They were, insisted one with a guffaw, Rebel nags now.

'It is in the lining. Please cut it carefully.'

The Captain obliged, snorting as he reached into the lining and produced the sealed letter. He peered curiously at the seal - a five-pointed star - then whistled up a couple of Rebel troopers.

'Keep a' holt of him until I return.'

Off he sauntered to see the commanding officer, while I waited tremulously, hoping that the General's letter would have the desired effect. It did. Ten minutes later the Captain returned at a trot.

'Our Colonel Baylor wants to see you. Come with me.'

He led me through the ranks of the Rebels up to a tent which was obviously field headquarters. Pausing to announce my arrival, he ushered me in.

Before me on a makeshift stool sat a black-avised stocky man who looked like he was in his early forties. He bore a great resemblance to Sam Grant who I met later on, both in features and steely determination. Balding, he'd grown tufts of hair over his ears with a dark beard and moustaches covering most of his face. But like Grant it was his eyes which held the attention. Sharp, clear and direct, they turned on me and on the instant I knew; here's another one of 'em. I was right, too. Had I known what Lieutenant Colonel John R. Baylor, C. S. Army, was capable of, I'd have turned tail on the spot and taken my chances with a three hundred mile walk through the desert.

Mind you, he was civil enough to me.

'Sit down... Colonel,' he began.

So the General had written down my rank, I thought for a wonder. I had not read the letter, you understand. Showing a typically Southern sense of the dramatic, the General placed it under seal without my knowledge of its contents, lest I was taken prisoner. Under the severest interrogation I could deny being aware it was in my coat lining and could not break under torture. I didn't think much of this at the time, but on reflection it made perfect sense, so I resisted the temptation to break the seal myself. I daresay he signed it in blood with skull and crossbones. What else, I wondered, had the General said about me?

'Let me understand this,' says Baylor. 'You are a British army officer acting as an agent for the Confederacy. You have been sent by a certain organisation to contact members of the United States military who hail from the South or are believed to have Southern sympathies, make them known to each other and organise a takeover of the forts, and thereby the Territory of Arizona.' He paused, lips curling into a thin smile.

"You are behind the times Colonel. We control many of these forts already. Anyhow, it seems you are more than simply a British colonel. You are none other than Colonel Armstrong VC, senior intelligence officer, hero of Crimea and China, damn your eyes. You've met the Queen of England and she has bestowed a knighthood upon you.'

Sweet Jesu, the General had boosted up old Tom, hadn't he just? I knew he admired my glorious military record - that's all *he* knew - but was it necessary to broadcast it to his Southern sympathiser friends? Then it came to me; the General knew it was vital the sympathisers respect my political and military credentials, and jump when I tell 'em to. When I said take the forts, they needed to trust that I knew what I was about. My guts heaved as I thought what might have happened had I been fool enough to actually show it to them.

'Most impressive...' Colonel Baylor hesitated, studying the letter, while I sat mum. What happens now?

He let me stew a full minute, then carefully folded the letter, placed it in his side pocket and to my eternal relief, broke out in a broad grin.

'Well if that don't beat the band. A British officer, no less, an emissary for... well you know, coming out here from California to support the South against those no-account bluebelly bastards sticking their great Yankee noses into our way of life. Let me congratulate you Sir.' With that he leant forward, clasped my paw in both of his, and shook it till it nearly fell off.

'Why Colonel,' he growled amicably, 'you sure are a sight for sore eyes. I had no idea there were agents like you working for the South. And your Yankee friends here don't know who you really are?'

I nodded. 'I call myself George Jeffreys, newspaper correspondent for the London *Times*.'

He grunted approvingly. 'Then that's who you are... George. Doubtless your military whiskers are just for show. Now, I have a patrol about to return to Mesilla to let them know we have settled the Fort Fillmore garrison. You will travel with them and I will catch up with you in a day or two. You an' me have heaps to talk about.'

Gratified if puzzled at his welcome, I smiled solemnly, as though I had serious matters on my mind - I had too - thanked him warmly and stood by while he instructed one of his captains to fetch my horse and take me along with him to bear the glad tidings of victory to Mesilla.

'And don't let any of our prisoners spot him leaving, y'heah?'

With that, he dismissed me and turned back to his staff. As I crept out behind the tent with my Rebel Captain I heard Baylor talking to his subordinates.

'What, you mean they are too worn out to move..?'
#Note 6

I kicked my heels in Mesilla, waiting for Colonel Baylor to return, furrowing my brow deep enough to plant potatoes and wondering what I should do next. I took the opportunity to sew my George Jeffreys London *Times* introduction into my coat lining, while I reflected that things could have been much worse. Whatever the General had written in the letter to the Rebels certainly impressed Baylor, and his officers back in Mesilla couldn't have been more friendly. They treated me as a guest - and watched me carefully - when I could have been crawling through the desert with the rest of Lynde's beaten command.

I was not too concerned at the Colonel's parting shot that we had heaps to talk about. Most likely he wanted to pump me about the General, and how I came to be working for him. Well, that was easy enough. Having discharged my British military duties in China, and knowing that war between the American States was looming, I had rushed to San Francisco and offered my services to the South. Our plan to take California had failed due to circumstances beyond my control, so I had volunteered instead to stir up rebellion in New Mexico before returning to England to espouse the cause of the South there. He could thank me on behalf of the Confederacy and set me on my way. Question was, where to? Not back to Frisco, that much was certain. And I could hardly ask him for an escort to New York. Could I travel southeast? Maybe I could get a ship from Confederate New Orleans. But with war engulfing the land and the Southern ports possibly blockaded, would there be passenger ships sailing anywhere? It was all so uncertain, so in the end I gave up conjecturing. We'd just have to see what the Lord provided. As it panned out, the Lord got it right in the end, but he took his time about it.

Baylor didn't return for several days. After paroling the defeated Union garrison at Las Cruces as advertised, he learned of a Union force from Fort Buchanan in the vicinity and formed a defensive line near the village of Picacho, to repel attack. However, word reached the Union force from Federal-held Fort Craig telling them of the defeat of Major Lynde's command, and ordering them to burn up their transportation and supplies lest the Rebels capture them, then flee the Territory.

The loss of the garrison from Fort Fillmore sent shock waves through the whole region, causing the Federals to abandon Fort Stanton - so much for Lynde's safe haven - and much else besides, leaving the Indians and bandits to loot the remains and clearing the way for the Confederacy to annex all of New Mexico and Arizona. And the Confederate commander, John R. Baylor, reckoned he was just the man to do it.

He finally returned, heading a caravan of wagons full to bursting with captured Union supplies and equipment. His men, I noted, were buoyant, high-stepping and ragging each other - and their officers - good naturedly. A far cry from the sullen Union troops under Major Lynde's command. That's what victory does for you, of course.

They were singing a ditty about Dixie. Not the famous song so much loved by Lincoln which later became the anthem of the South, but a reflective little number pining for the ol' plantation. Sounded odd coming from Texans, but one of the fellows had a banjo and they fair crooned it out. I found it in one of my wife's music books the other day and put down part of it here:

I'se Gwine back to Dixie,
I'se Gwine no more to wander,
My heart's turned back to Dixie,
I can't stay here no longer;
I've left the old plantation,
My home and my relation,

128

My heart's turned back to Dixie,
And I must go.

Baylor had work to attend to, and I heard nothing from him during the day, but as the afternoon faded a lieutenant called at my quarters, presented his commander's compliments and requested me to do Colonel Baylor the honour of attending dinner at his quarters that night. Naturally I said yes and in due course found myself ushered into his presence.

'Good evening Colonel,' says he. 'Pleasure to see you again. Now I have been out chasing Yankees for weeks, so I deserve a break. Come on man, let's eat.'

To my surprise, when he practically manhandled me into his dining room I saw the table was laid out only for two. I had expected all the off-duty officers would be there, plus hopefully a gaggle of the town's ladies (must keep friendly with the civilians, you know). It was an honour, I suppose, to be considered important enough to dine alone with the chief. On the other hand, what was so important about me? I felt a twinge at the base of my spine, warning me of danger ahead. My mission to stir up rebellion and take the forts was receipted and filed, thanks to this enterprising chap now breaking open a bottle and producing two glasses, helped in no small degree by the ass Lynde. All I wanted from Baylor now was a handshake for services almost rendered and an escort to a safe port.

'A toast, Colonel Armstrong. To the new Confederate States of America.'

I hear-heared appropriately, and downed the spirits. Whiskey.

'Colonel, let me once more thank you on behalf of the Army of Texas, and the whole South. As I said the other day, I had no idea we were employing such undercover agents as your good self.'

'Ah well... you know, it just fell into my lap, d'ye see...'

He dished out the food from its central plate. Roast chicken with trimmings.

'Tell me Colonel,' says he through a mouthful, 'how came you to be working for our... organisation?'

This brought me up with a start. What organisation? He'd referred to it before, I now recalled, in his tent when Lynde's bluecoats had hollered uncle, but it hadn't sunk in. So far as I knew, the General was pretty much a freelance, concocting his lame-brained schemes for taking California and stirring up the west all on his lonesome. My spine twinged again, causing the chicken to dry in my mouth.

'Well Colonel, it happened like this.' I went into my prepared account, claiming I had rushed to the South's aid after dealing with the Chinks and so forth, and enlisted with the General. I told him I was travelling back to England to campaign for the Southern cause, but stopped by Fort Fillmore en-route to sign up the Southern sympathisers so they could stir rebellion in Arizona and New Mexico. He whistled appreciatively as I got to the most important part. Now that he had practically captured the Territory single handed, I added toady-like, there was nothing to keep me.

'My mission here is over,' I concluded, 'thanks to you and your sterling fellows, so at your convenience I would like to go back east and board a ship to England, where I will do my utmost to bring Britain round to the South's side. Perhaps next time you send a party in that direction I might be allowed to join them...?'

His eyes bore into me like a snake at a mouse.

'Of course Colonel... in good time.'

The hairs on my neck tingled anxiously.

'You say that we have control of Arizona. Well, we have taken several forts, and cleared the Yankees out of the Territory for the time being, but we are a long way from establishing a new Confederate State. Our aim is to claim Arizona for the Confederacy. We want Arizona to comprise that portion of New Mexico lying south of the thirty-fourth parallel of north latitude, all the way west past the Colorado River to California.' He tore off some more chicken while I wondered what this was leading up to.

130

'Fact is, we don't have the resources to police the Territory and fight the Yankees at the same time.'

I asked him what policing the Territory involved.

'You see Colonel, the Yankee presence here kept the Indians and foreign bandits at bay. They had the devil of a job, but they kept some semblance of order. With the South seceding, Lincoln's Black Republicans in Washington are ordering troops back east to threaten our lands there, leaving the good folk of Arizona ripe for the plucking. With the Yankees departing, the tribes have broken out from the reservations, those that were in them in the first place, and bandits from Mexico have started plundering the settlements. We must put a stop to that, and we will. But this is not just a military affair, it is a political one. The social and political condition of Arizona is presently little short of general anarchy, and the people are destitute of law, order, and protection. Well Colonel, we are the government now. We must set up political and legal institutions, enforce law and order and civilise these lands for the benefit and future of the Confederacy.'

'Well yes... we mustn't have anarchy, must we? It's a tough job, but one I am convinced you and your splendid Texans can handle, and when I am back in England you may be sure I shall give you full credit...'

'We fear no pack of Indians nor Mexicans,' he roared, slamming his glass down on the table while his eyes bore into me. I shuddered at the force behind them. 'Your pardon, Colonel,' he simmered down to my relief. 'When I think what those red savages have done to God-fearing white folk...' I gathered he wasn't what Kit Carson called *soft on the redskins*. '...but no matter. My point is that chasing about the Territory avenging Indian outrages and hanging Mexicans will not gain us the hearts and minds of the people, nor cement the notion of Arizona as a permanent Confederate State.' He paused and refilled our glasses. 'Only law and order will do that. Your health Sir.'

We drank to my health, sincerely on my part, while I prayed that this lecture was merely his idea of polite dinner talk. Somehow I doubted it.

'This is where you come in.'

I spluttered into my glass, and threw an accusing glance at the whiskey bottle.

'Strong drinking liquor you Texans favour, Colonel. Beg pardon, what were you saying?'

He rose and strode towards the door. Peering out, he satisfied himself we were not being eavesdropped, and returned to the table.

'God has sent you to me.' He chuckled while electric bolts shot through my spine. 'Or more prosaically, in case you are not a religious man, you have been sent to me by the Knights of the Golden Circle.'

It is difficult to reel while sitting down, but I gave a fair imitation. Those blasted Knights again! How did he mean they sent me to him? I hadn't even met one, not officially anyhow.

'Your letter explains it all. As well as an accomplished military man, you are schooled in political intelligence. This includes administration, I'm sure. And we both know your coming to Arizona was not just to awaken our Southern brethren and help them take the Territory.' He smirked knowingly, like a priest after confession. 'I congratulate you on your reticence, by the way. You did not even hint at the true nature of your mission. That shows political savvy.'

I stared at the man. What in Hell *was* my true mission then?

'You can drop the reticence now, Colonel. Cards on the table.' He took a pull from his glass. Mine was empty already.

'Your letter from the General explains that your real talent, your true mission here after taking the Territory, is to help the new Confederate Governor set up a system of administration to permanently establish Confederate rule.'

If the General had walked in now I would have spat in his eye. So that was his true plan. No wonder he counselled against my reading his confounded letter. He knew I wished to travel east at full speed, to enlist in the Southern armies, as he thought. Now he'd duped me into applying for the job of Governor's aide-de-camp and unless my poltroon's instinct was sadly out of kilter, I had a shrewd idea who the first Confederate Governor of Arizona was going to be. Mistaking my look of horror for once of caution, Baylor sought to allay my fears.

'You need have no concern.' He lowered his voice. 'I too am a member of that esteemed organisation. So are many of my officers.'

Texas! Of course, that's where these crazed Knights were at their strongest. I should have known. He sat there beaming at me now like a turkey on twelfth night as I struggled to find words. Well, what could I say? Thanks to the General's lying letter, Baylor obviously believed that I had volunteered to offer my services to the Governor to help set up his fledgling State. I could hardly reply that I had changed my mind, if you please, and may I have an escort to the nearest salt-water port?

'I intend, Colonel, to proclaim myself temporary military Governor of the Territory of Arizona, until such time as Congress may provide civilian governance.' He leaned forward and I leaned back a bit. 'I am a soldier, Colonel. I have some experience of law, and a little business management, but I cannot pretend I know how to set up an administration to run a Territory. I confess I have been at a loss to know how to proceed. On setting out to take Arizona I sent word to the Knights of my predicament. Clearing out the Yankees is one thing, establishing the rule of law - Confederate law - is a horse of a different colour.' He paused and ran his finger around the top of his glass. I half expected a genie to appear, then realised I was present already. 'Word reached the General, and he did not let us down.'

Ye gods, it was all some fiendish conspiracy. My respect for the confounded Knights of the Golden Circle rose, along with the gorge in my throat. I could see it now sure as sin. The General knew of the Texas expedition into Arizona and sent me there first to help it succeed by rousing the Southern sympathisers within the forts. Then when the Rebels took over, why, Tommy the political advisor was on hand to collect the taxes, clean the drains and generally run the administration while Colonel blasted Baylor took all the plaudits as Governor.

And not a thing to be done about it. Baylor didn't look the kind of man who would take no for an answer. As military Governor, he would have power of life and death, and would probably regard refusal to serve as treason. And if I accepted *pro tem*, as it were, and cast off while he was busy out governing, I would find his Knights, who plainly had tentacles everywhere, joining the great movement of North Americans who wished to have a word with me. Besides, I was miles from anywhere and effectively a prisoner in this two-bit town.

I snapped out of my reverie as I realised Colonel Baylor was still talking at me.

'So, Colonel Armstrong, tomorrow I intend to proclaim myself Governor of the Confederate Territory of Arizona, and I want you, behind the scenes, to be my political advisor.' Smiling determinedly, he stretched out his hand. 'Do you accept my proposal?'

Plainly I couldn't refuse, so that meant I must accept. Meeting his handshake sinew for sinew, I nodded manically and looked towards the bottle.

'Colonel Baylor, in my country we settle matters over a glass. I have the honour to accept your generous and flattering proposal. Let us drink to a rewarding partnership.'

This is how your loyal correspondent became the political brains behind the Confederate Territory of Arizona. You will scarcely credit it, but as I lay on my cot in a house commandeered by the new Governor (starting tomorrow), I concluded that things had not fallen out too badly after all.

You see, I did not expect this civil war to last any length of time. Nor, will I say in my defence, did Lincoln or anyone else, bar Jeff Davis and a few far-seeing U.S. senators. I had seen the Northern troops in action, if you can call it that, and it was clear they would not risk their lives to free the Negroes. Nor did they care overmuch about States Rights, whatever those were. A few more skirmishes like Fort Fillmore and the Yankees would let the South go its own way. They were two countries after all, and with peace between them the business of making a profit could resume. Northern entrepreneurs could buy up all the cotton they wanted, turning a blind eye to how it was produced in the fields. Southern gentlefolk could buy manufactured goods in return, and turn a blind eye to how they were produced in the factories, and everyone, bar the slaves and poor whites, could live happily ever after.

With a short war in the offing, all I need do was advise Baylor on how to set up a civilian administration - child's play - and keep my head down until peace broke out once more. Meanwhile I could enjoy whatever perks came my way as the Governor's chief bottle washer and permit issuer. Once the State was established there would be perks aplenty. My imagination flew. Want to set up a brothel but don't have a licence? Why, go see Chief Administrator Tommy, and he will give you the State's blessing in return for a fair price; say ten percent of the profits plus regular inspection of the goods. Bismillah! By the time I'd finished, Arizona would put Sodom and Gomorra to shame.

Alas, I could never claim the credit, or the cash. Baylor and I agreed that the less anyone knew of a British army officer involved in American politics, the better. Publicly I would remain *Times* Correspondent George Jeffreys, following the fortunes of the new Territory for my readers. Meanwhile I'd give all my political advice offstage. Still, it meant I could live relatively well for a few months, then take my leave - southeast to New Orleans and a ship home for preference - with Baylor's best wishes. You can never have too many powerful friends, and I could see this John R. Baylor becoming the second president of the Confederate States. If I couldn't make something out of a personal friendship with such a figure, I was not the man I thought I was.

So on August first, 1861, Baylor declared himself Governor of the Territory of Arizona, if you please. I looked it up t'other day and the important part reads as follows.

"The social and political condition of Arizona being little short of general anarchy, and the people being literally destitute of law, order, and protection, the said Territory, from the date hereof, is hereby declared temporarily organized as a military government until such time as Congress may otherwise provide."

Naturally, he said a lot more. I was at the inauguration, near the back of the stage taking notes.

'I, John R. Baylor, Lieutenant-Colonel, commanding the Confederate Army in the Territory of Arizona,' he bellowed at the good folk of Mesilla, 'do hereby take possession of said Territory in the name and behalf of the Confederate States of America.' So there. He went on to specify the shape of his administration in the new Territory. This was where I had to help him, for in the matter of day-to-day administration he was clueless.

'We will keep the laws of the old U.S. Territory of New Mexico unchanged,' says he, 'save where they clash with the laws of the Confederate States. In particular, we guarantee the right of all free men to hold slaves, and will maintain this guarantee for all time.'

This saved me countless hours pouring over the law books, trying to conjure up a functioning Constitution out of a hat. Baylor wanted district and probate courts at Mesilla and Tucson, and on my prompting appointed a raft of territorial pecksniffs to run the new administration. Down the pecking order from Baylor came Secretary of the Territory, Attorney General, Treasurer and Territorial Marshal. Junior positions to follow.

He finally wrapped up to thunderous applause. 'The capital of the Territory will be here in Mesilla.'

We'd spent all day designing our New Jerusalem, so nothing would do but our leader must invite all the local bigwigs, plus our off-duty officers, to an impromptu dinner in Mesilla town hall. There he regaled us all with speeches commemorating this, the first new Confederate Territory, soon to become the first natural born Confederate State of America, or he would know the reason why. I joined in the fun, and the booze, and roared him on with three cheers and a tiger.

'Come on you fellows, t'aint every day you get to see the launching of a new State. And the first Rebel one, to boot. So let's hear it for our new Governor and leader of this new, free, democratic Territory. Sing up!'

And didn't they just? The evening was a great success, and the two of us topped it off with a nightcap back at his rooms. He was affability itself now, thanking me profusely for my help in setting out his Territory's Constitution, while I pooh pooh'd his thanks and said t'was nothing really, all in a day's work don'tcha know. We chatted for a quite some time, first about how his Knights of the Golden bollix would lead the South on to greater glory and a South American empire, then eventually on to my own military record. He took great interest in my Afghan and Indian exploits, especially when I described sneaking through enemy lines several times dressed as a native. I confess that, high flown with whiskey, I may have given him the impression I saved India for the British practically on my own, but well, I'd been behind the scenes all day, pretending to be a mere newspaperman, so it was good to remind the new Governor of my past heroics. And safe. For all I need do now was sit back in my office as supplied by the Confederate Territory of Arizona, giving advice to Governor Baylor until peace was declared or until he gave me an escort to a safe port. This being the case, I gave my tongue free rein. Fool that I was.

Chapter Nine

With the Yankee forces scattered, Baylor's immediate concern was bringing law and order to the Territory. This meant taming the Apache Indians, who had taken advantage of the White Man's conflict to don the war paint and flood down from the hills to murder, scalp and pillage. Well good luck in sorting *them* out, thinks I. Off you go, patrolling the vast, deathly spaces of Arizona and I'll cheer you on from my office window.

T'weren't just the Apaches, neither. Thieves and bandits lurking along the Mexican border could steal, plunder and intimidate to their hearts' content, for our Rebel forces were far too thin on the ground to deter all but the most timid.

Fortunately, the newly-ordained Confederate citizens did not hold this against their self-appointed Governor. Just the opposite, in fact. The departure of the Union troops from the Territory stirred up the populace against the cowardly Yankees who had deserted them first chance they got. Resentment set in among the settlers in and around Tucson. That summer they held a mass meeting and voted to make Arizona a part of the Confederacy, and even elected a delegate from the Territory of Arizona to the Confederate States Congress. So with peace likely to break out soon, or failing that, Baylor not needing my services much longer, all looked plain sailing for good old British Tommy.

The waters weren't so calm for Baylor. The people looked to him to establish law and order p.d.q, not appreciating that he had scarce resources to deliver. Baylor had just 450 men at La Mesilla and Fort Bliss with which to control the whole vast Territory. On my urging, he conscripted the local militia companies, adding about 200 more men to his strength. With this skeleton force he sought to counter raids by Mexican bandits from Sonora and attacks by marauding Apaches just about anywhere, not to say enforcing civil law in a land where side arms were as common as clap.

Encouraged by the departure of the Yankees, the Apaches imagined that it was their doing, and let rip in an attempt to drive the Whites forever from their lands. They ambushed wagon trains and butchered their occupants; slaughtered the miners in their mines and burnt ranches, and even assailed the large settlements of Tubac, Tucson, and Pinos Altos. The entire Territory was in a state of panic and chaos, and all looked to Governor Baylor and the Confederate Army for their salvation.

Baylor certainly had his work cut out, but like an ass I did not think it was any concern of mine. My job was to sit comfortably in my office and collate reports of civil matters such as minor property disputes, licences for mines, and collecting taxes, though we did precious little of that. I soon found out my error, and I set this warning down here for those who come later. Never, never, brag of your military exploits to a military man, especially one who is short of conscripts. It ain't safe.

I told you earlier that the Federals had evacuated Fort Stanton. Baylor sent a scout party of four Confederate soldiers to spy out the area surrounding it. The Apaches ambushed them, killing three. I was on hand when the survivor reported to Baylor at Fort Davis, where he had dragged me to check supplies, and I wished I'd been safe back at Mesilla.

'Killed you say? All three?'

'Yessir. They done chased us ten miles and only let up when they kilt the three of us.'

Baylor looked fit to be tied. I knew he detested the red race but I had not bargained for his virtuous rage at this attack on white men by those godless devils, as he called them.

'By all that's holy, raise their hand to our soldiers will they?' he turned to his lieutenant. 'Go chase them. Find their camp and wipe it out. Muster as many men as can ride right away, and get going. Now!'

He fairly bellowed at his lieutenant, who scurried off on his errand. Then he turned to me.

'We need every man, Colonel...' Something in his voice raised the hairs on my back.

'You must be pretty frustrated here, a man of action like yourself.' He grinned manically. 'Here's your chance to shake off the cobwebs and get back into the saddle. I know you've been itching to. I cannot spare many men from the garrison here, so I'll be obliged if you will accompany the party that's going out to do justice to them murderous savages that think they can fire on white men with impunity. Go saddle your horse, Colonel.' So help me, he clapped me on the back. He thought I'd be delighted.

This was desperate. I cudgelled my wits to think of a face-saving way to turn down his lunatic proposal, and came up with a deuced good one.

'Thank you Colonel, you are right. I'm not made for filling in forms and meeting citizens' delegations and... and so forth when there's killing to be done. But,' I frowned, as though in an inner turmoil, 'duty must come before pleasure. I am your political advisor, and in this capacity I must regretfully inform you that it will not do for a British officer masquerading as a newspaperman to ride to battle with soldiers of the Confederacy. Folk talk, and if my true identity were to be discovered it would cause an international incident. The Yankees would play it up, you may be sure.' I shot him a wry grin. 'A plague on politics.' I limbered up my sword arm. 'And I haven't had a good set to since China.'

I thought that would fox him, and it did for a moment. His face fell, then brightened as he found a way to drop me in the soup without risking political complication, rot him.

'But Colonel, there is no need to fear disclosure as a British officer. You have a great talent for disguise, remember?' He lowered his voice and came over all confidential. 'This is what we'll do.'

Thirty minutes later, loafers about the fort saw fourteen Confederate soldiers trotting through the gates, accompanied by a Mexican guide. You will have guessed, no doubt, that the Mexican guide was poor Tommy, dolled up like a gaucho *par excellence*, a vaquero with his scarf wound up around his face and blanket covering his quaking form.

I couldn't defy Baylor's order. Due to my idiotic bragging he imagined I was as mindlessly fearless as himself, eager to charge, guns blazing, into an Apache camp dealing White Man's justice to the savages. And with just fourteen soldiers. That's all the garrison could spare, its troops being fully occupied trying to control the huge Territory. I could have wept at my misfortune, but there was nothing for it but to ride alongside the lieutenant and make helpful suggestions as to where the Apaches' camp might be. If I had my way we would be searching for it still.

No such luck. Our party contained several expert trackers of the Kit Carson vintage, and in no time we were on the Apaches' trail.

'How many of them do you suppose there are?' says I coolly.

'Fifteen, mebbe twenty. They cannot be far ahead of us, the trail is fresh.'

Lord knows how he worked out the freshness of the trail, but experienced trackers can do this, you know. Kit Carson could probably have told us their birthdays and shoe sizes too.

We camped out briefly that night, and in the morning resumed our chase. Hours passed, and as the morning drew to a close our leading scout reined in his horse and galloped back towards us.

'Apache village ahead, just over the ridge, Lieutenant,' he reported, as my bowels tightened into my stomach.

'Right.' He pointed to a nearby copse. 'We'll leave the horses in there, then dismount an' go forward on foot. Mr. Jeffreys,' he turned to me. 'We're gonna circle the village an' take them from two sides. I want you to stay here an' guard the horses. You got your rifle. If'n things go awry we may have to retreat in a hurry so I want you to cover us and be ready for anything.'

Relief surged through me like a slug of rotgut. The lieutenant was unaware of my reputation as valiant Tommy, and knew me only as a newspaperman, of little use in a mêlée and fit only for remounts. I would be spared this insane attack and have fifteen horses alongside. We wouldn't need all of them for the return journey, that was certain. If the fools were going to attack an Apache village we might need just one.

Looking grim, as though I had hoped to lead the charge like Cardigan, I saluted obediently and we all cantered to the safety of the trees. There we dismounted and I shook the lieutenant's hand and wished him and his fellow idiots good hunting. Not one man raised any objection to the suicidal folly of attacking an Apache village with just fourteen men. Off they went over the hill towards the village as though on peacetime manoeuvres, while I pointed the horses in the right direction and awaited developments. They were not long in coming. The horizon shimmered in the desert sun through an uneasy silence broken only by the occasional caw caw of scavenger birds. Oh Jesu, thinks I, here it comes, any time now.

A volley of shots rent the air asunder, followed immediately by shrieks and shouts from the surprised Indians. Apache are lazy buggers when off duty, and seldom keep lookout, sensibly reckoning that nobody in their right mind would dream of attacking them. The volleys were joined by random crack-cracking in reply, accompanied by whoops and yells, as the 'Pash got their second wind. The discordant clatter mingled into one great cacophony of noise; guns, screams, cries and whoops and all sense of peace and order gone. My heart was thumping like a steam hammer as I steadied the horses and watched anxiously for signs of yelping Indians.

All my instincts screamed this was no place to linger, but I daren't obey them and flee, as the Rebel survivors, supposing there were any, would tell the tale. Even if the entire attacking force was wiped out, the Indians themselves, having no comprehension of cowardice, would spread the word of the Mexican deserting his comrades in the heat of battle. Baylor would soon learn of it, and I knew him too well by now to doubt the reckoning. All I could do was hold my horse's bridle and stare anxiously at the ridge of the hill.

The volleys had stopped. A worrying development as it suggested our force was in disarray and firing independently. My fears were confirmed when two of our soldiers came running full pelt over the ridge, followed far too closely by a horde of 'Pash, whooping and whirling their slingshots. One fellow went down, and a mass of red devilry flung itself upon him. The leading soldier was less than half a furlong ahead of the pack as I, bleating in terror, loosed off a couple of rifle shots.

He nearly made it. I slapped a horse in his direction and made ready to mount my own as he reached the outskirts of the trees. By hellish bad luck he tripped, maybe on a tree root, and flew sprawling into a tree. He stumbled up quickly, but he'd lost time. An arrow caught him in the shoulder and he spun round and fell to the ground.

'Help me mister, for God's sake hold 'em off!' He cried out to me as he scrambled to his feet. Too late. The Indians were closing on him now, whooping triumphantly as they cornered their quarry. I fired once more at the mob with no effect that I could see, then at last came to my senses. Flinging my rifle away in terror I darted back to where my horse was loosely tethered and without ceremony leapt astride her, released her bridle and was off through the far side of the copse lickety-split. As I cleared the copse I could just hear the howls of the unfortunate trooper as the 'Pash caught up with him. I hope they killed him quickly.

The Apaches did not follow in pursuit. Perhaps because I was only a Mexican, and there was no kudos in killing me, but more likely because they found our horses, and would have a jolly afternoon arguing over who had won them. I made straight for Fort Davis, not stopping to rest, and arrived back exhausted in the early hours. Baylor was staying overnight so I roused him and still in my Mexican

attire gave my report like the last survivor from Troy.
#Note__7

'Dead? All of them? How many Indians were there?'

'We attacked their village, Sir. I warned against an all out attack but your lieutenant... well he was a brave man Colonel, as were his men. You can be proud of them all.'

Steadily I explained how we split into two groups and attacked simultaneously, our lieutenant guessing they didn't have many modern rifles so they wouldn't show fight. We found they had good weapons and bullets aplenty, probably stolen from the Yankees, and after initial success their numbers began to tell.

'Most of my detail was wiped out first, save two and myself, so I told them to make for the copse and I would cover 'em. I was pinning the Indians down when my rifle jammed, and the 'Pash leapt forward. Our men were trapped as other Indians had sneaked around the flank.' I stammered a little, manfully, then composed myself. 'I couldn't save them. The lieutenant and his men were caught in a defile on the other side. I managed to fix my gun and circled round to surprise their attackers. They turned on me and I shot three or four of them, but I ran out of bullets and had to retire. The redskins turned their fire back on our boys in grey. I guess they thought me only a Mexican and not worth risking their hides over. By the time I got around to their side the lieutenant and his men were all dead. Meanwhile the Indians had rushed the copse where we stowed our horses and overpowered our guard. I arrived as they were squabbling over the horses and by great luck my horse was standing alone. I smashed my rifle butt into the nearest Indian's face and leapt onto her. They chased me for a distance but I managed to shake 'em off. The rest you know.'

An honest account, you see, a modest soldier reporting back to his commanding officer.

Baylor hit the ceiling. I thought I'd seen him in a rage before, but that was just grace before meat. He slammed the table twice and swore vengeance on the

144

whole Indian race, vowing to wipe them off the face of the earth, starting with the local Apaches and working his way through the rest in alphabetical order, finishing with the Zuni tribe of New Mexico, or words to that end.

'You need more men Colonel,' says I, when he had simmered down to red hot.

'Deed I do,' he agreed. So resuming my role as political advisor, I penned a request in his name to General Van Dorn, his superior officer in Texas, and to the new Confederate capital at Richmond, pointing out the importance of holding Arizona against both Yankees and Indians.

"The Indians are exceedingly troublesome" I wrote. *"And the Sonora Mexicans are threatening to rob Tucson, and have robbed Tubac. I cannot, with the limited force under my command, keep the enemy"* meaning the Yankees *"in check and protect our citizens. I also believe that Yankee troops are on the way from California to reclaim the Territory for the Union."*

He signed the letter and I wondered if I might be allowed to take it, with an escort, back east. He grinned, humour restored now that he had plans to kill more Indians, and offered me a nightcap.

'Thanks Colonel,' says he, pouring the whiskey, 'I know you are willing to take the risk but I need you here. You did sterling work getting back the news of our terrible losses yesterday. Why, you are nearly as brave as a Texan and I cannot spare such a good man. Besides, I know you will be looking to kill a few more red savages before you leave. And by the gods I will be right there beside you. Now, go get some sleep. We'll talk again in the morning.'

Next day we returned to Mesilla. Baylor prosed incessantly all the way about his lack of resources and what he wanted to do to the Indians, but beyond convincing me he detested Indians even more than Yankees, nothing to the purpose. We sent off the letter that day, and several more in the weeks following, but were told the South could spare no men. All were needed elsewhere, Van Dorn wrote, so

Baylor must make do with his small force.

The weeks passed slowly. Baylor's scattered forces had several run-ins with the Apaches and the Navajo, who joined in the fun when they saw the White Man with his tits in the mangle, as well as with the Mexicans. This defiance of Confederate rule enraged Baylor yet further, if such a thing was possible, but fortunately I wasn't involved in any of them. I kept my head down in my office, poring over land applications, business disputes and similar nonsense.

Meanwhile, the Federals had finally noticed what was going on while their eyes were turned east, and they regrouped at U.S. Fort Craig, one hundred miles north of Mesilla. They boasted a force of approximately 2,000 men under the command of Colonel Edward R. S. Canby. I was there when Baylor got the news of the new Federal threat, and had the satisfaction of watching him practically bite the furniture in his rage.

'How in Hell am I supposed to run this Territory with a handful of men and barely enough guns to mount a salute?'

'Send back to Texas, Colonel. Not to Van Dorn. Get a reliable man to recruit a force of men along the lines of the Texas Rangers. These Arizona Rangers could police the Territory and hold off the Indians while your soldiers give the Yankees the right about.'

I was hoping he'd give me the job. Once in Texas, I'd continue south to Orleans and wave the west goodbye. He nodded in agreement.

'Not a bad idea, Colonel. Not bad at all. I'll look into it.' And that was as far as I got with that one. Worth a try.

Baylor sent reconnaissance patrols along the Rio Grande to spy out Fort Craig, and began a series of guerrilla actions against Yankee patrols who were sniffing about the Territory trying to gauge our strength. These were effective in that they prevented the Yankees discovering just how thinly stretched our Butternuts were.

Then came the news I had been dreading. Baylor received reports of a Yankee force about two hundred

146

strong heading towards Mesilla.

'Right Colonel, now's your chance to get in on some real fighting. I'm sending one hundred men under Captain Coopwood to engage the enemy before they can threaten the town. You will accompany them in your Mexican get-up and see how Texans fight.' His eyes were glistening at the thought of death and carnage and all I could do was grin enthusiastically. Aloud I hoped that if I was killed, not that death worried me, the Yankees wouldn't discover I was really a British officer.

'No chance of that, Colonel,' says he. 'The Yankee who can knock over the saviour of India ain't been born yet. You go along and enjoy yourself, y'heah?'

We rode towards a place called Canada Alamosa, some forty miles south of Fort Craig, where the Union forces were camped. Once again my luck held; I was kept back behind the fighting, taking notes for the *Times*, and had the doubtful pleasure of watching our Texans route a force twice their number. My opinion of the Union army fell still lower, and I wondered hopefully just how long this war could last. If the Yankees back east were as poor specimens as these fellows, old Abe would have trouble holding on to Washington, never mind bringing the errant States to heel.

Baylor laughed uproariously when he heard Captain Coopwood's account of the skirmish. Clapping his hands in glee, he poured us both a drink and we toasted his Texans.

'This'll teach them Yankee blowhards to keep their distance for a while, ain't that right Captain? You too Mr. Jeffreys?'

And it did. This and several more minor skirmishes (fought without my assistance, I'm glad to say) along the border between Confederate and Union-held land, kept the Yankees from discovering our shortage of men and prevented their cautious commander, Colonel Canby, from mounting any serious attacks on Confederate Territory.

With most of Baylor's force now busy keeping the Yankees at bay, the Apaches stepped up their raids on the settlements. At my suggestion he had recruited the local militias into the Confederate army, and they kept the lid on Indian outrages as best they could. But as autumn turned to winter it became clear that they were too few in number, and the Apaches attacks continued more or less unabated.

'How in Hades am I supposed to fight the Yankees and those red savages both?' he carped at me for the hundredth time. 'I've taken your advice, since you asked, and I'm scaring up a force of Arizona Rangers to take on the Indians, but not from Texas; right here. Lieutenant Hunter is in charge of recruitment and we are aiming to raise six companies.'

God knows where you'll find that many men, thinks I. In fact Hunter raised only one company and by the time he did, they had their hands full fighting a Union invasion from California. That's by the by, but it scuppered my slim hopes of getting sent away to Texas.

'Do you think that will be enough?' says I, for I knew as well as Baylor that our position was deteriorating. Our numbers were being slowly whittled down; as winter drew on, sickness became rife among our overworked troops and with no reinforcements in the offing it could only be a matter of time before our depleted force collapsed.

'I'm not croaking, Colonel,' I added hastily, 'but we must face facts. Without more men we cannot hold this Territory much longer.' Hinting at withdrawal, you see.

He didn't explode, as I had feared, but sighed and shrugged his shoulders.

'That's not croaking Colonel. You are doing your job, which is to face facts and offer your frank views without angling for my job. That's why you are so valuable to me; as a foreigner you have no axe to grind. I won't admit it in front of my officers, but you're right. We just don't have the numbers to quiet the Apaches and keep the Yankees away at one and the same time. The Yankees are gathering at Fort Craig and it won't be long 'till they get their nerve up for another go at driving us out. I don't doubt our men's courage, but without reinforcements we can't hold out forever.' He took a pull of his drink while my hopes soared.

"You won't like this, Colonel, but I may have to get you to draft a letter to General Van Dorn saying I am making preparations to abandon Mesilla and fall back into west Texas.'

At last! Wearing my stern expression I nodded mutely. I wasn't going to risk any word or look that might suggest I thought he should stay and fight it out for the glory of the South. He sighed once more, stood up tiredly and held out his hand.

'Thank you Colonel. I was unsure about this course of action, fearing it might be looked upon as cowardice. But with the bravest soldier in the British Army agreeing with me, why, I know it is the right course. Thank you.'

Baylor was as good as his word and after sending the letter back to Texas he began to recall his scattered troops back to Mesilla preparatory to withdrawal.

This didn't go down well with the local citizenry, for we couldn't hide our withdrawal preparations from them, and our troops found themselves spat at in the street and getting into fist-fights with outraged Rebel supporters who saw their withdrawal as desertion in the face of the enemy.

One man went too far. Robert P. Kelley, editor of the *Mesilla Times*, the biggest selling newspaper in Arizona, launched a campaign of abuse against Baylor and his men. I had met Kelley on a number of occasions in my capacity as London *Times* correspondent, and found him a pompous bore as so many newspaper men are, but a rough and ready frontiersman and no coward. It took guts to dare to lambaste a military Governor, least of all a man of his hands like this one. I wouldn't have done it, but then I am not a newspaper man. When I told Billy Russell the story, Billy said Kelley was right.

Baylor first ignored the insults, teeth clenched, but in December Kelley published a red-hot editorial slating Baylor personally. He all but denounced him as a traitor for ratting out on his responsibilities, hinting Baylor's actions were due not to military reality but to fear of the Yankees.

That did it. Rising from his sick bed, for he had joined the ranks of the ailing and looked like death warmed up, Baylor ordered me to accompany him to the miscreant's office. As a supposed newspaper man, he thought my presence would add weight to his demands for a printed and verbal apology.

'Where's Kelley,' bellows Baylor at the surprised clerk in the newspaper office.

'He's not here Sir,' cries the clerk. 'He's down the town.'

'Well tell him I'm seeking him, and he'd best show his face if'n he wants to keep it at the front of his head.'

I followed close behind as Baylor stomped down the main avenue, relishing this chance for mischief. Despite my predicament I had become bored with my jack-in-office employment, punctuated by bouts of terror, and looked forward to the explosion when Baylor caught up with his quarry. Baylor was the Governor, fighting mad despite being unwell, and looked about ready to set this town on its ears.

We found Kelley in Bull's store, gathering provisions.

'See here Kelley,' demands Baylor in a voice to shake the foundations, 'I want a word with you.'

Kelley, as I say, was no coward. A tall man of middle years, beardless with stocky black hair, he stood rock-steady as the other customers scampered aside (but kept near enough to see the fun). He looked into Baylor's pallid face, weighed the odds, and faced up to him.

'What can I do for you, Governor?' he sneered.

Baylor told him in unmistakable terms to lay off the insults and withdraw his suggestion that he was a coward, but instead of cowering and humbly apologising like any sane man would have done, Kelley laughed in Baylor's face.

'You say I suggested you are a coward, Governor? Only suggested? Well now...' Kelley puffed out his chest ready for action. 'Let me put things straight. You are a coward pure an' simple and t'aint no more to be said.'

Baylor roared and went for him but Kelley slipped nimbly aside and to my horror drew a huge bowie knife from his waistcoat. He rushed forward and Baylor sprang sideways, grabbing a rifle that was leaning handy against the wall. He swung it round, striking Kelley on the back of the head, knocking him face down. The Queensbury Rules were yet to be written, not that Baylor would have taken any notice of them, so he dived down on top of his opponent and tried to wrest the knife from him, rolling over together in the sawdust. Kelley fought back savagely. He was strong, and Baylor just risen from his sick bed, and as the fighting continued upright it was plain that Kelley was getting the upper hand,

'Drop the knife Kelley or you're a dead man,' cries Baylor, heaving heavily. Kelley grunted and made a lunge at Baylor's stomach. Baylor warded off the blow with his right arm, and stepping back a pace, drew his revolver with his left and shot Kelley through the neck.

This was enough entertainment for anybody, even for me. Ignoring the screams and sensation, Baylor put away his gun, tilted his hat, bade the shoppers a good day, and with me following, strode out of the store. Kelley died several days later, and people stopped objecting to the Confederate withdrawal.

I thought that nothing now would stop us departing Arizona and retreating to Texas. Once there I could join one of the many parties travelling east to safety. But I rejoiced too soon, for at the last, Arizona got its reinforcements.

They weren't however, for Baylor's command. In January, Brigadier General Henry Hopkins Sibley arrived at Mesilla with three regiments of Texas Cavalry calling themselves the Army of New Mexico, if you please. At first delighted, Baylor soon realised that Sibley had no intention of obeying him as Governor but planned to take over and run the military himself.

Sibley intended to attack the Federals at Fort Craig, and then march north to capture Albuquerque, Santa Fé, and the important post at Fort Union. Far from reinforcing Baylor, he ordered him to turn over half his men to help Sibley achieve his objectives. Baylor protested vehemently, but Sibley placated him in part by explaining that he would take on responsibility for keeping the Union forces at bay, leaving Baylor a free hand to take care of the Indians.

Smarting at what was effectively a demotion, Baylor threw himself wholeheartedly into pacifying the lands. His problem was that with his force halved, he still had not the men to clear up the Territory as he wished. He led many patrols himself, and it was after one such patrol, fruitless, that he confided his difficulties over dinner.

'Its frustrating, Colonel. We can't keep chasing these savages up and down the Territory forever, but what can we do?'

'Make peace?' says I, for I was tired of Arizona, tired of stewing in my office pretending to work, and tired of bloody Baylor. When taking up the job, I'd had visions of lustful women approaching me on their husbands' behalf for help with land licences, civilian disputes, permissions and suchlike. I intended to accommodate them Tommy style. Not a chance. The menfolk here guarded their women like gold-dust, chaperoning even the crinkliest old biddies like they were a combination of Lily Langtry and Lola Montez. I'd have had more luck in a convent.

'Make peace with them red murderers? Over my dead body.'

'Well pretend to. Offer them some of their land back as part of a treaty. When they turn up to discuss details, massacre the lot of 'em.'

Baylor's eyes widened like Moses when the sea parted.

'Why Colonel, that's a humdinger of a plan. I knew you were too valuable to send back east.'

Cursing myself for accidentally giving useful advice, I tried to retrieve the situation.

'Of course, if you massacre the Indians through trickery the Yankees will tell the world that the Confederates are a bunch of barbarians who butcher women and children just because of their skin colour. Jeff Davis and the Confederate government are sensitive about this issue and won't look kindly on anyone who brings this to the world's and especially England's attention.'

'Sensitive be damned. Nobody cares about a pack of savages, least of all the Confederate Government, nor the Yankee one neither. No Colonel, I know you English are squeamish about killing women and children, even these red animals, so I won't hold that against you. But your idea stands.'

'You know best Colonel' says I, 'but perhaps if you spared the children...' Not that I cared, you understand. They could wipe out the entire Indian nation and the French too, while they were about it, and it wouldn't spoil my dinner. But I had no wish to be known in London as Tommy Herod, slayer of the innocents. If word ever got out...

'That's it! Colonel you inspire me.' He tittered. 'We shall invite the Apaches to parley, then when they are in our grasp, wipe out the warriors and the women, but spare the children.'

Well that's something I suppose, thinks I. Doubt it will satisfy the liberals though. Then he spoilt it.

'We'll sell the children as slaves. Plenty of Mexican land owners aren't fussy what trash they buy, and use the money raised to defray the cost of the operation.'

By God he meant it. Well, I'm pretty callous, and slavery don't bother me, but Baylor would have Satan himself refusing him entrance to Hell in case he lowered the tone. Aloud, I took a line from Pontius Pilate, a kindred spirit if ever I met one, and acquiesced.

'You know best, Colonel. T'aint for me to say.'

He chuckled jovially at this. I had noticed in my time with him that the deeper the damnation, the merrier his moods.

'You English never cease to amaze. Squeamish over a few savages, but you got yourselves an empire. Seems like you're not always quite so soft when there's a buck to be made, eh Colonel?'

153

'Pass the bottle Colonel, there's a good chap.'

We got on well, really. Maybe had I his courage I would be as bad as he. Well, his extermination policy got him fired in the end, while the Confederacy rewarded me with a medal, which shows that villainy is not always its own reward.#Note 9

Sibley, meanwhile, was as susceptible as most to the prospect of getting a good write up in the newspapers. Baylor introduced me as George Jeffreys, *Times* correspondent, and Sibley professed delight in meeting such a distinguished newspaperman. I played along, partly because it was amusing to note that Baylor was resentful at having to share me with his new commander. Sibley asked me to write something about his mission to take New Mexico for the Confederacy. Had I known what a fool he was, and the trouble he would cause me, I'd have burnt my pencils and told him I couldn't read.

Chapter Ten

Sibley brought us news of the war back east.

'It is going well, gentleman,' he proclaimed. 'We whipped them at Manassas. The Yankees tried to march on Richmond, but we met them thirty miles south of Washington, turned them around and whipped the curs all the way back home with their tails between their legs.' He laughed. 'Gentlemen, I almost felt sorry for them. Our General Beauregard showed the Yankees what Southern fighting men can do. They thought they outnumbered us, but what they didn't allow for is that one Southerner is worth ten Yankees.'

Cheers from the officers. Sibley had asked me to be on hand so I could witness his plans for claiming New Mexico for the mighty Confederacy. His triumphs in the west would match their triumphs in the east.

I thought Sibley was exaggerating the Confederate victory at the battle of Manassas, which the Yankees call Bull Run, but he wasn't. Thirty-five thousand bluecoats marched out from Washington to advance on the Confederate capital of Richmond, 120 miles south, but they were stopped after thirty miles by a force of twenty thousand Rebels. More than stopped. The Union forces won the early exchanges and looked certain to carry the day, but on the very cusp of victory, Nine thousand Southern reinforcements arriving by train attacked the Union's right flank, broke it, and with the Confederates advancing on all fronts the Union soldiers panicked and turned tail faster than a bishop in a brothel when the peelers hove in sight.

Would you believe it, well-to-do Washington citizens, including at least one senator, crossed the Potomac river and drove to Manassas to watch the fight. As their troops fled in disorder, the panic-stricken citizens about-faced their carriages and fled alongside, causing the most unholy muddy jam as thousands on foot, horse, ambulance and carriage tried to cross the same mile-long stone bridge and fly back to Washington. Alarm spread as

155

the routed soldiers, many without their weapons, flooded Washington's streets shouting the Rebels were coming, so flee for your lives. Billy Russell was one of the spectators, reporting for the *Times*, and damn near got himself lynched in the street for telling the truth of the debacle. Had the Confederate forces advanced on the capital that day they would have captured it along with most of the U.S. Government, and won the war in the first over. Unluckily for the Confederacy (and me), they were too exhausted, or too timid say some, and the chance passed. Washington and the Union survived to fight another day.

This victory bucked up the South no end, and convinced them that recognition of the Confederacy was within their grasp. The North was demoralised, they believed, and had no stomach for fight. In fact it had the opposite effect. You see, until Manassas, nobody in the North thought the Rebels had any chance of victory. They were outnumbered three to one excluding slaves, had no navy to speak of, barely any industry, shortage of uniforms, shoes and just about everything else, and precious little ability to manufacture guns, bullets and the accoutrements of war. They can't run an army on cotton and baccy, the story ran, so we will stroll down to the sunny South and teach 'em the error of their ways. Such was their complacency, the North called for volunteers to sign up for just three months. Plenty of time, thought they, to show the South who's master.

What the North now realised, to their astonishment and dismay, was that the South meant business, and had proved it by whipping them on the field of battle. And worse, if anything; the South's victory gave hope that the Powers - Britain, Russia, France and Spain, mainly - would recognise them as a new country, break the blockade and maybe even join in on their side.

The North woke up. Orders went out to recruit 500,000 three-year volunteers, with another 500,000 to follow. The South, seeing the North mobilise, called for 400,000 volunteers themselves. All was set for a long, arduous war, and poor Tommy stuck right in the middle.

'We are winning in the east, now we are going to win in the west.'

I saw Baylor sit up at this. He was under the impression we were winning in the west already, thanks to him, and plainly resented this Johnny-come-lately turning up to grab the plaudits.

'My intention is to take New Mexico for the South. Our first objective is Fort Craig at Valverde, both to eliminate the garrison as a threat in our rear and to capture their supplies. With precious little supplies of our own, we must take the fort quickly. We have a force of about three thousand men, cannon and horse, which is more than enough to defeat anything the Yankees can put up.' He peered around the room at the officers, his own ones looking keen and Baylor's regulars fairly seething at his attitude, for he gave the impression that up until now the Confederate forces in Arizona had spent their time building sandcastles.

'Any questions?'

I nearly asked him what experience he had of besieging forts, but thought better of it. Everyone stayed silent.

'Good. Tomorrow we will cross the Rio Grande and move up the eastern side of the river to the ford near Valverde, north of Fort Craig, and cut off Union communications between the fort and their headquarters in Santa Fé. We'll place artillery on the heights overlooking the river and fort, then attack with all guns blazing.'

While the Federals lounge behind their walls whistling Dixie, devil a doubt. It always amuses me to see these tin-pot Caesars with their well thought-out military schemes, where all goes to plan and they win an easy paper victory. Nine times out of ten they come adrift when the enemy unsportingly refuses to lay down and cooperate. His next announcement was less amusing.

'We'll drive the bluecoats back to Colorado, boys, then its ho! for Santa Fé. By the way,' he smiled to show this bit was light-hearted. 'Be on your best behaviour you fellows. No cussing,' he sniggered pompously, 'because we will have a gentleman from the London *Times* marching with us to record the battle for his folks back home in England.'

We set off the following afternoon. About three thousand troops, cavalry and infantry, cannon, wagons and a small cattle herd for rations. Plus Tommy in his Mexican get-up, heart aflutter, keeping as close as he reasonably can to Sibley and his staff officers. I had spent most of the night trying to conjure up reasons to be excused boots, but couldn't think of anything convincing. Besides, I didn't get the chance to speak to Sibley again until we were off. Baylor stayed behind, by the way. There was no love lost between him and his new commander, and he claimed he couldn't march with Sibley as he had Indians to kill. Sibley didn't object, so I found myself with Sibley's command, comforting myself that once again they were unlikely to thrust me into the firing line. My job was to toady our great commander and let the world know of his tactical brilliance. The price men put on fame! He was another officer with political ambitions, of course. Which one hadn't? Only the best one, General Lee.

Meeting Lee was still to come. For the moment my chief concern was staying well clear of trouble while pretending to be as eager as Sibley to win the fight. As we neared the river crossing, Sibley found the first hiccup in his great plan.

We halted, sending our cavalry across to secure the ford.

'Hold the advance,' shouts Sibley. The order was hardly necessary as our men had stopped at the first sign of opposition. For facing us was a large body of bluecoats on the east bank disputing our progress.

They opened fire and sent their cavalry across the river, forcing our advance guard to withdraw rapidly. The Yankees had set up artillery, and began to rain shot down upon our troops. Under this lethal cover the Yankee infantry advanced to where our troops were sheltering in a cottonwood grove. Fierce hand-to-hand fighting broke out under the branches. We could hear the screams and cries alongside the popping of musketry and hammering of cannon. Sibley and his staff officers were dangerously close to the firing, which meant I was too. An artillery shell landed nearby, stirring our General to action.

'Back,' cries he, 'we must send out a force to outflank them.'

He ordered a detachment of infantry to occupy their left flank and a force of cavalrymen to threaten their right. Both ran into opposition and the battle now became widespread and disjointed. A suicidal direct attack across the ford by the Texas Lancers was repulsed by grapeshot, canister and musketry, most of our men dying in blood on the spot. It wasn't as crazy as Picket's charge, in which I got entangled later at Gettysburg, but bad enough for that. It reminded me in miniature of the Taiping storming the Imperial Chinese stronghold of Soochow heedless of casualties, and as the Yankees made to advance in return I inched my horse back from our little coterie of staff officers, ready to turn tail on the instant.

Our whole force save the rearguard was now engaged in combat along a wide stretch of river. Chaos reigned, with neither side appearing to have the advantage and no semblance of order whatever. So much, thinks I, for General Sibley's great plan. I had backed off further from the battlefield, along with the staff officers, sensible chaps, when I noticed our gallant commander was missing.

'Where is he?' I asked a Captain. Not that it mattered, but our forces were wholly disjointed and it seemed to me that Sibley should be rallying them, preferably for an immediate withdrawal.

'He's sick, mister,' answers the Captain, spitting in contempt. 'Seems the cannon is too loud for him. He's back behind our lines in an ambulance.'

So help me, he had deserted in the face of the enemy. Sick my eye. I felt a kindred spirit for him and had a capital notion.

'I'll check if he's OK. Do you have any messages for him?'

The Captain had, but I'd best not repeat them.

Surging with relief, I left them to their carnage, and cantered through the pretty cottonwoods back to the rear. The trees soon muffled the noise of battle and I could almost have imagined I was ambling though English woodlands. There was one thought uppermost on my mind. Now that our brave leader had retired from the action, how would this affect Tommy? I briefly considered trying to reach the Union lines and declaring myself a British neutral, and when's the next party travelling to New York, but dismissed it out of hand. Risk aside, I'd met sharp-eyed Yankees before, and didn't fancy weeks of questioning, explaining how I came to be accompanying the Rebels disguised as a Mexican, and who in Hell was I anyway? No, my best chance was to nurse Sibley, agree the Yankees are too strong right now, and persuade him the honourable action was to call off the attack. Once back at Mesilla I would persuade Baylor that my work here was done, and tell Sibley I must take my account of the battle, vindicating his actions, back to London. Having decided on my course of action, I slowed down, letting my horse find its way through the dense foliage at its own speed. With luck I need never see a bluecoat again.

'Halt!' Hands grasped at my bridle and bodies surrounded my horse. Before I knew what was happening they pulled me roughly from the saddle and I sprawled helpless on the ground.

'Who're you and what you doing here?'

Heart palpitating wildly, I stuttered my reply in English, forgetting my Mexican garb.

'...Armstrong. British army officer.'

'You're what?'

'I'm a British officer.'

Looking up I saw rifles pointing down at me, bearded faces atop blue tunics peering in wonder.

'Why're you got up like a Mexican?'

'I... I... I'm escaping from the Rebels.' Lord it sounded lame, but in my confused state I blurted out the first words to come to mind.

'Stand up.' They stood back to make room. Climbing slowly to my feet, for I'd taken quite a jar, I tried to collect my wits. Their uniforms told me this was a Yankee patrol sneaking behind our lines causing mischief. Mischief to me, anyhow.

Their lieutenant looked closely at me.

'Well you're no Mexican, that's for certain. British officer, you say? With the Rebels?'

'Rebel deserter more like,' cries a voice. 'Saw we wuz whipping them and ran up the white flag. Ain't that so?'

'Or mebbe a spy,' says another.

This was desperate. No army likes spies or deserters. If they thought me either they might kill me just to do the Rebels a favour. Soldiers think like that. Unless they thought I had information? Then they'd take me back to their headquarters for interrogation and I could talk my way to freedom. Or would they interrogate me brutally and shoot me on the spot afterwards? These thoughts passed through my mind in an instant. I was in a fearful fix, such foul luck, just minutes from safety. My best hope was to put on a bold front and bluff my way back to their headquarters. Summoning up my most authoritative voice, I breathed in and addressed their leader.

'I must speak to your commanding officer. I've just escaped from the Rebels' camp and have vital information for him.'

This took him aback, as the voice of authority usually does, but he rallied, blast him.

'Any information you got, you can give it to me.'

'No Lieutenant,' says I, sticking fearfully to my guns. 'What I have to say is for your General's ears only.'

'Say Lieut'nant, are you gonna believe this skulking spy? Shoot him an' let's be going. 'T'aint safe to linger.' Others mumbled in agreement. There were about twenty of them, possibly pickets caught behind our lines when we first advanced. The lieutenant glared them to silence while

161

he decided whether to shoot me or not. An uncomfortable position for old Tom you may be sure.

'Don't rightly know what's best.' He turned back to me. 'Say mister, can you prove you got information for us? Quick now.'

'I've been trailing General Sibley and his troops for three days and I can tell your General Canby his numbers, dispositions, military objectives, amount of supplies and oh, all manner of things.' I strove to keep calm. 'Lieutenant,' I glanced at his men. 'I cannot say further here. I must talk with General Canby.'

'How'd an Englishman dressed up like a Mexican find the Rebels' military objectives,' haw hawed one of the men. Shut up shut up, thinks I. You're only a private, mind your own bloody business.

'OK,' decided the lieutenant, 'we'll take you along, but mind; one false move an' you're a dead man.'

I could have wept with relief as they surrounded me and we traipsed warily through the woods, one of them leading my horse at the rear. We crept parallel to the river, intending to cross upstream past the scene of battle, and rejoin the Union ranks. As we made our way up-river I worked on my story. I was a British officer who had found himself in California when the war began. Chased by the Knights of the Golden Circle for espousing Northern sentiments, I'd fled east to get to New York and back home to England, where I would campaign against England recognising the Confederate States. I sneaked through Rebel lines to reach Fort Fillmore and offered my services to Major Lynde. Helping with the evacuation, I'd been taken by the Rebels after Lynde surrendered, as I was not in uniform, and threatened as a spy. I convinced Rebel commander Colonel Baylor that I was a *Times* newspaperman and used this position to learn the Rebels' strengths and military objectives. I slipped away from them when they marched on Fort Craig and by great good luck, found a Union patrol. Now Sir, I would say to U.S. General Canby, the Rebel strength and objectives are...

It didn't sound half bad. I truly did know the Rebel strength and military aims, thanks to the fool Sibley demanding my attendance at his briefings so I could write up his tactical brilliance. I could give Canby much vital information. By George, my information might well save Arizona and New Mexico for the Union. What's that General? A medal? Why thank'ee Sir, but my work here is better kept under the rose, dy'see? A swift horse and escort back east is all I require. And best of luck beating those damn Rebels.

Well he might not go that far, but he'd surely set me on my way with the next eastbound party. New York was a far better bet than New Orleans, too. On balance, I reflected, meeting these bluecoats might have proven a blessing.

'You lousy spy. You fooled the Lieut'nant but you don't fool us no how. One wrong move mister an' yore dead meat.'

Just a malcontent slackjaw throwing his weight about, but it reminded me I wasn't out of the woods yet, whichever way you look at it. I nodded at him and grunted quietly to show I understood.

'What's the matter mister, cat got your tongue?'

I saw I'd have to answer the brute.

'No soldier,' says I in a low voice. 'I'm keeping quiet in case there's any Rebels about.'

'So's they kin rescue you?' Don't bet on it mister. One sniff of a Rebel an' I'll finish you myself. I'll...'

He screamed as a volley of shots smashed into our ranks. I dived into the undergrowth in panic while bullets zinged through the trees around us and further screams rent the air.

'Ambush! Down men!' cries someone. His order was wasted on me. I hugged the ground for my salvation as the world erupted in chaos. We had stumbled into as fine an ambush as you could wish for. Musket balls and bullets were flying in from every direction as the bluecoats took what cover they could and tried to make some order. Half a dozen must have fallen in the first volley and it was clear the survivors stood no chance against an enemy they couldn't see. Luckily my lieutenant agreed.

'Quarter!' he yells. 'You got us fair n' square. We surrender. Stop firing.'

To my surprise, they did. The war was not as savage in the beginning as it later became. Three years on the Rebels would have butchered us where we lay.

'Stand up slowly. Leave your arms on the ground.'

The bluecoats obeyed, and seeing they were not shot down where they stood, I gingerly copied them.

The Rebels appeared from all sides, quickly collected the fallen guns and herded the Yankees together. They ignored me at first, beyond a curious glance or two, but with the bluecoats corralled, their lieutenant turned to me.

'Why its Mr. Jeffreys, is it not? What are you doing here Sir?'

By the holies, he knew me! I couldn't tell one junior officer from another, you understand. I didn't want the Federal lieutenant to dispute my story so I beckoned him to one side.

'Thank heavens for you and your men, Lieutenant. These bluebellies captured me as I was taking a message to General Sibley, back securing the ambulances. They were going to shoot me out of hand - just what you'd expect from Yankees - so I had to spin 'em a yarn. Don't listen to anything they say. Now it is vital I get to the General. Can you spare me a few men for escort? I've been delayed too much already. And,' I gave him my Tommy grin, 'I'll be sure to report your great action here. Why, if my message hadn't got through we might have lost the battle. You are to be congratulated Sir. Now I must be on my way.'

Don't let them get a word in edgeways, you see. It worked; the officer blinked, then snapped an order to his men, and in no time I was off with a small escort, my horse and gun restored.

We cleared the cottonwoods without incident. Approaching our rearguard with the ambulances I bade my escort goodbye and cantered to safety.

'Where's General Sibley?' I asked an officer.

He pointed me to an ambulance under a hospital flag without comment, and I made my way to one of the carriages set up to cater for the sick and wounded. Knocking politely and getting no answer, I announced myself and entered.

There was our sick General lying face up on the bed. Drunk to the world.

Napoleon used to say "give me a lucky general". When he said it he cannot have had General Sibley in mind, but truth to tell, General Sibley was the luckiest general I ever came across. For would you believe it; with him no longer directing operations the Confederates reversed their early setback and went on to win the battle of Valverde. And he got the credit.

With Sibley indisposed, command passed to Colonel Thomas Green, a man who knew what he was about. The battle raged for some time, neither side getting the advantage, when Green formed two storming parties. One charged the Union batteries to the right while the other went for the Union left. The right attack was repulsed with heavy Confederate losses (one of the Union defenders was Kit Carson, no less, so I'm not surprised). The other charge took the Federal batteries, through vicious hand-to-hand fighting with pistols, bayonets, clubs and knives, and drove the Federal left flank back into their main body, throwing the Union forces completely out of kilter.

General Canby threw up the sponge. The bluecoats withdrew from the field in a disorderly manner and scampered to Fort Craig, leaving much of their artillery and other equipment behind. The day belonged to the Rebels.

Well, this was the best tonic Sibley could get. Next morning, recovered from his malady, he resumed command as though he had never been away. He pronounced Fort Craig still too formidable to take (though it transpired that many of its cannon were in fact "Quaker Guns"; wooden dummies) and he would bypass it and march on up the Rio Grande, leaving it in enemy hands.

Where was Tommy during these great events? Safely with the rearguard, you may be sure. I found myself a shelter behind Sibley's ambulance and spent my time writing up the day's events newspaper fashion, placing a patriotic Confederate shine on all that occurred. Nobody disputed my presence, and I remained there until the battle was won.

Baylor arrived during the night, and a fine old set-to he had with Sibley after his Texans had told him the story. From behind the ambulance I heard a still half-drunk Sibley insist he was unwell while a blood-angry Baylor panned him as an infamous coward and a disgrace to the Confederacy. Sibley took no action against his junior officer, preferring to let sleeping dogs lie, but this split between the Arizona Governor and its chief military officer weakened the Confederate position in the far west. As if I cared.

So the Confederates won the battle but failed to take the fort, which was their objective in the first place. Sibley moved north up the river towards Albuquerque - without me, thank the Lord - driving smaller Union garrisons before him, and mopping up their supplies where the Yankees didn't burn them first. They occupied Santa Fé, then Sibley made a proclamation to the people of New Mexico, claiming the Territory for the Confederate States of America. He assured the populace that he came with the best of intentions, and so forth, so knuckle down, pay your taxes and we will all live happily ever after.

General Canby, who between you and me was little better in the field than Sibley, though sober so far as I know, carried the can for the defeat. A bit harsh, as he kept the fort, but there you are. They knew each other well, by the way, and even trained together, which explains a lot. Canby blamed his militia regiments for the failure to hold the line, retreating in disarray in the face of our Texans. The militia protested they only followed the example set by Canby's regulars, who ran first, so there. The usual military excuses; I daresay the Romans are still squabbling over who lost them their empire. #Note_8

Most of this I learned much later, for at long last I was soon to be on my way back east.

I returned to Mesilla with Baylor, Sibley's enthusiasm for press coverage being temporarily abated, and informed him flat that I had spent quite enough time in Arizona and wished to go back to England and campaign for the Confederacy there. To my surprise, he agreed straight off. It seems Sibley's usurping of his role as military commander of the Territory had cooled his enthusiasm for the post of Governor, and he was ready to let me go.

At our final dinner together Baylor prosed about how he intended to deal with the Indians. He would take up my flippant suggestion and pretend to offer peace, lure them into a trap and wipe the adults out, selling the children into slavery to defray costs. I didn't object; I'd seen the results of Indian raids and would lose no sleep over their demise. I couldn't have changed his mind anyhow, so I let it be.

'Well Colonel,' says he through a mouthful of chicken, 'I guess you are gonna miss us when you're back in England, huh?'

'I certainly will, Colonel, especially the heat and dust and Indians and bullets flying and heat and dust.' Keeping it light, you see.

He laughed, and poured me a drink.

'You health. Colonel, and the health of Her Majesty Queen Victoria.'

I stood. 'Her Majesty.'

Later in the evening he became more serious.

'Do you think England will recognise the Confederacy any time soon?'

I'd wondered about this. I had learnt in my time here that England's recognition was of first importance to the Confederates. Should England recognise the Confederacy as a beleaguered country, our navy would break any blockade the Yankees might put up, in order to obtain Southern cotton. This would enable the Rebels to buy arms, ships and other equipment and quite probably ensure victory. On the other hand, should England break the North's blockade we might well find ourselves at war with the United States, delighting the Confederacy but putting British Canada at high risk of invasion.

England, I knew, would back the winning side.

'Depends how you do in the field, I believe. If you look like you can hold your own, then England and the other Powers will recognise you soon enough. If not...'

'But we *are* winning, Colonel,' protests Baylor. 'And you want cotton an' we got it. You need it for British jobs, so your ordinary folk will be yammering for war with the Yankees if they stop us selling it you.'

'The ordinary folk don't count, Colonel. Not in England. But like I say, you keep winning your battles and we will recognise you soon enough.'

It was true, too. Those Northerners who weighed up the odds and decided the South couldn't win due to lack of numbers and industry failed to realise that war is politics by other means. If the North couldn't conquer the Confederacy quickly, England might well recognise her and all bets were off. It damn well near happened too, as you will see in my later recordings.

Soon after I'd left with Baylor's thanks and handshakes, he tried a dry run at his *sell the children* policy, when for once he caught the redskins in the act. Chiricahua Apaches ran off 100 horses belonging to the Confederate Army. He set out after them with a large force, crossing the border into the Mexican State of Chihuahua and overtaking them outside the town of Corralitos, one hundred miles into Mexican Territory. He took nine Apaches alive, one man, three women, and five children. Recovering the animals, he executed the adults and sold the children to a Mexican landowner. This act disgusted even the Confederate government, sensitive to foreign opinion as I'd warned, and from then on Baylor was walking a fine line,

Perhaps Baylor sniffed the wind, for entirely out of character he negotiated treaties with the Pima and Papago Indians, long-time enemies of the Apache. Surprisingly, this worked, and the Tucson area had peace for the first time since the civil war began.

There was another reason for his unexpected willingness to talk to the Indians. His new-found love for one part of the red race didn't stop him progressing with his plan to exterminate the rest. He ordered his officers use all means to persuade the Apaches and Navahos to meet him to discuss peace. Well, thought the Indians, he made peace with the Pima and Papago tribes, maybe we can talk.

So the Confederates tried to lure the Indians with promises of food and whiskey. Baylor offered them grain to feed their people, leaving it in handy deserted warehouses. He poisoned it first. Meanwhile, one of his officers persuaded about a dozen Indians to come into camp to discuss a peace treaty. Once in gunshot range, the Confederates slaughtered them. Word of the poisoned grain and killings got out, and the Indians became reluctant to cooperate, even declining the whiskey. Either they feared it was poisoned or they had taken the pledge.

I missed all this, being safely on my way to New Orleans, there to enlist the help of the British Consulate and catch a ship anywhere away from this war-infested land. I guessed the Yankees would be blockading the port, but felt sure arrangements could be made through the Consulate to ferry neutrals to safety, and being the bold Tommy, they would pull a string or two to arrange this.

Did I miss Baylor, La Mesilla and his Confederate Territory of Arizona? Like a dose of pox. #Note_9

Chapter eleven

I wouldn't recommend travelling from Arizona to Memphis by stagecoach. For one, the company is too mixed. The seats are hard, the rattling over harsh terrain shakes your bones, and you get precious little sleep. Stifling hot, too.

Mind, it helps if you have a strong escort of Texas's finest riding alongside to teach the local Indians and bandits to keep their distance. This means you can take a break from the carriage and ride out in the open when the sun is down.

Baylor at last was able to spare men as escort, for reinforcements trickled in to help Sibley, and Baylor siphoned off some for himself. Many of his men were due leave in Texas, so he sent back a fair-sized armed group under a Lieutenant Joe Roberts to escort the invalided, a few civilians and one distinguished newspaper correspondent back to Texas and all points east. With the war humming along nicely, the Wells Fargo and Butterfield stagecoach lines were no longer functioning, so he scared up a few private carriages for us instead.

I travelled in a light celerity coach, drawn by two pairs of dry-boned mules, with eight other passengers in three rows, and a tight squeeze we made of it. We sat with our knees folded double, our baggage on our laps, not that I had much, and mail bags containing letters home from the remaining troops beneath our seats.

We trundled forward through the relentless heat and choking dust of the day, and icy cold of night, with brief stops at way stations for what passes in this wilderness as food. We even had to get out and help the mules pull the carriages across strips of desert, and wade through many small rivers. No wonder I have arthritis today.

One of the way stations had a Butterfield warning up on the wall.

YOU WILL BE TRAVELLING THROUGH INDIAN COUNTRY AND THE SAFETY OF YOUR PERSON CANNOT BE VOUCHSAFED BY ANYONE BUT GOD.

All due respect to the Almighty, but I was glad we had armed troops to help. Arriving in mid-Texas, we dropped off our invalids. This was a blessing, for these men were a constant reminder of the true reality of the glorious wars our politicians are forever dragging harmless folk into. They were returning home to Texas with fewer limbs than they had set out with, and a pitiful group they made. A few patriotic idiots struck up Rebel songs on the way and clearly expected a hero's welcome. Poor fools, many of them would soon be begging cap-in-hand in the streets. The rest sat snivelling, wondering how they would earn a living with only one arm, or disfigured or blind, and would their sweethearts stand by them. Probably not; served the asses right for volunteering.

The train rolled on with a smaller escort, but strong enough for that, and nobody bothered us. I even managed to enjoy some of the finest views and natural wonders in the world, and the most beautiful sunsets ever, better even than the African coast. We followed much of the Butterfield stagecoach route, stopping at Fort Chadbourne, Abilene, Colbert's Ferry to cross the Red River, Fort Smith, Madison, Des Arc, Cadron, Plumer's Station, Norristown, Little Rock and Lord knows where else, and fetched up at Memphis without incident after about a month.

As I say, I don't recommend you try it.

We arrived early and Lieutenant Roberts dismissed the escort. He was travelling downriver to his uncle's plantation in Louisiana. I had intended to take the railroad straight to New Orleans but Roberts persuaded me that the railroad prioritised ferrying troops and supplies north. South-bound passenger trains were continually interrupted and left in sidings, sometimes overnight. Better, says he, to steam down the Mississippi. It sounded sensible, so the Lieutenant and I checked into Gayoso House, a huge hotel-cum-military headquarters, situated along a bluff overlooking the Tennessee side of the Mississippi. The Lieutenant's uniform ensured we were welcome, and I spent some joyful hours bathing - despite the muddy bathwater straight from the river - relaxing, having my clothes laundered and generally becoming my own man again.

It was not yet time for dinner, so I took a turn around the town. After so long stuck in the wilds, Memphis came as quite a busy surprise. It was a large, bustling place with a population of around thirty thousand, including many Europeans, Negroes and even half-tame Indians. Saloons selling *forty rod* and *sixty rod* gut-rot whiskey abounded, with dancehalls and gaming rooms on every corner. It wasn't all play though. Criss-cross streets thronged with horses, wagons, omnibuses and citizens hurrying to and fro. The wide, tree-lined esplanade along the river sported stores, warehouses, rows of shops some several stories high, imposing buildings for the purpose of trade and commerce and civic works, all bustling fit to make you tired. It quite unnerved me after my month on the plains.

This enterprise could not hide the fact that the citizens were involved in a war to preserve their way of life. All along the riverbank, fortifications had sprung up and were being added to constantly. No shipping was allowed north, and the inhabitants were expecting Yankee riverboats to come raiding at any time. They were all fervent secessionists, and the talk was of *Lincoln's mercenaries*, and *abolition hordes*. It was a centre for volunteers, and I passed any number of makeshift companies dressed in the most outlandish uniforms, some even draped in blue, which seemed to me to be asking for trouble. Grey and butternut predominated, with a variety of weaponry to drive the quartermaster to drink. Handguns, rifled-muskets, breech loaders and repeating weapons, as well as a fantastic variety of swords and knives. Spirits were high, and talk was of States Rights and what they intended to do with Lincoln once they's ketch'ed a'hold of 'im.

I spent a pleasant afternoon watching preparations for other folks' war, and in good humour made my way back to Gayoso House for dinner. Lieutenant Roberts had gone to investigate riverboats going south and I had hopes of us being on our way tomorrow.

'Fraid there's no passenger steamers running just now, Tom, on account of the Yankee war. But I used my rank,' he pointed at his Lieutenant's insignia, 'to cadge us a ride on a small boat running as far as Baton Rouge. 'You kin find a boat from there to New Orleans easily enough. Or...'

'Yes?'

'Or why not ketch a boat there to my uncle's place? He likes to entertain company, an' it will please him powerful if I bring you along. Bide a day or two and there's sure to be a boat to Nawlins. Why, he may even rustle you up one his own self. An' his spread is dandy, with fine food and the best cellar in the South.'

Joe Roberts was a likable sort and it didn't sound half bad, so I accepted on the spot.

'Be glad to Joe. Now, where's that waiter?'

I'd steamed along the Mississippi before, in the other direction, and nothing had changed. The river wound up and down like a French military parade, and apart from the great bastion of Vicksburg and a few smaller works, nothing to see on either bank save flatland and marsh, with the occasional hamlet and landing post.

We arrived at Joe's uncle's sugar plantation on a Sunday, at a place called Cahabanooze, the Indian term for duck's sleeping place. The boat ran alongside the levee and landed us on the eastern bank. I followed him through a gate in the paling into his uncle's grounds. The house was very near to the river, on account, says Joe, of the Mississippi breaking off a sizable portion of the bank some years back. One day the house would follow.

It was a solid, two-storey mansion with a verandah right the way around it, surrounded by ancient trees and Magnolias.

Joe told a Negro servant to run ahead and announce our arrival. As we neared the front door Joe's uncle appeared, wreathed in smiles. His name was Mr. Roman, though he insisted everyone called him Governor. He was a former sea Captain, and gave us a rousing welcome.

Joe introduced me.

'What's that? A newspaperman from the London *Times?* Why, if'n that don' beat everything. And how is your Mr. Russell, Suh?' Astonished, I said he was well, to my recollection.

'Mr. Russell was here, not nine months back. Stayed for a few days as I hope you will too. Mind, I'm none too happy about his reports on the South, but we speak freely here, and I guess his editors back home mangled his stories up to please your government.'

I mentioned this to Billy later. He told me both sides were highly sensitive about what outsiders wrote about them. They expected uncritical support and bridled at even the tiniest criticism. But the Governor was right about the *Times* editors. They mangled Billy's accounts to suit their editorial policy, which changed like the weather. Sometimes for the South, sometimes against. #Note 10

The Governor parked us in sumptuous quarters. Joe and I shared a detached house in the grounds surrounded by shady trees, with servants, four bedrooms, library and sitting room at our disposal.

After we had dined and rested, he showed us around the plantation, and asked me if I cared to see the slave quarters. I didn't, but he seemed eager and one must show willing, so presently he led me to a high compound within which the slaves lived.

We heard the distant caterwaul of fiddles, and I was surprised to see young black women emerge from a wicker gate dressed to the nines in pure white dresses, crinolines and pink sashes, with gaudy handkerchiefs on their heads. They curtsied prettily as they passed, suddenly reminding me I still hadn't had a sniff of a woman since China.

'They're off to their Sunday dance,' explains the Governor. It seems he was one of the more indulgent slave owners, as few permitted such recreation on a Sunday, though most planters did give their slaves the day off for rest and sometimes worship. The planters were split on whether or not to spread Christianity to the Negroes. Some held it might make them resent their bondage, others that the promise of pie in the sky when they die kept them in line in this world. Of course, the Sunday dances were merely to encourage them to produce future slaves, but then, aren't our own workers' entertainments for the same purpose?

Passing through the gate, we encountered a square enclosure, containing lines of small wooden huts. They had no windows, but gratings allowed a little light inside. Each hut had two rooms. One was a bedroom, containing a mattress stuffed with cotton wool or dried Spanish moss. Clothes hung from nails driven into the walls. The other room boasted kitchen utensils, sometimes a table and couple of chairs, and a fireplace constantly aglow no matter how warm the day. Around the huts, a squabbling of pigs, poultry and mangy curs fussed over fragments of clothing, bits of shoes, feathers and general debris. Further along stood a stagnant pool, where dozens of mules cooled themselves against the hot sun on their day off from the fields.

I also saw two huge chained dogs, which the Governor informed me were let off their chains at night and roamed the enclosure to enforce the nightly curfew and protect it from intruders.

'Care to see the field hands' quarters, Mr. Jeffreys?'

I had been thinking that, what with fine clothes and a weekly dance, there was not much wrong with the slaves' conditions that a broom wouldn't put right. Certainly nothing worth a war. What I hadn't realised was that these were the quarters of the house slaves, the cream of slave society. Field hands were the real thing.

We passed through another wicker gate into the enclosure penning the less fortunate field workers. They stood up with alacrity as we approached, the children hiding behind their elders, females curtsying, dead-eyed men bowing humbly. No finery here, just the minimum to keep them decent. It suddenly occurred to me that I had seen few flies in the upper enclosure; this was explained now, as the entire fly population of the lower Mississippi seemed to live here. They swarmed around the tin cooking utensils, dining on remnants of cooked molasses. The field hands' furnishing consisted of old and broken crockery on dressers, field rags lying any old how, and not a decoration, ornament or book anywhere in sight.

Slaves are not allowed to read, of course, as reading might give them ideas above their station. Liberal-inclined slave owners who try to improve the slaves' lot by teaching them find themselves on the wrong end of popular opinion and sometimes the wrong end of a barrel.

Looking at these degraded people, I understood the human yearning for freedom. These slaves were better treated than most. Adequately fed and housed; one day off per week; seldom whipped (but whipped good n' proper if they deserved it, says the Governor. They stole from each other but never from white folk if they knew what was good for them). They were even allowed to raise families and stay together, more or less. But the abject, soulless dejection, especially in the children, revealed the melancholy that replaces *joie de vivre* where humans exist in a world without hope.

It's all one to me, and if the price of comfort for the privileged is misery for the wretched, you won't catch me burning the bullwhips. But for some reason this wretchedness put me thoroughly out of sorts. When the Governor insisted I inspect the slaves' hospital I near as a toucher told him what he could do with his Negroes and sugar and the whole kit and caboodle. But of course I didn't, and presently wished I had, as I found myself in a long, bare room with five beds, all containing sufferers of pneumonia or the fever. An old Negress tended them, mopping their brows, and looked likely to carry off the lot. I was glad to be out of there, and my final port of call was the happiest, for it was the sugar room, where they held their dance. Several Negro couples were cavorting to fiddles, reminding me of an Irish reel, and a high old time they were having of it. How they danced in that heat was beyond me, but then they were used to it I suppose.

I was relieved to get away from the slaves' quarters and back to the gardens, which were as fine as any on an English country estate. The quiet shade relaxed me and I found my foul mood evaporating as I cast the slaves from my mind.

I retired to my quarters for the rest of the afternoon and arrived at the dinner table in the cool of the early evening.

The Governor had company, as I learned was usual on a Sunday. As well as me and Lieutenant Roberts, several neighbouring planters turned up for their vittles. We ate on the verandah, Negroes keeping off the mosquitoes, and with the cigars the talk soon came around to the war.

'Looks like we'll break the blockade pretty soon,' says one.

'True enuff. That's if'n you kin call it a blockade.'

They laughed at this, and I learned that U.S. Secretary of State William Seward had proclaimed a blockade of the Southern ports and coastline when hostilities began. This proclamation was a political blunder, as it was recognition that the South was a separate country, something the North could not admit. Well, you can't blockade your own country, can you? The blockade was *de facto* recognition of the South, and increased Lincoln's fears that the Powers would recognise the Confederacy, and the Lord alone knew where that might lead. It was futile at this stage anyhow. The North did not have the ships to enforce it properly, and blockade runners broke through almost at will. Trouble was, equipment for war is heavy and expensive to transport, and therefore not very profitable. So instead of importing guns, powder and the essential materials of battle most needed, the blockade-runners favoured luxuries such as French cognac, Madeira wine, Belgium silk, laces, perfumes and cigars. Meanwhile the Rebels had a new reason to dismiss the blockade.

'Say Mr. Jeffreys, have you heard of the CSS Virginia?'

'CSS?'

'Confederate States Ship. Our navy. Only this is a ship with a difference.'

'Really? What is different about it?'

'Well Suh, the Virginia is an ironclad. A ship clad entirely in iron. No Yankee gunboat can do more'n scratch it. Its done sunk two Yankee frigates at Chesapeake Bay with more to come.'

'Ironclad? How does it float?'

They laughed.

'Low in the water, Mr. Jeffreys. The Yankees can hardly hit it with their guns, and when they do, why, cannon just bounces off. When it comes out to sea it will clear the blockade in a jiffy. Those Yankee boats will run back home or we'll sink 'em.'

This was nearly true. The Virginia sank two frigates as he said, but when it went to finish off a third the following day, blowed if the Yankees didn't challenge it with an ironclad of their own, the USS Monitor. The two monsters fought themselves to a standstill, neither managing to see off the other, and both retired for repairs, dented but afloat. They never fought again, each guarding the other, and in time the Rebels were forced to scupper their ship to prevent the Yankees capturing it.

The battle's significance was that it brought in the new era of steel ships. Great Britain and France halted further construction of wooden-hulled vessels, and others followed suit. We were entering the modern age of warfare.

Incidentally, the Virginia could never have broken the blockade. Suitable for river-fighting, it was wholly unstable and would have sunk at the first seaworthy wave.

I'd had a good dinner, and with the drink was feeling neighbourly, so I thought I would flatter them a little.

'Well, I see us British will have to look to our laurels. If your Confederate navy cannot be sunk, we shall have to place extra cannon in the Tower of London.'

There was a good deal of laughter and joshing at this, but the Governor reassured me.

'Don' fret yoursel' Mr. Jeffreys. The South is a good friend of England. An' England is a good friend to the South. Why, 'thout us, your good folk wouldn't have a shred to wear. It's our cotton that keeps y'all respectable.'

I joined in the haw-hawing jollity, then stuck a pin in him for devilment.

'But can your merchant ships get the cotton to England?'

This sobered them up.

'That's the nub, Mr. Jeffreys. We kin if we really want to, but do we? What if we jes hold on to our cotton? Seems England and France will go mighty short, and mebbe they'll blame the Yankees fer stopping us sending it you.'

This confused me a mite. Well, I'd been out west, and was not up on the latest political manoeuvres. Cotton was the South's biggest money spinner by a long shot, and I could not see any advantage in them withholding it and forsaking the cash. They enlightened me. The Southern planters had had the bright idea of starving Europe of cotton in order to force England and France to attack the North. The Confederate government backed the idea, forgetting that the previous year had seen a bumper cotton harvest and Europe had enough cotton to be going on with. Undaunted, the South calculated that if the war was a long one, cotton shortages would begin to bite, and Europe would in turn bite the Yankees. It seemed to me that starving Europe of cotton would more likely encourage us to help the Yankees bring these ornery troublemakers to heel all the quicker, but then, I'm not a politician.

'Don't you need the money?' asks I. 'Surely the money cotton brings in will help you buy arms and warships and suchlike.'

'We got enuff guns to last us awhiles,' pipes up Joe. 'Sides, we pick 'em up off'n the battlefields every time we chase the Yankees, an' that's a lot of chasing.' The table erupted at this remark by the man in Rebel grey.

'This war will be over before the next cotton season.'

More haw-hawing, but I have to say I agreed with them. I'd seen and heard the Southern sentiments in Memphis, and it was plain as the nose on Secretary Steward's face that the Southerners wanted no truck with the North. They would go their own way whatever Washington did. The Northern taxpayers would bridle at stumping up to drag such recalcitrants back into the fold, losing many of their sons in the process, and would vote for any politician who promised peace.

The wiseacres look back and say Lincoln was never going to recognise the South, but at the time it seemed clear that he would have to, and soon. The South were going to win their war for independence, it was just a matter of months or even weeks. Certainly the planters thought so.

'Yep,' says one, a man called Perrin. 'I got a son captaining the Mississippi Horse up in Virginny an' I reckon he'll be home in time to bring in the harvest.'

This brought the subject round to States Rights and you'll think I am bragging, but I spotted a major flaw in the Confederate strategy right there and then.

You see, the North were one, united country, with a national army. Every State was equal and governed from Washington, fighting for the same cause. When Washington gave an order, within reason they jumped. The South, on the other hand, resisted Jeff Davis's calls for a national army. They were a collection of States each determined to rule itself, united in a loose association, or Confederacy. Hence the call for States Rights. No State felt obliged to obey commands from the Confederate government in Richmond if it didn't feel so inclined. Each

State fed and clothed its own soldiers, so you got one regiment eating well, and the one over the hill starving because it's State hadn't got supplies to it. They cooperated much better as the war went on, but in the beginning it was virtually every State for itself.

Meanwhile, their policy of withholding cotton from Europe to encourage the Powers to intervene presupposed a long war. After all, it would take two years for the shortages to really bite. But the secessionists knew that they had to win quickly or be ground down by the superior Northern numbers and industrial might. This meant fighting a short, sharp war, so withholding cotton made no sense. They attempted to fight a short war and a long one at the same time, and this contributed greatly to their undoing.

'I don't think it right thet yore boy has to go to Virginny to fight,' says a man called Andrews. 'No man should hev to fight outside his own borders.'

'Don' you think we have to go help Virginny?'

'The Virginians ought nevah to have let the Yankees on their soil in t'fust place.'

'What do you think, Mr. Jeffreys?'

'Well... I'm not a military man,' I never spoke a truer word, but the Governor shot me a keen look which disconcerted me a little. 'But I recall we English fought the Scots and Irish in the past. Now we are all together and fight as one county. Unless you work together the Yankees can pick off each State piecemeal.'

'Mebbe yore right, Mr. Jeffreys,' says the Governor. 'Them Yankees fight together an' so should we.'

'Well, I respect yore views, Mr. Jeffreys,' protests Andrews, 'but I jes' don' think it right to bring war outside off of yore own borders.'

'I doubt it will matter much, anyhow,' says I, not wishing to argue when I knew I was right, but didn't care, 'as Lincoln will have to recognise your Confederacy before November's mid-term elections anyhow.'

They all agreed on this and they toasted the South, and our Queen Victoria, and a rousing good evening was had by all. As Joe and I strolled back to our quarters at evening's end, I gazed up at the stars twinkling merrily through the tall trees and thought, about time I was home.

I stayed at Cahabanooze for three pleasant days, until a boat was found to take me to New Orleans, resplendent in new attire generously gifted to me by the Governor, who was full of concern for my appearance. The journey of about fifty miles got me to the city late afternoon, so I took the Governor's advice and checked in to the St Charles Hotel. It was a noisy, bustling establishment of American design, unlike the French hotels nearby, with many uniformed officers relaxing in the hall on chairs with their legs up against the wall, smoking, spitting and reading the newspapers.

I'd been to New Orleans before, ten years earlier, and liked it then. Known as the crescent city for the way it hugged the Mississippi, it seemed busier now, with diverse Rebel flags poking out of many buildings, but I was pleased to find it had kept its charm. Prices had soared, however, and I was now almost cleaned out. This did not worry me overmuch, as the Governor had told me where to find the British Consul, a Mr. William Mure. Once I declared myself as Tommy V.C. he would be sure to set me right.

I walked along to the French area to dine splendidly at a Creole restaurant, or "restaurat," as they are called here, and noticed most of the townsfolk were well-dressed and seemingly affluent. No sign yet of war-hardship. The poor lived mainly around the railway station, in row upon row of dilapidated one-storey houses. From what I saw of them, they were a miserable and sickly bunch, but they did their job, which was to cater for their betters.

Here on the right side of town, spires appealed to the heavens and wide avenues boasted fine French architecture. French influence reigned everywhere; with shops called *magasins*, people speaking French in the streets and even the Negroes out carrying their masters' purchases talking in Frog. There were oyster and European lager-bier saloons, exclusive billiard rooms and even hair salons for the better classes. If it hadn't been for the war and the fact that my pockets were hanging out once more - not that I looked it in my fine clothes - I would have liked to stay for a week or two.

I returned to my hotel and after exchanging pleasantries with the loafers in the hall, retired for the night. I would find the British Consul in the morning and see what help he could provide.

Next day I breakfasted and paid my hotel bill and, confirming directions from the desk, set out to find the British Consul. His place of work was not far from the St Charles Hotel and as I traversed the badly paved sidewalk adjacent to St Charles Street I expected to find him in short order.

I approached a likely looking building near a street corner. It seemed a place of some activity as there were a fair number of people milling around outside, with a few stationary carriages opposite. I approached the throng and asked a group of young men if this was where I might find the British Consul.

'What d'ye want him fer, mister?' replies one of them briskly.

Well it was no business of his, but the last thing I needed was a brawl on the steps, so I answered him politely.

'I'm looking for the British Consul. I am a British citizen and am seeking his advice and assistance.'

'What advice an' assistance do ye seek?'

For the first time I noticed that several of these rough looking men were staring at me intently. I felt my buttocks tighten but I'd gone too far now so I pressed on.

'That's between me and the Consul. Good day to you Sir.'

I made to pass but the group closed around me.

'Yore business is gitting out of here, ain't it?'

'My business is no concern of yours,' I replied, wondering what the devil this was all about. In broad daylight too.

'You ain't goin' nowhere mister,' says the spokesman, blocking my way as others closed in around me.

'And who the devil's going to stop me?' cries I sounding much bolder than I felt.

'We are mister.' He grabbed me by the lapel.

I may not be strong in character but I am damned strong in body, or was then. Seeing there was nothing for it. I stabbed my finger in his eye and as he pulled back in pain, smashed him fully in the face. Leaping sideways, I dodged the swinging blackjack that was meant for the back of my head, and screaming out loud - it helps - spun around and darted down the way I'd came. Once safe at the hotel I'd lodge an outraged complaint about trash in the streets.

So I thought. I'd barely made two yards when several toughs spilled out of one of the opposite carriages and blocked my way. Panicking, I swerved aside and, confound it, tripped over a jutting paving stone. I flew sprawling and in an instant they were upon me. Many hands pulled me roughly to my feet and held me secure, hemmed in by the villainous crowd.

The man whose eye I had nearly put out approached.

'What do you want with me? I have no money.' Without answer he drove his fist into my face.

'Take him away boys,' he called to the others. They whisked me along, bruised and helpless. Halting outside one of the carriages, they produced rope and rapidly secured my hands and feet. In a trice I found myself bundled inside, and to my amazement and fright there were three other men already inside, like me, feet and hands securely bound.

I gaped at them, mind struggling to understand what as happening. The mob, whoever they were, had made no attempt to rob me. Mass kidnapping seemed to be their game, but why? And in the middle of town?

My confusion must have shown, for one of my fellow victims spoke up.

'Welcome aboard, Sir. I noticed you through the window. You certainly put up a show. Sorry to see you taken. Do you understand me?'

My astonishment grew, for this man was as English as I was.

'You're English begod! What in Hell is happening? Why have those scoundrels attacked us and trussed us up in here?'

His looked surprised. 'Don't you know?' He shook his head sadly.

More confused than ever, I begged him to explain.

'It is simple, Sir. The gentlemen who accosted you - and all of us - wait near the British Consulate for people like you and I to pass by. People who are attempting to leave this green and pleasant land. They don't like it Sir, not one bit.'

'What do you mean?'

'Desertion, Sir. Why should we be allowed to flee the bold new Confederacy in their hour of need?'

A worm of understanding was growing in the back of my mind. I didn't want to hear what was coming next.

'We are to be taken to the nearest recruitment centre and made to take the oath.'

'Oath? What oath?'

'Why, the oath of allegiance to the Confederate States of America. You see, Sir. They need all hands to the pumps. They stop every man who tries to take a ship out of New Orleans and conscript them.'

'Conscript them?'

'Yes Sir.' He gave me a wry smile. 'Welcome to the Confederate Army.'

Chapter Twelve

'I, George Jeffreys, do solemnly swear that I will bear true faith and allegiance to the Confederate States of America and that I will serve them honestly and faithfully against all their enemies or oppressors whomsoever; and that I will observe and obey the orders of the President of the Confederate States and the orders of the officers appointed over me, according to the Rules and Articles of War.'

I took the oath without demur. My English compatriot refused, swearing he wanted no truck with their war. This defiance earned him a savage beating *pour encourager les autres*. I needed no such encouragement.

Our kidnappers collected upwards of twenty victims in all, of various European nationalities, and marched us all off to the nearest Rebel recruitment post. There they gave us the simple choice; swear the oath or be beaten to a pulp until you do.

We were helpless in their hands. They congratulated us jeeringly and informed us we were now volunteers in the Confederate army. The recruiting officer told us our fate.

'We're enlisting men for the 25th Louisiana infantry regiment, but we don' want you on account you is deserters. Instead, we're gonna send you nort' to Virginny, where they ain't so fussy, haw haw.'

Our guards hollered at this. It seems he gave the same address to all impressed soldiers, and got a laugh every time.

'We will take you to the station an' put you safely on the train to Atlanta. Don' want any of you boys gitting lost now, do we?'

Another roar from our guards.

'When you land there they'll tell you yore regiment an' send you on yore way. Now git,' says he, and the vigilantes frogmarched us along the back streets to the station.

This was appalling. One moment I had been strolling happily on my way to the Consul and home, now I found myself herded through the town to be sent north to fight for the wretched Confederacy. It was impossible to take in at first, but as we were placed in a warehouse of sorts beside the station to await our train, the fearfulness of the thing began to home in on me.

Once I recovered my wits, I began to consider my options. I couldn't escape here; even if I lost my guards I would be stuck in New Orleans without money, and I daren't try to contact the Consul as all paths to him were watched closely. So presumably I would have to make my break elsewhere. Not in Atlanta. It was slap bang in the middle of the South. There would be no escape from there, that much was certain. I also ruled out our destination of Richmond. This was the capital of the Confederacy, and right in the firing line, being just downwind of Washington.

On reflection, the best place to decamp looked to be north of Atlanta, but before we reached Richmond. Once again I could have wept. What an unholy mess I'd landed myself in. Or rather, others had landed my uncomplaining self in. What I needed was a portion of Tommy enterprise to get me out and home, safe and sound.

Had I been more aware of how the civil war was shaping up, I would have trod more warily, perhaps sending the British Consul a note from my hotel and sneaking out to meet him in the dark. What I didn't know then was just how determined the Confederacy was to maintain its independence. They would suspend any law, trample individuals underfoot and conscript anyone with two legs to help them achieve victory.

Foreigners were fair game, as I discovered, and were regularly forced into the Confederate forces at gunpoint or, as in my case, for fear of a beating. Southern-born officers who remained loyal to the North had their land and property confiscated, and their families faced harassment and suspicion, if not worse. Anyone foolhardy enough to cast doubt on the South's ultimate victory faced six months in the calaboose with conscription to follow. All of which mattered to me less than my shoe size.

The following days were among the most hellish of my life. We were packed in with genuine volunteers and spent hour upon hour chugging slowly through the Southern States, crammed together in stifling wooden carriages throughout the day and night, short on water and fed cornmeal and salted meats. Our escort let us out for much-needed breathers, heavily guarded, at some of the major stops, where we picked up more volunteers. These breaks allowed us to escape the blistering heat of the carriages for a while, which I am convinced kept us alive through the journey, but I swear I lost a couple of stone in pure sweat. And my face had come up in a fine bruise around the eye from the blow given to me in New Orleans.

As a troop train of sorts we were given priority over returning traffic so we made good time, considering the roundabout route we had to take.

There is no direct rail line from New Orleans to Atlanta, or wasn't then. So we took a circuitous course north to Jackson, then Granada, turning west at Grand Junction, and all the way across Alabama, through Decatur and into Tennessee, halting at Chattanooga. We had been told we would assemble in Atlanta, but in fact we halted about thirty miles north, at a town called Big Shanty. There we found a great mustering of Rebel troops, preparing to travel north up to Virginia.

With a great whooshing of released steam, the train halted, and at last we were permitted to disembark and, being early morning, given our first hot breakfast in a week.

Big Shanty was a temporary military base where new recruits were assembled into regiments and put into some kind of order, prior to boarding trains north to Virginia or wherever they were required. Row upon row of white tents ran along the west side of the road, with the railroad station and a huge shed to accommodate passengers opposite on the right.

All was chaos, with three or four thousand troops scattered about the area. It was raining steadily as our guards deposited us in the middle of this confusion, near the shed where a train with the imposing name of the General emblazoned in gold on the side plaque was just pulling in from the south. It was another General, I recalled angrily, who had brought me to this pretty pass.

'Here's the train in from Marietta,' calls out the station manager, and as I watched, the train halted and the engineer, fireman and conductor, along with a fair crowd of passengers, got out and made for the shed, probably for breakfast.

Soldiers and civilians were swarming everywhere, with no order that I could follow, and suddenly I noticed that my fellow volunteers were nowhere to be seen. They must have been taken along somewhere, and whoever was now escorting them had somehow overlooked me.

What luck! For the moment I was alone in this huge crowd, with nobody paying me the slightest heed. I knew this happy situation would not last, so I must grasp the moment and turn it to my advantage. But how? Not knowing what to do, I wandered casually towards the General, noticing that there were few passengers left on board. Soldiers were idling a short distance away, but taking no notice of the train or me. I'm not sure what I had in mind; perhaps I could sneak on board undetected, but it was facing north and might well be our troop train, which would have made me look a fool. Still undecided what to do, I ambled around behind the train to the far side, putting it between me and the tents, trusting to inspiration and my stars for something to turn up.

Fortune favours the brave, they say. Well we poltroons have our share too. Would you believe it, something turned up indeed. A few fellows in civilian rig were loitering around near the engine, and as I neared them, they climbed aboard. This meant nothing to me, but as I overtook the passenger carriages and came alongside the rear goods boxcar - there were three of them behind the engine and tender, followed by the passenger cars -

someone in the engine threw the steam valve wide-open, the wheels screeched piercingly, skidding in protest at the sudden release of pent-up energy, and taking a moment to grip, thrust the train forward as if shot from a cannon.

There are instants when you cannot stop to think. The second the engine fired and the wheels began skidding I rushed forward and hurled myself between the back and middle boxcar and held on for dear life. It was a spur of the moment decision and I had no notion where the train was going or what I should do next, but it was heading north, away from this Confederate camp, and that was what mattered right now. Time enough to make plans when I was over the hills and far away.

The train picked up a little speed and in no time it had cleared the town and was chugging steadily through the countryside. I was surprised to hear sounds of men yelling in what sounded like triumph from the front of the train, too many people to fit in the engine, and wondered who they might be. I recalled the men climbing on to the train were dressed in civilian garb, and I couldn't even make a guess. Never mind; as soon as we reached a station I would disembark quietly and be on my way to somewhere the Lord would provide.

Before we had gone much further the train began slowing down. We were in the wilderness and I couldn't see any reason for this. Once more I wondered who the Hell was driving, and what would they do if they discovered me. I was about to find out.

Suddenly the breaks squealed, forcing me to cling on anxiously, and we came to a full stop. Before I could collect my wits, the front boxcar opened and several men jumped out.

'What's happening Captain?' Cries one.

'No bother boys, seems the engineer back at Shanty closed the dampers. Bit of oil and wood will put us right. Jus' take a minute.'

By which I guessed the fire had gone out, though I couldn't be sure. But what was going on here?

'Hoy!'

I'd been seen. While I dithered, one of the men had walked down the train behind me and spotted my rear end jutting between the boxcars.

'Captain! We got ourselves a stowaway.'

Many footsteps, and before I could explain that I was there to oil the axles or something equally useful, there were half a dozen revolvers pointing at me.

'Now you just come down from there mister, nice and easy like.'

I obeyed, and found myself facing the man they had called Captain. He was six feet tall, medium build, clear complexion with grey eyes, dark hair and a long curling beard. I should put him in his mid-thirties. He ignored me at first and gave out orders to his men.

'Scott. Take care of that wire.'

'Right Cap'n.'

To my astonishment the man Scott shinned up the adjacent telegraph post like a squirrel, and proceeded to cut the wires.

'The rest of you keep an eye out.'

The Captain now turned to me. He looked me up and down carefully while his men held their guns menacingly, then spoke.

'Who are you and what are you doing here?'

I had been keeping my eyes and ears open wondering what to say I was about while he was weighing me up. Sabotaging the telegraph aside, it was plain these men had stolen this train. The engineers were in a desperate hurry to get it started as quickly as possible, shouting encouragement to each other while they stoked the fire. At the same time the edginess of the men in front of me, along with their military demeanour and immediate obedience to orders, said that these were not civilians. Nor were they common thieves with more ambition than sense. I saw with a start that the passenger cars were not with us. They must have unpinned them. And they did not sound as though they came from the South.

I decided to risk the truth; well, sort of.

'I'm running from the Rebels.'

'Go on...'

'They were trying to conscript me into their army so when I saw your train moving off I jumped on board to escape.'

'Engine's ready, Cap'n,' came a voice from ahead.

'Right.' He turned to the others. 'We'll have to take him with us. Ross, Dorsey, he's in your charge. Find out who and what he is and we'll decide what to do with him next time we stop.'

'He admits he's a Rebel deserter. Why not shoot him now, Cap'n? If he's been there all the time he must have heard our plans an all.'

'No I didn't,' I almost squealed. 'I couldn't hear a thing above the noise of the train. 'Sides, I ain't an eavesdropper...'

'Save it,' says the Captain. 'Dorsey, you should be ashamed of yourself. We are soldiers, not murderers. And this man is a civilian.'

I didn't care to mention I was sworn in to the Confederate Army. It was lucky the New Orleans folk kept their uniforms for their own men. Had I been in Rebel grey or butternut they might have shot me out of hand.

They bundled me into the first boxcar and the train took off once more.

'Alright mister,' says Ross. 'You heard the Captain. Who are you and what are you doing here?'

Now, when the Captain said they were soldiers not murderers, a mighty relief had stolen over me. I'd run the rule over these strange men. They appeared pretty pleased about something, and I guessed that they were Union Army escaping from the South, perhaps from captivity. It seemed my best policy was to travel along with them. And all I had to do was convince them I was on their side.

'Speak up.'

'It's all right Mr. ...Ross?'

'That's right. Now for the last time, who are you?'

The revolvers were pointing menacingly at me again, but I was no longer worried, on the outside at least.

I held out my hand and exclaimed jovially.

'Mr. George Jeffreys of the London *Times*, Sir. Lately from Fort Fillmore, Arizona, or New Mexico, I'm never quite sure which.'

Ross ignored my hand.

'What's that mister? You're an Englishman? From the London *Times* and Arizona?'

There were some amused snorts, but I was ahead of them.

'If you will just let me open the lining of my coat, I can show you proof.'

'We'll do better than that, mister. We'll open it for you.'

My other protector, Dorsey, retrieved my coat wrapped in my holdall and carefully cut a hole in the lining.

'It's a letter of introduction to the commanding officer at Fort Fillmore, Major Lynde. It gives my *bona fides*.' Fortunately I had sown it in my new coat at the Governor's in case it was again needed. Us intelligence officers always plan for the worst.

'Your what now?'

'My name and occupation. I toured the western States reporting on the war from the North's side.'

Dorsey handed the letter to Ross and he pored over it slowly. The other men, I noticed with relief, had put away their guns. Ross finished reading, said doubtfully that it looked convincing, and passed it to one of his comrades. He turned to me with a puzzled expression.

'If this is right, Mr. Jeffreys, how come we find you clinging to our train in the middle of Georgia?'

I was ready for that one.

'Fort Fillmore was taken by the Rebels. They captured Major Lynde's garrison, but as I was not in uniform they refused me parole. Instead they sent me back to the South where they said they'd make me fight for the Confederacy. I was taken back to Texas with their wounded and then under guard to their camp at Big Shanty where they ordered me to take the Rebel oath. Well, of course I refused,' I gave a wry grin and pointed at my face, still bruised from where I'd been punched, 'so they gave me twenty-four hours to change my mind, or...' I let it hang. 'Then I saw your train start up, so I shook off my guards and dived onto it.' I shrugged modestly, 'and that, gentlemen, is my story.'

Dorsey turned to one of his comrades.

'Hey, Wood. You're English. Ask him something about England.'

Wood lobbed me a few easy questions. Easy, that is, if you are English, including the name of the man on the column in Trafalgar Square, and how many innings in a cricket match, and what does LBW mean. As a bowler myself I quite warmed to him.

My story convinced them. My accent suited and the letter was impressive, so they relaxed and gave me some much-needed water.

'I'll tell the Cap'n you seem on the square, Mr. Jeffreys, though the Lord himself knows what we are gonna do with you.'

This raised an interesting point.

'I've told you who I am and how I come to be here, gentlemen. Suppose you do the same?'

Just then the train began to slow down again. The men shushed me to silence and took station, ready to spill out guns blazing on a signal from their Captain. It wasn't necessary, thank the heavens, as it was merely a wood-stop, where they could load up with wood for the engine. We stayed down as we heard the Captain asking some nearby workmen for a loan of an iron bar they evidently had with them, and they obliged. He seemed a cool hand, this Captain, and just the man to see us all safely back in Union Territory, for I'd decided I wanted to travel back to the North with them, if they'd have me.

Loaded with wood, the train began moving again as the heavens opened. Meandering around the many curves and corners, the General made its way slowly northwards. I still didn't know who these men were as they decided to show the Captain my letter first and let him decide what to do. I did learn that they were Union soldiers, as I guessed, and I knew they numbered about twenty, but nothing more. I imagined their aim was to get back home to the North, avoiding trouble on the way. Well I soon discovered my error.

'Here comes a bridge. Must be the Etowah River.' One of the men peering through a gap in the car informed us. This news put them on alert.

'Get ready.' The train slowly crossed the bridge and came to a halt. We stayed silent until one of the men from the engine opened the door.

'Job's off, boys,' says the Captain. 'We just spotted another train on a side track. It's not harnessed to any cars but it is puffing steam, so it could be used against us. There's a few loafers about too, so we will pick up some water and take off slow and steady. No point in us raising suspicions too early.'

He glanced at me, then back to Ross.

'It's OK, Captain. He's cleared himself.' He passed the Captain my letter.

'A reporter from the London *Times*?' He hopped into the boxcar.

'I reckon you got quite a tale to tell, but keep it short.'

I did, and he whistled and said if that don't beat all.

'Very well Mr. Jeffreys, its best you stay with us. Don't want you picked up by the Rebels, anyhow. My name is Andrews. They call me the Captain though in truth I am a civilian, but for now I am in charge of these soldiers here.'

I didn't understand why a civilian was commanding soldiers, but now was not the time to ask.

'Thank you Sir, and may I say how pleased I am...'

'No you may not. You know our strength so we cannot allow you to be captured. You're not a soldier, and you shouldn't be here at all. Very well. Men,' he called the others to attention. 'Mr. Jeffreys does not exist, d'ye hear? We don't want the Rebels saying we bring English newspapermen on our raids. Washington is having enough trouble with England as it is. So you don't know him, never saw him and you will not mention him to anyone ever.' He turned back to me and held out his hand with a smile. 'Welcome aboard Mr. Jeffreys. Like I said to the boys, you are not here. If ever I see this story in the London *Times* I will shoot you dead.'

'But who are you? What are you doing here?' My heart had started thumping at his mention of the word *raids*. That's a word to give me sleepless nights.

'The boys will explain. I'm a bit pushed for time.' Someone begged his pardon.

'What's that Mr. Knight?'

'That train, Cap'n. We had better destroy it, and the bridge.'

'Leave them both,' replies Andrews. 'We don't want to show our hand too soon. It won't make any difference. Now let's go.'

Back in the closed boxcar I learned the truth behind this strange journey. And wished I hadn't.

Far from fleeing the South, these men were volunteers on a death-or-glory mission. They had stolen the train at Big Shanty in order to drive it to the North, burning bridges behind them to paralyse the South's transport system from Atlanta to Chattanooga. You can imagine what I thought about *that*. With the bridges burnt, the Rebels could not reinforce Chattanooga when the Federals attacked it, and without reinforcements it would fall. This would be a dagger into the South's belly and, they hoped, help bring the war to a swift end.

So while Rebels stood aside and watched admiringly, the twenty of us were to chuff our way through the Confederacy, burning Lord knows how many bridges, for the two hundred miles north to Chattanooga, which was itself in Rebel hands.

'Now don't fret, Mr. Jeffreys, there's a fork before we get there. We will turn west and steam away on up to join with our General Mitchel, who is somewhere thereabouts.'

Bad enough, you'd think, but there was worse. You need to understand that this was a single track railroad with traffic running in both directions. The railroad people had designed a complicated system whereby trains adhered to a strict timetable in order to avoid head-on collisions. At certain stations a northbound train, say, would shunt into a siding and wait for the southbound train to pass by, then continue its journey north. If they ran an unscheduled train, for example due to the demands of war, then the first southbound train would fly a red flag from her rear, to let everyone know there was another southbound train due soon. So it was vital to keep to the timetable, which was why we had travelled at a slow rate so far.

The General was an express train, so once past Big Shanty the number of stops was limited. This meant giving fewer explanations to curious stationmasters and a faster ride to Chattanooga, not that that was much consolation.

Once again I was caught by the short hairs. I couldn't make my excuses and leave, Captain Andrews had made that plain. I was stuck with these heroic maniacs and not a thing to do about it. I raised an important military question.

'The Rebels must have noticed by now that they are a train short. What happens if they send one after us?'

'We'll run if we can, else we'll fight.'

That's what I feared. There was nothing for it, I must stay put and pray we and the Rebels keep to the timetable. On top of my fears I was dog tired. I thanked them for the information, begged their pardon and curled up in a corner, finishing with a Tommy *bon mot*. 'I've got sleep to catch up on. Wake me up if there's any shooting.'

We sped through Cartersville, leaving disappointed passengers on the platform in our wake, then stopped at Cassville. Rested, I was up again now. I had found a handy spy-hole in the corner of the boxcar, and watched anxiously to see how things went.

Andrews and Knight got out of the engine, and Andrews demanded wood and water. The aging wood tender (who astonished me by introducing himself as William Russel; for a moment I thought Billy had gone undercover) was suspicious as we had no passengers or morning mail, and we were not one of the regular crews. #Note_11

'I don't recollect ever seeing you fellows before,' says Russel. 'What have you got in there?' he pointed our boxcars.

'We are taking ammunition and powder for General Beauregard, and I have passes to prove it.'

Beauregard was at Shiloh, contesting a ferocious engagement with Union General Grant. Where, as I mentioned earlier, my old pal from California, General Albert Sidney Johnston, kicked the bucket.

Russel stared suspiciously at our boxcars.

'You just drop a few sparks from that pipe of yours inside,' continues Andrews, 'and you'll find out what's inside soon enough. There's powder an' more in those cars to blow you and your station into the middle of next week. We're hustling it through to Beauregard to shoot holes in Yanks with.'

'Oh, that's your lay is it?' says Russel. 'Hope you get through with it all right. The Federals ain't far off, and if they stop that peanut burner of yours, you're pretty sure to find out what the inside of a prison looks like.'

'We'll take our chances,' says Knight the engineer, 'but I'd hanged sight rather have the Yanks get me than run into a head-on with a southbound train. We've lost our schedule and if we don't get one pretty quick we're going to have trouble. Haven't you got one we can have?'

'Sure,' says the tank tender. After searching his pockets, he finally located a soiled piece of paper, which he handed to Andrews.

They jawed a bit more and Andrews's apparent sincerity won the old codger over. He even let Andrews take his railway map. I was beginning to like our Captain, as convincing a liar as me. Unluckily for him, he had courage too. That was his downfall, as I am still about the place while he has mouldered in his grave this many a year.

Much later I learned that he was engaged in buying contraband merchandise and smuggling it into the South for large sums of money, which made me like him more then ever.

The rain was still falling in buckets. Next stop Kingston. We were expecting a train coming in the opposite direction so, keeping to the railway practices, we passed slowly through the station, halted, then shunted back into a siding to await the southbound train. We stopped on the west side of the station.

The station crew eyed us uncertainly. They had been expecting the General with passenger cars and mail, and seeing we had neither their engineer approached our locomotive and challenged Andrews, standing alongside.

'How is this? What's up? Here's the engine with none of the passenger cars and a strange crew.'

Andrews replied 'I have taken this train by government authority to run ammunition through to General Beauregard, who must have it at once.'

He waved his hand at the boxcars and they nodded in agreement, and asked when the passenger train would be along.

'Soon enough,' responded Andrews indifferently, 'Don't suppose it can be long, they were readying a train when I left Atlanta.'

The southbound freight train was late. We couldn't leave until it had passed so we had no choice but to remain quiet in the boxcar while Anderson and Knight, him smoking a cigar, and our engineers, lounged nonchalantly on the platform. One of the boys, Wilson as I recall, gave me a snatched meal of buttermilk and cornbread.

Eventually Anderson went into the telegraph office and returned saying the southbound train should be here soon. He sympathised with the telegraph operator that the line from Atlanta was down, but he could do nothing about that. He refused to allow any telegraphs north, he told them, for fear the Yankees would intercept them.

Time was our enemy. The station crew and several waiting passengers regarded our train, and began to

199

wonder. This man had promised there would be a northbound replacement for the General, they were thinking, so where is it?

Suspense was high as the rest of us cowered in silence, awaiting the southbound train. Eventually it arrived, and slowly pulled up for wood and water on the main track. Seeing Andrews strolling about and apparently accepted by all, they had no reason to doubt his story and agreed to back up into another siding while we progressed. Then Andrews spotted the red flag on the back.

'What does this mean? asks Andrews. 'I am under orders to get this powder through to Beauregard and you are signalling for another train on the track.'

'Sorry Suh,' the southbound engineer apologised, 'its on account General Mitchel has taken Huntsville and is moving eastward towards Chattanooga. Our men there are sending goods to safety and the extra train is to get the rolling stock and goods out the way.'

Andrews thanked him for the information, and asked him to move further up the sidings to make room for the second train.

'But what will you do about Mitchel?'

'I do not believe Mitchel would be such a fool as to besiege Chattanooga, but if he does Beauregard will sweep him off the road. Now I have my orders, which are to get this powder north, so I'll be obliged if you can move your train up the siding.'

So we waited and the second train arrived. And damned if it too didn't have a red flag. Our boys were boiling fit to bust by now, cooped up in the boxcar, and I wasn't feeling too good myself.

Knight strolled back over to us and quietly related the position through the hatch, telling us to be ready for trouble at any moment.

'Boys,' whispers Knight, 'we have to wait for yet another train. Folk around here are getting suspicious and uneasy. Be prepared to leap out if we call you, and let them have it hot and fast.'

We looked around at each other in the crowded semi-darkness. One of our fellows, Robertson, fingered his pistol impatiently. He was just a lad, and looked ready and eager for a shoot-out. Sooner him than me. The suspense grew, along with the bile in my stomach. In silence the men shared out ammunition and primed their pistols. I still had a Colt Navy revolver, given to me by Baylor, and with shaking fingers I loaded five of the six cylinders, praying to God I wouldn't have to use it.

The passengers outside grumbled because the replacement northbound train had not showed, and why had Atlanta not warned them before the signal was lost? Andrews stayed cool, blaming slack-jawed Atlanta railroad officials.

'Listen out for whistles,' whispers Ross. 'From the north it's the southbound train, from the south it means they are chasing us.'

My bowels shivered at this, and they were not improved when almost as he said it we heard the distant tooting of a train whistle, sounding like the cry of a hawk hovering above. I was not the only one to stiffen, and we were relieved when we realised it came from the north. The third train arrived and once more Andrews ordered it into the sidings.

'Adjust the switch right away,' orders Andrews, but the switch driver folded his arms in defiance.

'Unless I get authority from Atlanta your train stays where it is.' With that he stomped back into his office.

Andrews followed him good-humouredly. Reaching the door he practically yelled at the man, making it plain for everyone to hear.

'I have no more time to waste with you. If you won't throw the switch I'll do it myself.'

He marched into the office, collected the keys and calmly went off to do the job. I'll say this for Andrews, he was as brazen as a snake-oil salesman in a cattle town.

The switch driver followed him, buzzing like a mosquito around a bull elephant, threatening to arrest Andrews, report him and have him gaoled. Andrews ignored him and went about throwing the switch. He displayed such calm, authoritative confidence that nobody dared move to stop him.

Our train finally squealed into action, and pulled slowly along the siding to the main line. As our engineers shunted it along, Andrews continued his bluff.

'It's a disgrace that civilian jackanapes obstruct the war effort,' he snarled at the station crew, 'and by God unless you shape up we must introduce martial law.' He glared at the passengers. 'That goes for you too.'

He said he'd remember Kingston and its unpatriotic staff, wouldn't he just. That quietened them. Some passengers even applauded, agreeing the army came first.

Andrews and Knight climbed aboard the engine, and at last we were on our way.

Our pursuers arrived at Kingston four minutes later.

Chapter Thirteen

Once beyond the station we stopped and Andrews ordered the telegraph wires cut, and placed rocks and debris on the track.

Now we were clear of any scheduled trains coming towards us until we made the next station, we were able to stoke up the fire and put on speed.

'Push it boys,' says Andrews, 'from now on we'll burn any bridge we cross.'

The rain was getting worse and we feared it might derail us should we take one of the many winding curves too fast, but Andrews hurtled us along and the men in the carriage cheered him for it. All but one, and you may have three guesses who that was. We halted a mile or two further on to cut the wires again and lift a rail. It was warm work and I had to lend a hand to lever it from the ground. As I perspired in the pounding rain I couldn't help thinking that these clowns should have thought to bring along the proper bars for rail-raising. Brute force eventually did the trick, but we lost time, and suddenly heard the sound I dreaded.

Like the plaintiff cry of a lone wolf in the mountains, the whistle of a locomotive in pursuit echoed through the trees.

'How far?' asks Andrews quietly. I sat still quaking, for the sound had put the willies up me.

'Must be 'bout two or three miles.'

'All aboard,' yells Andrews. I'll swear he was enjoying himself.

We bounced swiftly along the track and in short order arrived at Adairsville. Again we shunted into a side-track to await the southbound train and Andrews bluffed his way confidently through the usual questions. The station crew believed him without demur but this time presented him with a new problem.

'The extra trains from Chattanooga have torn our schedule to shreds, Captain Andrews Suh. The reg'lar train ain't due for a whiles. She's running a fair bit late.'

This was a facer for Andrews. We cannot have been more than fifteen minutes at best ahead of our pursuers. We'd sprung the rails but if they knew their work, that wouldn't hold them long. I should have known his response.

'You'll have to wait here 'till the passenger train comes through,' continues the station manager.

'No, I must go at once. The fate of our army depends on my getting through promptly with these carloads of ammunition. Suppose the Yankees attack Beauregard? He has not powder enough for three hours fight.'

The manager bridled a little, but seeing Andrews was not to be gainsaid, finally replied.

'Get through by all means, but you will have to run very slow and put a flag-man out on every curve or you will have the most awful collision.'

'I will attend to that,' snaps Andrews. He stepped back up onto the engine and motioned to our engineer to open the throttle. The General chuffed slowly out of the station, but once clear we felt the engine heave and the train surged on up to breakneck speed. Andrews had decided to race it to the next station.

Had I not been imprisoned in the boxcar, I would have shaken Andrews warmly by the throat. The maniac was trying to dash north while another train was rolling south on the same track. Devil a doubt we would smash into each other, leaving nothing but kindling. I had a vision of my Julie laying my headstone; *hereabouts lies Tommy, smashed into a thousand little pieces all over Georgia, April twelve, 1862. Never did find most of him.*

We sped on at full steam to reach Calhoun, the next station, before the southbound train collided with us. We were thrown about the boxcar like dice in a tumbler as the General rocked and reeled fit to frighten the thundergod. How the train stayed upright I'll never understand. With the train whistle blowing constantly we ran nine miles in seven and a half minutes on light track, at least one of us expecting death at every moment.

For a wonder we made it. The southbound passenger train was about to leave the station but seeing us approaching, slackening speed and whistling for our lives, it backed up the track and let us into the platform. With the train in front of us, however, we could not pass. The train and station crews were stunned by our arrival and demanded an explanation.

'I must press on without delay,' says Andrews, after explaining how Beauregard needed our ammunition and the whole war depended on us getting through pronto. I think by now he was believing it himself. 'Pull your engine into the siding ahead and let me out.' He looked and sounded like a man who would brook no argument and they obeyed on the instant. He tried to convince the southbound conductor it was now safe for him to progress down the track, which would have sold our pursuers good and proper, but the faintheart was so shaken by our sudden arrival that he refused to move until he had clearance from Adairsville. Andrews gave up and we started forward once more.

At last we had a clear road to Chattanooga. Just past Calhoun we broke the track and the telegraph wires once more. Again we heard the whistles of our unseen pursuer. Why they were advertising their presence baffled me until one of the raiders explained it was to clear the track of travellers at the many blind corners. Our engineers weren't so fussy.

Excitement in the boxcar was growing. The boys had been cursing a frustrating day hiding silently in station sidings. Now at last it was getting time to fire the bridges.

After a long, straight road, the General crossed a river and halted. We jumped out of our boxcar as Andrews and Knight climbed down from the engine.

'Oostenaula Bridge,' cries Knight. 'Come on boys, this is what we're here for.'

'Train!'

I swung around and my stomach gave a lurch. Not two miles away a locomotive was puffing towards us. Andrews thought fast.

'Jettison the last boxcar.' We'll take off and leave it to slow 'em down.'

Willing hands unpinned the last car and we climbed back into the first one. We hadn't time to derail it and the pursuing train, its engine running in reverse, simply pushed it along in front, making it nothing but a gesture. We could see this clearly as the train took a wide, arching circle giving us a panoramic view through the still thunderous rain. We had no time to burn the bridge either. It would have taken an age to ignite the sodden wooden struts.

We raced through a nearby town, dropping our second boxcar in the station, with identical results. For all Andrews' calm under pressure, it struck me this raid was turning into something of a farce.

'I'm sick of this running,' says one of the boxcar boys, 'let's stand and fight.'

This was the worst news I'd had all day, which was saying quite something.

'We don't know the strength of the forces on the chasing train,' replies Ross.

'We daren't take the risk.'

Spoken like a man, thinks I. They should place those words on my headstone.

Past Resaca we dropped boulders and rubbish from the boxcar onto the track behind us to slow pursuit, and Scott shinned up the telegraph post and cut the wires again. We stopped at a wood-station to stack up with firewood, and quickly lugged a number of heavy wooden sleepers to drop behind us onto the rails.

We had only half-filled the tender when our pursuers steamed into view, and we had to board the engine and remaining boxcar at speed. The chasing train was now so near it had to slow up so as not to hit us and its occupants opened fire with shotguns, but the pellets fell wide. We sped on, throwing sleepers in our wake. Some of the boys began hacking at the boxcar itself and hurling bits of it overboard.

I was struggling to control my fear. The enormity of what we were doing closed in on me and I knew any of us caught by the Rebels would face the noose, if not immediate lynching. Could I claim they'd kidnapped me? Aye, that was it. They held me hostage at Big Shanty and had taken me along against my will. Would the Rebels believe me? It was damned unlikely; I wouldn't have done. My best hope was that we managed somehow to stay ahead of our nemesis until... until what? As the boys cracked yet another piece of the boxcar and spilled it on the rails, I could only cower in the far corner and hope for the best.

Our obstructions slowed the pursuers, and darting through the many twists and turns of the track we managed to lose sight of them. We raced through Tilton without stopping then halted at a water-station. Andrews related our Beauregard tale once again, even though we only had one boxcar and that was looking like a good night out in bedlam, battered and beaten with splintered sides and most of the back missing. We were only half-filled with water before our chasers approached and we fled, dropping obstructions behind us. Past the water-station we stopped and cut the wires as usual, hurled more ties and sticks of firewood on the track and quickly resumed our crazy race.

Again some wanted to fight, but others yelled we only had revolvers against shotguns and rifles. There was much grumbling at this; and I wondered why they hadn't thought to bring rifles along before launching their suicidal venture. And dragging me along, rot them.

We approached Dalton, a fair sized town. Here the road forked west, avoiding Rebel-held Chattanooga, and Andrews himself flicked the switch. There were many townsfolk about, but he threw them easily.

'I am running this train to Corinth and have no time to spare.'

God knows what they must have thought, for our boxcar was open to the world now, with sixteen damn-your-eyes men looking menacing at them, and your correspondent at the back trying to burrow underneath, but no-one dared challenge us. There was an enclosed station shed over the track, and we rolled through just as another whistle announced the pursuers. We approached a great tunnel, a perfect place for an ambush, but to my relief went right through, and on past the village of Tunnel Hill beyond.

The rain still fell in torrents. I'll say this for Andrews, he didn't give up easily. On his orders attempted to set the last boxcar ablaze as we drove, and climbed into the tender. With some difficulty we got the drenched boxcar smouldering, well, they did, using the last of our engine oil and blazing faggots from the engine. We removed the pin and left the smouldering boxcar behind. The rain put the fire out and the chasers simply pushed it to safety.

The mission had failed. It had failed through bad weather, bad planning, the relentless pursuit and plain bad luck. If only the Yankees had not advanced on Huntsville, scaring the pants off the Rebels and making them evacuate two trainloads of supplies and goods from Chattanooga, the raid would probably have succeeded and cut off the South's rail communications. Then they could have taken Chattanooga and much else besides, and the Rebels could have neither reinforced nor quickly retreated. Usual lack of military co-ordination, of course. It happens in every army.

All thought now was of escape. We threw splinters, papers and even Andrews's saddlebags into the furnace, but were fast running out of fuel. We needed to get to Bridgeport where the Yankees were advancing, we hoped, about thirty miles past Chattanooga.

'Right boys,' shouts Andrews over the noise of the engine, 'time to run. Our best bet is to split up and flee to the mountains where the Rebel cavalry cannot follow us. We each have a revolver and ammunition, so God bless you all and we'll met back at our lines in a few days.'

This was appalling. When talk had turned to escape, I'd imagined the whole twenty of 'em, with Tommy snug in the middle, crossing the mountain range together, a match for anyone we were likely to encounter. Andrews thought different. His plan was that we would all drop off the slowing train in ones and twos, and make our way back independently. This way we were changing from a formidable force to a smattering of refugees on the run. Some of the boys raised this point but Andrews gestured them to silence.

'We'll do it my way. No arguments. When I give the word, jump off and scatter.'

Over the next uphill mile or so the raiders jumped over the side of the tender and sprawled into the bracken. The numbers were getting low and, with a charming smile. Andrews glanced at me.

'So long Mr. Jeffreys. Remember what I said. Good luck.'

That was all. I'd had time to think, and it was plain I couldn't risk capture by the Rebels, so crossing the mountains and reaching the Federal army was my best hope. I didn't want to do it alone, though, so waiting for the next man to jump, I jumped with him.

I landed in a bush and rolled through it and onto soft, soggy ground. Shaking myself, I stumbled up and looked around for the man who had jumped with me. There he was, brushing himself down.

'Come on man, run!' shouts I, and crashed through the undergrowth in a westward direction. He took one look at me and followed.

So ended the Andrews Raid of 1862. #Note_12

We ascended a small bank to find a strip of woodland separated from a wheat field by a fence. Spurred on by gunfire behind us - the pursuing train must have caught up with the General at last - we tramped through the wheat, struggling with the thick, clinging mud. We arrived, chests heaving, at dense woodland, passed gratefully into the cover of the trees, and collapsed, panting.

I had struck lucky in attaching myself to this raider. His name was Jacob Parrot, not much more than a boy, but he bore an old head on young shoulders, and an air of quiet authority which belied his years. A carpenter by profession, of middling height and dark complexion, with black hair and eyes.

He was calm with an easy manner and knew what he was about. He also seemed to have studied the land he had gone stealing trains in, and his invaluable knowledge prevented me running around in circles, as would have been the case had I travelled alone.

We had to move quickly, as the hue and cry would soon be up and by tomorrow morning the woods would be buzzing with angry Rebels. We'd poked their beehive with a stick and they would be gunning for us and toting a rope.

Conserving our strength for putting as much distance behind us and pursuit as possible, we didn't talk much that first evening. We staggered up and down uncountable small hills and valleys with narrow woods. Presently we arrived at the bend of a small river.

'That's Chickamauga Creek, Tom,' says Parrot.

'Where does it go?'

'It flows into the Tennessee River just a mite above Chattanooga. We gotta cross it.'

That was what I feared. The creek was swollen angrily by the rains, and the bank opposite stood cliff-like, towering above us. I later discovered that had we followed it downstream, as alone I would have done, we'd have been cut off by another stream joining it. Knowing the terrain, the Rebels caught several of our men in this trap.

There was nothing for it. Holding his gun above his head Parrot waded into the frantic stream. Commending my soul to the Lord, I did the same with my holdall and followed him.

Clinging to rock and rotting vegetation, I stumbled after Parrot through the rain-swollen torrent, and finally fetched up at the far bank; a high wall of mud and moss extending in either direction as far as the eye could see. Parrot pocketed his revolver and began to ascend, clinging to the sparse vegetation. He looked down and saw me hesitating.

'Climb damn you. The Rebels ain't more'n five minutes behind us. If they catch us here they'll shoot us like dogs.'

I didn't need telling twice. Fear lent me wings and I scrambled up the bank after him, grasping clumps of grass and pulling myself up hand over hand by main strength.

At last we crested the bank, pulling ourselves over the top and lying flat out, panting till our lungs were sore.

We had hardly got our breath back when from close behind came a sound to fill us with dread; the doleful baying of bloodhounds.

'How come they got hounds on our trail so goddam fast?' cries Parrot.

Lets stay here while we figure it out, shall we? thinks I. Then when they catch us we can ask them how they did it. Aloud I replied.

'Come on man, the hounds can't follow us through that river. Let's go.'

I didn't know it then, but by the most confounded luck it was a muster day at the nearby town of Ringgold. Hundreds of mounted and well-armed men were assembled there for training. Our pursuers had alerted them and their exercise was now real. We had half a blasted regiment hunting us. The dogs would have belonged to local plantation owners, used to tracking runaway slaves over this very land. Those dogs probably knew every twig. And their owners knew which way we would run, damn 'em.

We sped off rapidly, through more woods, oblivious to our empty stomachs and sodden clothes. The rain teemed to swamp the Ark, which Parrot pointed out was a blessing, as it would make it harder for dogs to track us. True enough, the sound of baying faded and Parrot opined that none of our fellows can have been captured yet.

'Not heard any gunshot, anyhow,' says he.

This was a pity, since capturing some of the others would hold them up, but I didn't point this out. I just grunted, saving my energy for our journey.

As dusk gathered we slowed down to a careful walk, over shallow hills and across innumerable streams. We could hear nothing behind us and my hopes rose that we had eluded our hunters. The rain stopped at last, but with almost total cloud overhead we could not see the sun and had to hope for the best. We were aiming west, but Parrot had no compass - more bad planning - so we could only hope we hadn't strayed too far from our course.

We descended down a long slope into a valley concealed all around by woods. Suddenly Parrot grabbed my arm. I froze, and he pointed to a rough hut half-concealed by the trees, with a man smoking in a scrubby garden.

'I'll go an' ask him how far to Chattanooga,' he whispers. 'You got your gun?'

I nodded, and pulled it from my sodden holdall.

'Cover me. He can't know about our raid, and folks are generally helpful in the backwoods, but keep your gun handy jus' in case.'

He walked forward boldly, while I wondered what I should do if the man yelled for help and his ten armed sons rushed out of the hut. There was only one answer to that.

It wasn't necessary though. Parrot was right, and the man helpfully informed him that the town was eight miles north. This was good news, as it showed we were travelling in the right direction and had made fair progress. We weren't going to Chattanooga, of course, but that's what the man would say should our hunters ask him.

We were to circle around Chattanooga and make our way north to, if they were there, the Union forces. As dusk began to fall and I relaxed slightly, hunger began gnawing at my stomach, and I trudged on as if in a dream, and a nightmare at that.

I was roused out of it soon enough, when after about an hour we came across the very hut where Parrot had asked directions. We had walked in a bloody circle. I jumped as we again heard the cry of distant hounds.

Too done in even to curse, we set off again, this time determined to travel in a straight line. In due course we

212

arrived at a river, but Parrot said he knew of no such river hereabouts.

'It might be the Chickamauga,' says he, 'or one of its tributaries. With all this rain I cannot tell.'

To attempt to ford it was certain death, so we walked along the bank, hoping the skies would clear or Parrot would see some landmark he recognised. We daren't rest, though every limb in my body was screaming to lie down.

Presently we came upon a path running adjacent to the river. We were both too far gone to trudge through the trees, so heedless of the risk we walked along the path, making good time, though we didn't know where to. In the twilight we encountered a Negro driving a team. He told us we were but four miles from Chattanooga. So we had walked north instead of west. Parrot wisely asked the Negro the direction of Ringgold so we had two reference points with which to set a course, and we passed on. The Negro wasn't likely to betray us, even if anyone listened to him.

'It ain't too bad,' says Parrot. 'Six or seven miles will bring us to Tennessee if we can keep our way this time.'

Soon after, the river swung right, and we left the path and trailed over several steep hills and deep valleys. The sky had cleared, for a mercy, and with the North Star to our right we could steer a steady course. Eventually we arrived at a banked road, and skirting it carefully, we passed several houses and joined it when we were clear. The sky now clouded again and a light drizzle fell, dampening our spirits along with our clothes, which had all but dried out through our exertions. I was nearly done, and Parrot was hardly in any better shape. My teeth chattered with the cold which cut through to the bone.

There was nothing for it. We climbed some way above the road, and finding a gnarled old fallen tree, lay down on the lee side and fell into the ecstasy of blissful, dreamless sleep.

'You boys OK?'

It took me a moment or two to realise where I was. Parrot was quicker, and he jumped up at the sound of the voice.

Before us stood an elderly man cradling a shotgun, but not appearing aggressive in any way. Indeed, it seemed to me his voice registered concern. Parrot must have thought the same, for he replied humbly.

'Pardon us Sir, we are Kentuckians fleeing from the Yankee rule. We are on the way to enlist with the Confederate Army at Chattanooga as we hear there is a Kentucky Regiment there.' In fact, Parrot had already told me he was from Ohio, but he could hardly admit that.

Note well Parrot's story. It has a major bearing on the fate of the fleeing raiders. The elderly man sighed.

'This terrible war. I just wish our boys were at home. Come and let me give you something to eat.'

The mention of something to eat awoke my stomach, and I nodded vigorously to Parrot. He eyed the man suspiciously, but must have reckoned that with us both armed he dare not play us false.

He led us a short way, to not much more than a hovel, and cooked up some cornbread and bacon with coffee. We gobbled it greedily while the old man lamented the terrible state of things, and hoped he would live long enough to see better times. I kept quiet, mostly, lest I betray my origins, but I doubt it would have mattered anyway. We got chatting and the old man remarked that yesterday was the first anniversary of the beginning of the war. I could have found better ways to spend it.

The old man had a brush and razor, and after eating we made a fairly satisfactory toilet, cleaning our mud-stained clothes, and you would never have suspected we had spent the night under a log. Parrot paid the man in Confederate dollars.

'Don't let anyone know you've been here.' He pleaded, as we thanked him and took our leave.

Parrot said later he was sure he was a Union man, and would have helped us if he could, but directions to

Chattanooga - which we had no intention of utilising - were all we could ask for.

'Have you any money George?'

'Fraid not, I'm cleaned out.' I wondered if this was a touch. Seemed a deuced odd time to be borrowing money.

'They kitted us out with plenty. Here.' he unpeeled several notes from a wad of Rebel dollar bills and handed them to me. 'Case we get split up.'

We plodded on, and our road took us alongside a creek, swollen to the size of a small river by the rains, and made steady progress throughout the morning.

Eventually we spied scattered houses ahead, and I suggested dropping back into the woods, but Parrot disagreed.

'We must be ahead of the news here. Best we wander into town and ask directions.'

I didn't like it, but we were totally lost now, and couldn't stroll around the Confederacy like vagrants forever, and the morning's meal was wearing off, so I agreed.

We made our way to the edge of town just as church bells began ringing.

'Sunday worship,' says Parrot. 'Good news, as the street will be crowded and we won't stick out so much.'

I looked at our bedraggled clothes and doubted it.

'But these villagers all know each other,' says I. 'Any strangers will stick out like a sore thumb.'

'Too late now; let me do the talking.'

My innards did a summersault as I saw half a dozen rough-looking men approaching us, armed with two rifles and a shotgun. They had *search party* written all over their grizzled faces.

We couldn't turn back, so Parrot took a deep breath and faced up to them.

'Good morning gentlemen, what can we do for you?'

They gathered around us before replying, and I strove to look calm with my heart in my mouth.

'Kin we talk to you?' says a gruff voice.

'Very well,' answers Parrot in a relaxed manner. 'I will be glad to hear anything you have to say.'

His attitude seemed to calm the men, and their spokesman continued in politer vein.

'No doubt all is well, but strange things have been happening in these parts, and it is my duty to question every feller who passes through the area.'

'What strange things?'

'Best we discuss it inside. I'm the mayor in case you wonder 'bout my authority. Follow me, please gents.'

My face reddening in fear, I followed Parrot and the mayor, with the lads galumphing behind. There was nothing else to do.

He took us to a small office on the edge of town, and, beckoning us forward, turned and faced us. The lads of the village moseyed on in behind and stood or sat around us like an inquisition.

'Now Sir,' says he to Parrot. 'What are your names and where are you from?'

'My name is Jacob Hagan of Fleming County, Kentucky, and this is my friend George Wade,' says Parrot. 'Now what are these strange things of which you talk?'

He was a cool hand, I'll say that for him. A good fellow was Jacob Parrot, and just the man for a tight corner.

'The Yankees stole a train on the railroad, tried to burn our bridges then skedaddled. The hunt is up and we're gonna find them wherever they run to.'

We both expressed surprise, and Parrot said it was the darndest thing.

'So yore both from Fleming County in Kentucky?'

'And proud of it.'

'I see...' He reached in a draw and produced a book of maps of some kind.

'Tell me, where is the county seat?'

'Flemingsburg,' answers Parrot without hesitation. Give me a man who does his homework, thinks I. When you want to establish an alibi, first establish the facts.

'That's right. Now, name the counties surrounding your'n.'

Luckily the mayor seemed to expect Parrot to do the talking for us both. I looked down at the floor and tried to give my impression of a village idiot.

Parrot paused, and I thought Jesu, this is it. He finally replied, naming three counties.

'Let me jes' check.'

The mayor thumbed his maps, then began laughing.

'Sorry Suh, them's counties right enuff, but none of them border yore county of Fleming.'

The lads haw-hawed, but quite friendly, while I measured the distance to the door. Parrot was unfazed.

'I bet none of you folk here can name all your neighbouring counties neither,' says he, grinning.

They all laughed at this, and sparked off a great naming contest. Do you know, not one of the lads could name all their neighbouring counties? The mayor put away his book and became more conversational.

'And what brings ye to these parts, Jacob?' says the mayor.

'Well Sir, we fled Kentucky because we could not stand living under Lincoln no more. We came to enlist in the Confederate army and fight for our right to live free of Yankee interference.'

The mayor seemed to believe us, and the atmosphere, which had earlier seemed too much like a lynch party for my liking, relaxed. They stacked their pieces and eyed us in an almost friendly manner.

'This sounds well, Jacob, an' we'll be happy to speed you on yore way, but first we'll have to search you both to make sure yore possessions are in harmony with yore claims. As good Southern men you won't mind such an inconvenience for yore country's good.'

We could hardly object, and they checked our possessions and pockets, and my holdall, but found nothing amiss. My heart was in my mouth when they searched my coat pockets, but none felt inclined to check the lining so my letter introducing me to Major Lynde as

George Jeffreys of the London *Times* remained undiscovered. Lord knows how many holes it would have punched in our story. Our chief possessions were our guns and Confederate dollars, both normal in the circumstances, which they returned to us. I stuffed my dollars in my trouser pocket and reached for the holdall to store my revolver.

'Sorry to keep worrying you gents, but I gotta ask, where were you yesterday?'

'We'd been at Chattanooga, Sir, looking about for several days.'

'Then why did you not enlist there?'

You've blundered Parrot, thinks I. Face calm, but panicking underneath, I placed my pistol handily in my coat pocket instead of the holdall. If things went adrift, it might buy me a head start.

But Parrot was ready with the answer.

'We didn't care for those raw conscript regiments at Chattanooga,' replies he, 'but we heard tell the finest regiment in these parts is the First Georgia. They're over at Corinth and we are making our way there now.'

This was the best answer he could have given. We were in Georgia and it flattered their State pride to hear Kentuckians say one of their very own was the finest.

'Why that's dandy,' says the mayor admiringly.

'True enuff so,' adds one of the lads to much agreement.

'But say,' continues the mayor, who was beginning to get on my nerves, 'why did you not go d'rectly to Corinth instead of making a circuit out here?'

Parrot didn't hesitate. 'Because Mitchel has taken Huntsville and we want to keep out of his reach.' I could have kissed him

This satisfied them at last. The mayor turned to the lads.

'We may as well let them go, for they are all right.'

'Thank you Sir,' says Parrot while I grunted ingratiatingly.

The mayor shook our hands and we made to leave. We hadn't reached the door, however, when it flew wide open and in burst a flushed youngster with exciting news.

'They've caught the bridge burners,' cries he breathlessly.

Shouts and yowls of exultation. The lads whooped and hollered. I joined in immediately, and with my eyes urged Parrot to do the same.

When we had all calmed down the mayor and the lads pressed the boy for further information.

'Where? Who are they? What did they do? What were they after?' and more worryingly, 'did they ketch them all?'

'Jes' a few o' them,' cries the boy. 'They denied they wuz Yankees at fust, but our boys got it out of 'em.'

More cheering from the lads.

'They fust made out they wuz citizens of Fleming County, Kentucky.'

You'll think me fanciful, but for a moment I swear I could hear my own heart beating.

'...Why,' cries the mayor incredulously, staring from the boy to Parrot and me, 'but that's what...'

He stopped short, as he was looking down the barrel of my pistol.

'Get down!' says I, not too loudly. 'All of you on the floor. 'Jacob, collect their guns.'

Parrot wasted no time gathering up the three weapons. Luckily none had side arms.

'You cover 'em, Jacob, I'll get us some horses.'

'Keep it short, George.'

I stepped out of the office casually, so as not to alert the Sunday worshippers and loafers, and strode back down the road we had come up. The rain was beginning to fall again and the street was emptying. There were no horses handy, so I carried on back along the way, turned a corner and with nobody in sight, began sprinting frantically the way we had come, down to the creek. There was a house backing onto it, and I hoped beyond hope that where there was a house on the creek, there would be a boat.

There was. A dandy little canoe tethered but not tightly secured. A second to loosen the ropes and I cast off downstream.

Nice fellow, Parrot, and deuced handy in a jam. I'd miss him.

Chapter Fourteen

All of the Andrews Raiders, as they came to be known, were caught, and several were hanged, including Andrews himself. Others were exchanged and in later years wrote their accounts, some of which I have used here as crib sheets for my own recollections. They have helped me put names to the places and suchlike, though their accounts, and mine, differ in minor details. For example, some say there was a mutiny against Andrews when he refused to ambush our pursuers; well I heard grumbling, but no more than that. The best account for my money is by Corporal William Pittenger, but you have to watch him, for he uses my trick of the modest brag to inflate his own importance (he even had the effrontery to claim Parrot's and my interrogation in the mayor's office for his own - truly a man after my own heart). Beyond muttering to himself and telling the others to mind their cursing, during the raid I barely noticed him.

Parrot survived, you'll be relieved to learn. When the lads of the village finally overpowered him, they worked off their anger by dishing out one hundred lashes with rawhide, and threatening him with immediate shooting. They wanted Parrot to confess everything, including all he knew about me, but he defied them and was eventually imprisoned and exchanged. He later became a Union Lieutenant. Truly I had chosen him wisely.

None of the raiders' accounts mentions my name, or George Jeffreys's name rather, though some refer to me as an unknown accomplice. The Confederate newspapers reported that one raider escaped, which I suppose will have to do. I've had more than my share of undeserved praise, so missing out when for once I deserved some (well, I helped bust the rail you know, and I was there all the way) seems only fair.

Most accounts also recognise that sharing one background between them was an act of folly. I mean to say, with all of them claiming to come from the same county in Kentucky, it only needed the Rebels to catch a few and the rest of the raiders would give themselves away by making the same claim. It was all at one with the overall planning. Andrews was a dedicated Unionist whose courage and nerve under pressure got the raiders as far as they did, but such a raid requires the most detailed planning, and here Andrews let himself and his comrades down. No rifles, no proper implements for breaking rails to prevent the Rebels chasing them, not enough compasses and failing to persuade the Yankees to hold their advance until after the mission (though bad weather delayed the raid by a day, which made all the difference).

Worse, despite the pleading of his raiders, Andrews refused to turn on his pursuers. He had at least two ideal opportunities to do so, but he turned them down. Not that I blame him for that, but splitting us up when he abandoned the raid condemned them all. Together we (well, they) could probably have fought our way to safety.

None of this counts. What matters is that the raid failed, all the Yankee raiders were caught with several hanged, and if I have survived into a rich and debauched old age, it is no fault of theirs.

Within two minutes of escaping the mayor's office and his toughs, I was in a small canoe hurtling along a dangerously swollen creek that was close to bursting its banks. The rain flung itself down from the heavens once again, to add to the deluge of the past days and further swell the seasonal spring flood. I clung helplessly to the bottom of the canoe, head down as it bobbed and eddied to the whims of nature. I didn't fight it; all that mattered was that I put as great a distance as possible between me and danger, and this splendid little canoe was increasing that distance by the second.

I must have covered a mile or more when the creek ran through a deep gorge, narrowing down to a tithe of its former width. The banks either side towered menacingly above the foaming torrent, like gods pointing down in judgement, and you can imagine who was in the dock. The current squeezed through the gorge at rapid pace, jostling me every way to Sunday and crashing into logs, debris and general river flotsam.

After an age, the creek widened and the water calmed to a steady flow. I was able to engage the paddle and make an attempt at controlling the canoe's direction. The current now became manageable, and as the rain died down and the sun broke through the clouds I became less concerned with staying afloat and more with evading any pursuit. I had been chased quite enough for one lifetime, and needed a moment or two to collect my thoughts.

The creek was running through low-lying woods now, and I let the canoe float gently along, I saw we were about to join what looked like a fully grown river. Where there were rivers, there were people, so I carefully paddled to the Northern shore and, balancing precariously, stepped up onto the bank. With an effort I pulled up the canoe, upended it to lose the river water, dragged it behind some bushes and covered it with foliage. I sought now to find out exactly where I was and what in blazes I should do next.

There was a large, rounded rock under a spreading tree, and finding it dry, I sat down wearily, removed my sodden coat and collected my thoughts.

And such thoughts they were. Here I was, somewhere between Chattanooga and Corinth. Parrot had given me a general description of the area, and it seemed to me that unless I was completely out, this river must be the Tennessee. It flowed west, which was the way Parrot had wanted to go, so that suited me. My best course of action was to lie low here until nightfall, then launch myself along the Tennessee River and put many more miles between me and the furious Rebels of Georgia. Then what? Could I find the Union troops that the raiders insisted were somewhere about the place? Deuced risky. This was the South, so where there were Union troops, there would be Confederate troops disputing their progress. To come between them was asking for buckshot from both sides.

The Tennessee River flowed west then swung north towards Shiloh, where just a week ago the Confederates had kicked the Yankees up the arse. They had failed to follow through, though, and U.S. General Grant had got his second wind and was looking to get his own back. Both sides would be trigger-happy, so I decided I would not risk travelling north if I could help it. But where would travelling west get me?

Above the sun blazed hot. My spirits rose while my clothes began to steam with evaporating river water, and the warmth thawed the ice in my bones. Feeling more like myself, I became conscious of the fact that I hadn't eaten since morning and it was now late afternoon. I marked carefully the position of my hidden canoe, and began scouting the area to see if I could find something to eat.

I tramped uphill through the undergrowth and came to a well-worn path winding along the valley. Walking about half a mile, I arrived at a cabin set a little back, conspicuous by a slender stream of smoke rising gently from its stack.

Parrot had told me that itinerant strangers wandering the backwoods commonly knocked on doors begging for food. He claimed this attracted no undue attention. Well if they could do it, so could I. Checking my revolver was dry, I donned my most ingratiating smile and rapped gently on the door.

A middle aged man answered, and I gave him my prepared story about how I was from Texas, but travelling to Decatur in Alabama and had become separated from my companion when the Yankees chased us at Huntsville. I would pay willingly for a supper and directions to set me on my way.

The man seemed welcoming enough, and my manner was friendly-humble, so he admitted me without too much delay.

'What do ye call yourself, Suh?'

'Err... Jeffreys. George Jeffreys.'

'Well Mr. Jeffreys, you are welcome to sit down at our table.'

My luck was in, for dinner was about to be served, white tie optional. They hung my coat beside the fireplace to dry, and I took my place downwind of the family. After saying grace at the man's behest, we tucked in to some fine Sunday meat and vegetables. I was keenly aware of his wife and youngsters staring at my bedraggled appearance with a mixture of curiosity and disdain. It couldn't be helped. The main thing was that they didn't holler for a constable.

I handed over a Rebel dollar for the meal, which the man accepted without a murmur, and set me on my way. Here I learnt something to my advantage.

'Well Suh, if'n you follow the Tennessee River west you will come to Decatur and the railroad soon enuff. You din't say what you wuz goin' there fer, an' I ain't asking, but you best hurry if'n you want to get there afore the Yankees do.'

I thanked him kindly, then made my way back carefully to my canoe. So the river would take me to Decatur before swinging north? I knew the name. I had passed through Decatur on the troop train when I had been press-ganged into the Confederate Army. Thanks to the generosity of the sainted Parrot I had a fair amount of money in my pocket, and could afford to take the train ... where?

I pondered this while returning to my canoe. I didn't credit the man's fears that the Yankees would be near. After losing at Shiloh (or so I was told by Southerners at the time; it was really more of a draw) they would not be looking for trouble this far south yet awhile. I didn't dare try to find them as there was sure to be a Confederate army hungry for conscripts in the way. Besides, for all I knew, the Yankees might be conscripting men too.

I didn't suppose I could spend my Confederate dollars in the north, so that was yet another reason to stay in Rebel territory. The snag was, half the Rebel army wanted to hang me for stealing their train, while the other half wanted to conscript me into their ranks. Quite an interesting position, I can say from my vantage point in twentieth century England, but at the time I could only curse and kick the nearest tree, slaking my thirst for vengeance for the sins of the whole continent. All I got was a bruised foot. Funnily enough, I have always rather liked Americans; it's just their blasted politics I can't stand.

The more I considered it, the more there appeared to be but one course of action. One I shrank from but knew I must take. I must return to New Orleans and try my luck again with the British Consul.

My course of action decided, I felt a great wave of tiredness sweep over me. My coat was dry now, thanks to the fire in the hut, and the hot Alabama Sun dried off the rest of my attire, leaving me dry and warm for the first time, it seemed, in an age.

I found a patch of long grass not far from my canoe, and using my coat as a blanket to keep off the mosquitoes, drifted off into peaceful slumber.

'Hey look pap, there's a canoe.'

It was a child's voice, and on the instant I had crouched up from my grassy bed to see what was happening. To my relief it was merely the child and his father, nosing about the riverbank when they should have been working or at school. Sunday was a free day, I suppose.

'Hello there,' says I, 'what are you doing with my boat?'

'Your boat?' says the man in reply. 'I thought it had drifted here, I was going to take care of it.'

I'm sure he was.

'This is a government boat,' says I. 'And not to be touched.'

'Yessir,' answers the man. 'Come now Billy, let us be off.'

They walked away rather faster than they had arrived, I'll warrant. I cursed a little more at the inquisitiveness of children, and decided to leave at once. They were sure to talk of the strange man with the canoe, and once word arrived from upstream, someone would put two and two together.

I must have slept for several hours, for the light was beginning to fade. It wasn't yet dark, but I could take no chances. I waited until the man and his brat had disappeared from view, then dragged my canoe back down to the water. My aim was to reach Decatur, where I could, I hoped, catch a train back to New Orleans.

Somewhat to my surprise, I made it without serious mishap. I had a scare after an hour or so when a squad of Rebel cavalrymen beckoned me over to the northern bank, but by reprising my role as Tommy the village idiot I affected to misunderstand and they let me travel on undisturbed. The current transported me easily enough all night, with barely any river traffic. I was able to slip silently by the odd boat travelling upstream, and as dawn approached, I lay up on the bank once more, and again cadged a meal and a brush-up at a local cottage.

My closest call was in the early hours of the following night. I was rowing quietly past a lantern-lit house on the corner of the river and a stream, only to discover at the last that it was a patrol boat, nestling at the water's edge. Luckily the night was pitch dark with drizzling rain, and by lying low I managed to glide past unnoticed. It occurred to me that had Andrews and Parrot been with me, they would have swung aboard the patrol boat like Pirate Bill, and stolen it.

Early next morning I saw the railroad bridge silhouetted against the dawn sky across the river some way ahead, where the Memphis and Charleston railroad crosses the Tennessee River. I rowed to the bank and pulled my canoe up and out of sight, and prepared myself for the walk into town.

The town had a population of about six hundred, or eight hundred if you counted the slaves, which they didn't. It was the junction of two railroads, with track leading to Corinth to the west, Chattanooga to the east and Nashville to the north. I wanted Corinth and all stations south to New Orleans. It was something of a hub for Confederate soldiers as well as civilians, and all-in-all just the place for a reluctant absconder to avoid attention. With rumours of Yankee raiding parties and their main army not too far away, everything was in a state of bustle and excitement, and nobody paid me any heed whatsoever, being just another traveller in the crowd.

I found a cosy eating house in Lafayette Street, where I ate a splendid ham and eggs with coffee, and a washroom where I made myself as presentable as possible. My coat was a good one but it was struggling to maintain its dignity.

My luck held. There was a train due out this morning bound for Corinth, and I purchased a ticket. Nobody bothered with me and I sat quietly in a waiting room of sorts, sipping another coffee while I waited for my train.

The journey to Corinth passed without incident, but on arrival I discovered there was no southbound service for two days. I found a room and stayed there until my train was due, then made my way cautiously to the station.

I told myself that nobody would be connecting me with the stolen train; my only risk was that of forced conscription into the Rebel army. Luckily the Rebel troops and civilians were busy with their own affairs. The Yankees were rumoured nearby, and all was in uproar. Nobody raised an eyebrow when I purchased my ticket to New Orleans, and it was with much relief that I boarded the train and awaited the departure whistle.

There were spare seats, for a mercy, and I found one opposite two talkative young men. They were friendly, introducing themselves as a Captain Pegram and his companion, Francis Dawson, an Englishman. Hearing I was English too, they were inquisitive. I decided to be George Jeffreys of the London *Times*, and before long we were chatting away like old companions.

'Well Sir,' says Captain Pegram, 'as a neutral, may I ask you what you make of the Yankee blockade?'

'Dunno,' says I. 'I haven't tried to run an arms shipment past it.'

'Well George, you will be able to run as many arms shipments as you want, soon enough,' says he, laughing.

'Really? How come?'

'How come,' says Dawson, 'because the Captain is about to take command of the greatest fighting ship the world has ever known. It will drive the Yankees back home to New York sooner than you can say Jack Robinson. That's how come.'

'Hush now Francis,' says Captain Pegram. 'For all we know, Mr. Jeffreys here might be a Yankee spy.' He said it with a grin at me, steadying the spasm that gripped my stomach.

'Well it doesn't matter if he is,' argues Dawson, 'as the Yankees already know, and there's nothing they can do about it.'

Dawson, I realised, was a British convert to the Rebel cause. Englishmen were fighting on both sides, of course, and being volunteers in a war that was none of their business, were naturally more fanatical than the average bluecoat or butternut.

'What is this great fighting ship?' I was intrigued, and truth to tell, a little worried that this Yankee and Confederate knowhow might one day threaten Britannia's hold on the oceans. For the day Britain no longer rules the waves is the day we stop being the world's most powerful nation. That's why if the Kaiser doesn't stop building dreadnaughts he will find the British Lion biting his behind.

'The *Louisiana*,' replies Dawson proudly. 'And Captain Pegram here will take command of it when we reach New Orleans, and with him at the helm...'

'And Master Mate Dawson at his side...,' pipes up the Captain.

'Aye, and together we shall drive the Yankee fleet off the coast of New Orleans, clear the Mississippi all the way to Memphis and beyond, and sweep the seas clean of Yankee scum up to Washington itself.' #Note_13

That was all *he* knew.

The journey south was slow indeed. After nearly a week of delays and sitting in sidings while northbound trains took precedence, we set off on the last lap to New Orleans. Luckily, by clinging to my new friends, both in naval uniform, I ensured I was treated right royally, even displacing a colonel in a boarding house when we stopped over one night. It seems the navy were more popular than the army, at least with one boarding house owner.

We pushed on gamely, but about twenty miles short of the city the train pulled into yet another siding. Train after train passed us in the opposite direction full of soldiers and civilians. Then a guard marched along the corridor with stunning news.

'Ladies and gennlemen, train stops here. We ain't going further south on account of Nawlins is about to fall to the Yankees.'

'What's that?' roars just about everybody. 'What do you mean Orleans is about to fall? How can this be?'

'Don' ask me,' says the guard. 'I'm jes telling ye. Seems our forts done failed to stop the Yankee Navy. They are expected to sail up the river and take Nawlins next day or two.'

So New Orleans was under siege from the Yankees. Was this good or bad news? Good or bad for Tommy, I mean? My companions were in no doubt.

'We'll have to go back,' says the bold Captain Pegram. 'The *Louisiana* is not yet completed. If the Yankees take New Orleans our boys will destroy it to prevent it falling into enemy hands.'

Well said, thinks I. The perfect excuse to about turn to safer pastures. He was right, mind. There was no point in going forward to certain capture. Dawson wasn't so sure.

'But we cannot just give up Captain. Maybe we can take it upriver beyond the Yankee gunboats.'

'Not a chance,' Pegram shrugs. 'The Yankees know all about our two ironclads. They will make straight for them. Our navy boys will have to destroy them first. Knowing our boys, they will be burning them right now.'

They argued the toss for a few minutes, and finally Dawson gave in to the inevitable, and the two disembarked to await the next train north, the fair-weather sailors.

Not the intrepid Tommy though. I'd had time to consider the new position and decided that things could not have fallen better.

If the city fell to the Yankees I'd no longer fear conscription by the Rebels. Instead I could simply bowl round to the British Consul and press him for a berth aboard the next boat out. The blockade would no longer count.

Most of our passengers had left the train and were milling about in a daze, uttering impotent threats against the Yankees and wondering what to do next. No such doubts for me. Safety was a mere twenty miles away and all I needed was the means to get there.

I still had some Confederate dollars, but not knowing the situation on the ground in the city ahead, I preferred to hang on to my money. Stealing a horse was a hanging matter, devil a doubt, so I looked around the small village where we had stopped and enquired about hiring one. There was nothing to be had, of course. Many mounts had been impressed into the Rebel forces, and the locals would not part with the few remaining.

In frustration I returned to the railway sidings, to discover that some of my fellow passengers had persuaded a villager to drive them toward New Orleans in his buggy. It was pulled by mules, but it beat walking all ends up. By waving more dollars than I cared to part with, I persuaded them to let me climb aboard.

We passed several parties of refugees fleeing the city and urging us to do likewise, but our driver took us to within three miles of our destination, near enough to walk the rest. I arrived at the outskirts of town in the early evening.

You can learn all about the fall of New Orleans from the books, if you've a mind to. I have placed a summary here, to let you know how things stood when Tommy arrived.

New Orleans stands one hundred miles upriver from the coast. The city was sparsely defended, relying downriver on two forts, Jackson and St Philip, on opposite sides of the river. A land invasion did not worry them, as their swamps would protect them from any marching army.

The man in charge of the defences was a thirty-nine year old Maryland-born West Pointer called Mansfield Lovell. He had been the New York Deputy Street Commissioner, whatever that was, until the outbreak of war, when Jeff Davis made him a major general and gave him charge of New Orleans. Mind you, nothing surprises me. It was a political appointment designed to show the world that even New Yorkers could fight for the South.

He made the best of a bad job. The Frogs of New Orleans were full of Gallic enthusiasm for the war, but expressed this by throwing rousing champagne parties rather than volunteering to join the ranks of the Rebel army.

Lovell wrote to Richmond complaining that the city was short of arms, ammunition, clothing and supplies in general. It was short of men, too, which was why I had to watch my step. President Davis had just enacted the Conscription Act, drafting all white men between eighteen and thirty-five for three years service. I was slightly older, but looked every inch a soldier. Even if they believed my age, the Rebels wouldn't let a few years experience stand between me and dying for the cause. All Lovell had to defend the city, then, were three thousand short-term volunteers armed mostly with shotguns, and his precious forts guarding the way to its heart.

Lovell knew all about the Union fleet on his doorstep, but refused to believe it was coming for New Orleans. Why not? Why, because the General in command was a Democrat, a one-time supporter of fellow Democrat Jeff Davis. The Republican President Lincoln would never give such a general the command of any expedition which could result in the glorious prize of New Orleans.

Accordingly, he sent most of his tiny navy - eight converted paddle-wheel steamers - upriver to deal with the Federal threat from the north. The independent-minded captains spent most of their days arguing with each other, and were off the strength as far as defending the city from below was concerned.

On the plus side, the Rebels had a secret weapon. Or rather, two. They were constructing two ironclads; superior to their Virginia ironclad that had caused the Yankees so much trouble. They were the *Louisiana*, to be captained by my travelling companion, and the *Mississippi*, and if ready in time might well remove the threat to New Orleans both north and south, and afterwards steam out to sea and break the Yankee blockade. Time, however, was one thing the Rebels did not have. Showing a fine contempt for the patriotic speeches of their leaders, the shipyard workers went on strike. They did not recognise Confederate bonds for payment, so construction was delayed. The ships were not ready on time with fatal results for Confederate New Orleans.

The Yankee fleet attacked the forts, and after a Hell of a fight, the U.S. ships steamed past them and drove up to New Orleans itself. Being built around the river, the ships could drop anchor bang in the middle of town and, if they so chose, reduce the joint to rubble. News of the Yankee breakthrough reached the city on Holy Thursday, the day before the fleet arrived.

I have been in towns under siege or awaiting the conquering enemy more times than I care to remember, but nothing I'd seen prepared me for what I encountered those first minutes walking to the docks where the crowds were thickest. This was no longer the glad confident Orleans of just a few weeks ago. It was a city in chaos.

The folk were in a frenzy of anger and fear at the news that Yankee ships were approaching, brandishing knives and pistols and yelling resistance.

'We will fight to the death,' cries one.

'Burn everything, cotton and crops. Those damned Yankees shall not feast off our labour.'

The mob drove wagons rattling over the cobblestones, laden with cotton from the presses, to burn on the piers. They bust open consignments of rice and hogsheads of molasses, and dumped them in the river. I imagine this was what the Boston Tea Party must have looked like; an unpleasant thought for an English bystander.

There were fires breaking out everywhere, as the townsfolk destroyed anything they thought might be of use to the Union forces. You could barely see the night sky for the smoke billowing up to the heavens. Yells and oaths filled the air from folk who knew that tomorrow all defiance must end, or face oblivion under Yankee naval guns

I was pretty pleased, myself. Their actions proved beyond all doubt that the Yankees were coming, and it only remained for me to find a bed somewhere safely away from the town centre, and await developments. And in case you are wondering what I was doing in the centre of town while the mob were rampant, for fires burned unchecked and looters roamed at will, you must realise that when the mob is on the loose, the safest place is right in the middle. T'was only the shop owners and men of property who need worry. An itinerant like myself could roam at will in perfect safety.

So I repaired to the cheaper part of town near to the railroad station, and took my pick of the boarding houses there, as most guests had fled earlier. I had a good meal, excellent brush up, and restful night's sleep. Tomorrow I would lay low, in case of resistance, and afterwards scout out the land.

The Yankees arrived on the morrow, Good Friday, as advertised. After smashing easily through the few batteries protecting the river entrance to the city, their ships came slowly into view around Slaughterhouse Bend.

One witness called it "black with men, heavy with deadly portent." Aye, it certainly changed a few things around the town. But would the Rebels fight?

Surrender you fools, thinks I, snug in my room. You cannot fight the Yankee army and navy at the same time.

After last night's valiant cries of defiance, it came as no surprise that saner voices prevailed. In the cold light of day it was plain that the only option was surrender before the navy blasted the city to blazes.

Lovell was nowhere to be seen, having declared New Orleans an "Open City" and fled with his tiny Rebel force.

Yankee Admiral Farragut gave the citizens of New Orleans their choice. Immediate surrender, "Or I will return with my troops and not leave as long as one brick remains upon another".

With the city authorities helpless, and the absence of any organised resistance, the Yankees simply marched their men through the city centre to the town hall and took over the administration.

Resistance was sporadic but fierce in localised areas. Rioters stormed the mint and a Southern fellow, William Mumford, succeeded in tearing down the U.S. flag that had been put up on Farragut's orders. The mob dragged it through the streets and tore it to ribbons, Mumford and others wearing a shred of it on their lapels. As things turned out it was an unwise move.

An enraged Farragut ordered them to fly the flag over the town hall or he would bombard the city. The desperate mayor turned to the foreign consuls, including the British, for help, He begged them to send the four thousand five hundred-strong European brigade, a peacekeeping militia comprised of foreign bankers, merchants and the like, to stop them. Fat chance. The consuls would have their work cut out protecting their own lives and liberty, to say nothing of their strongboxes, but I'll come to that presently.

U.S. General Butler took command, backed by eighteen thousand men, and proclaimed several edicts along the lines of *do as I say or I'll hang the lot of you.*

He set up headquarters at the St. Charles Hotel. The management ignored his demand for breakfast so he threatened to annex the entire building. An infuriated mob gathered outside so Butler ordered artillery in to disperse them.

Butler placed New Orleans under martial law, ordered all firearms handed in, banned public assemblies and all Rebel flags. He got off to a roaring start by hanging the unfortunate Mumford. Serves the fool right for not skipping town. Any house used by sharpshooters will be destroyed, says Butler, all shops must serve Union officers or have their goods confiscated. Anti-Northern demonstrations would be punished - a woman who laughed at a Union funeral got two years imprisonment - and all businessmen were forced to take the loyalty oath or have their businesses auctioned off.

Northern troops took over public buildings, but allowed the mayor to run local affairs under Butler's orders. When, later, the mayor defied Butler, he had him arrested and gaoled.

He censored the local newspapers and closed one, The *Daily True Delta*. He arrested clergymen for refusing to pray for President Lincoln, cancelled a consignment of sugar bound for Europe, gave preferential treatment to Negro refugees, and generally went out of his way to show the citizens who was boss.

With martial law in place, commerce practically came to a standstill. Labourers no longer populated the levee as there were no cargoes to unload. The wharves lay idle and warehouses normally full to bursting with cotton and sugar and grain gaped hollow. With no trade there was precious little money about. Unemployment skyrocketed, not helped by Butler's hostility to the unemployed, who would find themselves exiled into Rebel lands, homeless and hungry. When taken to task by the mayor, Butler retorted, "Let the Rebels feed them". Townsfolk joked that an olive oil label would pass for cash as it was greasy, smelt bad and bore a signature.

The Southern women felt little obligation to respect the Union soldiers. They would shun them in the street, gathering up their skirts in disgust, and marching off street cars holding their noses when Yankees boarded them.

When Butler himself walked past a balcony on which six young women turned their backsides towards him, he remarked, "These women evidently know which end of them looks the best".

In retaliation he issued "General Order No. 28", which proclaimed that any female who insulted a Union soldier by word or deed would be held liable as a woman of the town plying her avocation. This enraged the South by trampling on their womenfolk's honour. One Southern newspaper put a $10,000 price on Butler's head. The London *Times* described his Order as a "military rule of intolerable brutality". Even our own lecher-in-chief, Lord Palmerston, got in on the act, condemning it as "infamous. An insult to the entire Anglo-Saxon race." So there.

As if that was not enough, Butler earned the sobriquet 'Spoons', due to rumours that he stole silverware from wealthy houses. Nothing was proven, and several letters on the subject mysteriously disappeared from the official files, which spoke plainer than words.

British and foreign consuls protested to no avail when he forced their neutrals to take loyalty oaths. Butler declared all foreign funds to be Rebel contraband, broke into the Dutch embassy and that was the last anyone saw of the eight hundred thousand dollars in their vault. He tried the same tack with the French, but the Frog ambassador, damned plucky, reminded Butler that the *Milan*, a French warship, was handily moored on the river, and Butler scurried off to easier targets. He accused the British Guard, part of the European defence force, of sending uniforms to the Rebels, arresting two and banishing thirty-seven. Consul Mure told Lord Lyons, who sent the British sloop *Rinaldo* to the city, but nothing came of it.

The general corruption under Butler's rule eventually forced Lincoln to replace him with a less controversial figure, and good riddance, for his hostility to the British scuppered my chances of a swift boat home. Damn him for a corrupt, arrogant scoundrel.

Chapter Fifteen

Most of the above occurred over the passing weeks and months, and I was not there to see much of it, though Butler's hostility to the foreign consuls, especially Britain's, started right away and affectedly me immediately.

I laid low for a couple of days, then on the Monday after Easter, when it was plain that the city was not under attack, sent a Negro with a note to the British Consul in St Charles Street. In it I announced myself as Tommy, in the hope that my name might stir them into a quick reply. It did, but not the reply I'd hoped for.

'Gennleman to see you Suh,' announced my roomkeeper. I dived for my holdall, seeking my navy revolver, but it was not necessary.

'Colonel Armstrong Sir? George Coppell, acting British Consul, at your service.'

Two well-dressed gentlemen crossed the threshold and I bade them welcome. He introduced the second man, barely out of leading strings, as a British officer, whose name escapes me.

'My apologies, Colonel.' Coppell turned to his companion. 'Well?'

'Yes Mr. Coppell,' the snirp grinned. 'That's Colonel Armstrong right enough. I've seen him at Horseguards several times, as well as in the newspapers of course. I'd recognise him anywhere.'

That made one of us, for I didn't know him from Adam. Still don't. The important thing was, he recognised me. Now all would be plain sailing, surely?

'It's not as simple as that, Colonel,' says Coppell. 'Quite the opposite. Your presence here could prove an embarrassment.'

'Embarrassment? How the devil can I be an embarrassment?'

'Due to your... esteem. We have had a visit from a representative of the new U.S. regime. Consul Mure has been left in no doubt that General Butler, the military governor with total power over this city, is no friend of the

239

British. He suspects all Europeans, believing we are supporters of the rebellion, and acts accordingly. You are well known Sir, well known in Washington, and should the American government find out you are here, well...'

'Well what for God's sake?' I didn't catch his drift.

'Lord Lyons in Washington has instructed all consuls as their number one priority not to give the American government, and Secretary Seward in particular, any excuse whatsoever to accuse the British of secret dealings with the South.'

'What the Hell's that got to do with me?' By George I was rattled. I knew something of Washington politics you see, and knew they could smell a conspiracy in a convent.

'You are aware of the *Trent* Affair?' #Note 14

I knew the tale. It was all the talk last winter. A Union naval captain had boarded a British mail ship and taken prisoner two Confederate diplomats on their way to Europe. Well, you don't do that to British ships, and a fine old row erupted, almost leading to war between Britain and the United States. The previous war between the two countries was due to British ships intercepting American ones (and also America threatening Canada by slaughtering the Indian tribes who formed the buffer between the two countries), so both sides had reversed their views in a splendid example of international hypocrisy. But again, what had this to do with me?

'Both the British and American publics are as stirred up as they can be, what with *Trent* and other issues. Seward and others suspect we are planning to recognise the Confederacy, and God knows what might come of that. Now, we have an understanding with Washington that whenever high ranking or important soldiers travel in the country, we inform them first. How then do we explain your presence here?'

'But I'm not that important. I'm only a bloody colonel.'

Coppell smiled. He continued, betraying just a hint of Liverpool accent.

'Not just any colonel though, eh? A political officer steeped in undercover work, including some for the United States themselves.'

'What the deuce do you know about that?' I was flabbergasted. I'd worked unofficially for Uncle Sam during the John Brown fiasco - who called me Joshua of all names - but I was in deep field, totally undercover. Coppell, blast him, enlightened me.

'When Consul Mure saw your note, he guessed it was the same Colonel Armstrong who Lord Lyons had mentioned to him when John Brown was hanged. Seems you were heavily involved in that.'

His junior gazed at me as though I were some kind of boyhood hero.

My face must have looked a picture. The sins of the past come back to haunt you, they say. Not half so readily as the so-called virtues.

When in doubt, bluster.

'All right Coppell, never mind what I might or might not have done in the past. What matters is now. So lets get down to cases, shall we?' Bluff, no-nonsense, you see.

'If Washington discovers you here, they will smell a perfidious Albion plot. They'll want to know why, for a beginning. What reason can we give?' He looked at me keenly. 'In fact, just how came you here, Colonel?'

I could see he was beginning to believe Washington's fantasies, and suspicioned that I might really have been here to broker a deal with the Rebels. My derring-do reputation had tripped me up yet again. If only folk knew just what a poltroon I really was. Luckily, I look and sound like a hero, and they have never found out, but it can be an infernal burden sometimes.

I couldn't tell the truth. For one, it was so deuced unlikely. Also, I'd be admitting to the very interference in American affairs that he and Mure suspected me of, if at a lower magnitude.

'Coppell, me lad,' says I condescendingly, 'you'd never believe me if I told you.'

I winked at his junior, and he was my slave forever. The great British Tommy, living up to his reputation.

'Well,' he sniffed a little at this. 'What counts is we want you gone from here, as quickly as possible'

Now he was talking my language.

'Couldn't agree more, so if you can find me some quiet berth on the first ship out...'

'It is not that simple. We cannot get you out by sea. The blockade is still in force, and Butler won't let any British ship simply sail out without checking who is on board first. We might be helping prominent Rebels to escape, you see.'

'So what can I do?'

'You must leave town, Colonel. The longer you stay, the greater the chances of discovery. Travel north to the Federal states. Once in the North, nobody will think you are conspiring with Rebels, and you can make your way to Washington where Lord Lyons will see you home quietly. And for Heaven's sake, don't ever mention who you really are until you're safely inside the British Consulate.'

'Travel north? In case you haven't noticed, the South is at war with the North. They're not sending many trains thataways.' By the Gods this was desperate.

'You can travel up the Mississippi. As a neutral you should be able to get through the Rebel lines without hindrance.'

'And how will I pay my way? I only have Rebel money, and precious little of that.'

'How came you by Rebel money?'

'Never you mind.'

'Now look, Colonel,' says he. 'I know you believe we are letting you down, but you must see that it is impossible for you to remain in New Orleans. General Butler wants all foreign nationals to present themselves to his office to account for their presence here. He insists all such people take the loyalty oath, which obliges them to report anything detrimental to the Union, in word or deed, an oath inconsistent with the ordinary obligations of probity, honour, and neutrality. As a British officer here

242

unofficially, they would order you to take this oath. Taking it would be an insult to the Crown and your rank, but refusal would place you in an intolerable position.'

I stared at the man. He was right; serving British officers cannot just swear allegiance to another country. If I swore the oath just to save my shrinking skin, I'd be disgraced. But if I refused... What would they do then?

'Almost certainly place you in prison for the duration. Or worse, if they discover your identity they will assume you are here on behalf of Her Majesty's Government, with serious consequences for Anglo-American relations.'

'Hang the Anglo-American relations...'

'Not to say serious repercussions for yourself. They might well consider you a British spy...'

That did it. This was just the sort of idiotic conclusion the Yankees would jump at. I could see there was no point in struggling.

'Very well. It is plain my presence here is causing you a problem. I never thought I'd see the day when the British Consulate... ah, but let it be.'

'Thank you colonel, I knew you'd see it is the only way.'

'So will you purchase me a ticket on the next boat up the Mississippi?'

'What boat? There aren't any right now.'

This was the final straw.

'Then what in blazes have we been discussing this past half hour? You say I cannot stay. Now you say I cannot go. Talk sense man.'

'There are still a few horses to be had, Colonel. You can ride upriver out of Federal control, and catch a boat north from, say, Baton Rouge.'

'That's a hundred miles away.' As I said it, I could see his thoughts, which were that a hundred miles away was not as far as he'd like Tommy to be, but it's a start. And as I considered Baton Rouge, an idea occurred to me. Perhaps I could look in at the Governor's plantation. That was only fifty miles away and I could expect a warm

243

welcome. Maybe I could sit out the war there, for with New Orleans taken, surely the South would throw in the towel soon. Aye, that was my safest choice. Well I've been wrong before.

'I'll need money to buy a horse,' I protested. 'That's if I can find one.'

'You can borrow mine,' says the snirp, toady-like.

Coppell smiled at me like a riverboat gambler holding five aces.

'Well that's settled then. Bring the horse here immediately.'

The snirp went about his errand while I worked off my spite by lamenting the shoddy state of British Consulates and how it wouldn't have done in my day.

'Touch a Briton anywhere in the world and we'd have sicced a gunboat on them,' says I, John Bull personified.

'Diplomacy doesn't work like that any more, Colonel. If we sent a gunboat to rescue you, like as not the United States would invade Canada.'

'That's hardly a loss, is it?' I argued, but he was right, damn him. I was an embarrassment.

The snirp brought his horse to my boarding house presently, and we said our goodbyes, though not before I had cadged fifty U.S. dollars from him, promising to repay the sum plus a fair price for his horse when I got back safe home. He wrote me a bill with his address in England, which I lost.

I had a quick meal to sustain me, and left that afternoon. Coppell insisted I made haste, before General Butler could seal the city off from the surrounding countryside. I insisted on a new outfit first, though. My clothes were a sight to behold, and I had no wish to be arrested as a vagrant. I'm pleased to say I got them out of consulate funds.

You can imagine the mood I was in, cantering west towards what I hoped would be a safe billet to sit out what remained of the war. I had no idea how the Governor would receive me, of course, but his nephew, Lieutenant Joe Roberts, had told him I been most useful to Colonel Baylor out in Arizona.

He added that I supported the South wholeheartedly and hinted I was more than just a newspaperman. The Governor would surely welcome me as a Southern sympathiser.

I passed the outskirts of the city with no alarms and found myself in open country, heading west with the great Mississippi to my right. All I need do was follow it and I would fetch up at Cahabanooze and the Governor's spread.

The land was as flat as a German orchestra, stopping abruptly at a continuous stretch of dense forest. Irrigated by the river, this area, called the Coast by the inhabitants, is rich, lush and fertile, ideal for growing maize and sugar. Plantations abounded, set at right angles to the banks of the river, and stretching all the way along to the forest several miles off.

This, I realised, was the true, slaveholding South, and what the war was all about. The plantation owners set up their majestic villas in the style of Roman coliseums, with porticoes, pillars, verandahs, and huge coloured blinds to keep out the sun. A distance away, where they wouldn't detract from the grandeur, lay rows of whitewashed huts, the slave quarters. The fields are the brightest green, with flourishing crops of maize and sugar.

I saw no boats on the river, and precious few people about. This suited me fine, of course, and when night fell I was able to find a niche under some trees to unroll my newly acquired blanket and sleep beneath the clear sky in the crisp air. Tomorrow would decide my future.

I arrived at Cahabanooze without incident the following late afternoon. It was very hot now, and I was glad to reach the levee where I recognised the top of the mansion over the paling which surrounded the estate. It was, as I recalled, right on the edge of the water, thanks to some fool building it near a river that keeps spreading its banks. The gate was locked, and I had to knock several times before a black servant opened it and enquired politely after my business. I told him, and a few minutes later the Governor himself arrived at the gate.

'Why bless my soul if it ain't Mr. Jeffreys,' cries he happily, 'if'n that don' beat all. Thought you'd be halfway round the world by now. Come on in, Suh, come on in. Jasper,' he turned to the Negro, 'take Mr. Jeffreys's horse and see he gets a good coolin' an' vittles an' water and the best spot in the stables.' He looked me up and down like I was his prodigal son.

'You shore are a sight for sore eyes. C'mon up to the house an' we'll get you a bath an' some good food inside you.' He lowered his voice slightly, 'then we can ketch up on old times, and what you bin doin' and so forth. Come on then, Mr. Jeffreys. You fixing to stay long? I'll put you up in the same quarters.'

He couldn't have said fairer, and as we approached the familiar two storey mansion with its overhanging verandah, my spirits rose. I had hoped for a good welcome, but the Governor's reaction on meeting up with me again exceeded my expectations by a country mile. We had dealt well together when I'd arrived here with his nephew Joe, but it was a short acquaintance, and were hardly bosom chums. Then again, some folk just take to me; Lincoln for one, more's the pity.

Maybe it is just my nature, but he appeared a mite *too* welcoming. My neck-hairs twinged uneasily, but I dismissed them. Doubtless it was just the famous Southern hospitality I had heard so much about, but found precious little of so far. Besides, as Joe said, he was always pleased to have visitors. I don't suppose he got many, living in a swamp.

That first evening was quiet. The Governor excused himself, pleading business at another plantation nearby, so I dined alone in my old quarters and took a welcome early night's rest in a sumptuous bed.

He was busy away the next day too, but home early evening. After a dinner of pre-war proportions, though not, alas, fatted cow, he proposed we sit out on the verandah with cigars and a glass for a prose.

'You'll think I have been neglectin' you, Mr. Jeffreys, but in these difficult times there's much to attend to.'

Looking over the verandah wall at the tall trees swaying gently in the cool breeze, breathing in the sweet, intoxicating fragrance of the magnolia blossom, I assured him he had been the perfect host, and a good rest was just what the doctor ordered, or words to that effect.

'Feel free to walk wherevah you wish on the estate, Mr. Jeffreys, but only during the day. In these dangerous times we keep extra hounds and loose them in the outer grounds every night. If they ketch anyone prowling they'll tear them to little pieces.'

I thanked him and said he was a wise man to take no chances in these uncertain days.

'Thank you Suh, thank you. Well now...'

I saw it was time for explanations once again. Fortunately, I'd had plenty of time to assemble my story.

'Nothing much to it, really,' says I, puffing on a Cuban cigar, 'I arrived safely in New Orleans and decided to stay for a while, informing our *Times* readers how the South is standing up to the blockade. Not that I could get my reports back to England,' I shrugged.

He gave me an odd look, then frowned. 'We jus' got the news on how the Yankees beat the forts an' took the town.' He showed what he thought of that by spitting cigar juice over the low wall.

'Yes,' I sympathised. 'That's why I left. The Yankees brought their ships right into the centre and threatened to leave not one stone standing on another unless the city surrendered. But I'm sure the Reb... the Confederates will take it back when they get their second wind.'

'Damn right we will,' says he, angrily. 'But you would have been pretty safe, Mr. Jeffreys, being a neutral an' all.'

'Safe enough maybe...' I looked him in the eye. 'But you know something Governor, one thing I cannot abide is Yankees telling honest Southerners how to live their lives. Couldn't stick it there with Lincoln's mercenaries strutting along good Southern streets. I was not quite sure what to do with myself, then I remembered your kindness to me when I visited with your nephew. Of course I know you are a true Southerner, so I begged to impose myself on your hospitality until I can get back to England.'

He gave me that odd look again, then planted his cigar and stuck out his hand.

'Mr. Jeffreys, you are welcome here jest as long as you want.'

I shook his hand firmly, relieved that he was ready to provide me with a snug hidey-hole for a month or two, until the South hollered Uncle.

Releasing my paw, he continued.

'It is an honour to know you.'

My neck-hairs twinged again at this remark, but I couldn't see any catch, so I thanked him simply, as a plain no-nonsense Englishman should, and we sank a few glasses.

The Governor brought me up to date with the fighting. Most of it was bad news for the South. He'd just heard that Fort Macon on the North Carolina coast had fallen after a month's siege. This was another blow to the South's attempts to beat the blockade. I tried to look stern.

'The Yankees tried to take our boys at Turnback Creek and Neosho, and at Montavallo, Diamond Grove and Walkersville up in Missouri, but most they got was a handful of prisoners.'

These were quite a distance away. They were only minor skirmishes too; the real fighting was going on to the east, mainly near the Confederate capital of Richmond, and on up the Mississippi itself.

'So,' says I, 'your sources are better than mine. How is the war progessing overall?' I hoped he would say the Rebels were close to calling it a day, but if the Governor wasn't simply farting in the wind, and he didn't seem the

248

type, they had a lot of fight in them yet.

'I take it you know about the Anaconda Plan,' says he, pouring the drinks.

'Yes. It's a military objective to suffocate the South into surrender.' This was the North's overriding strategy. They would blockade the South's ports all along their coast, and capture the Mississippi River, thereby cutting the eastern Southern states off from the western bread baskets of Louisiana and Texas, and the trade route to Mexico. The South called it Anaconda in derision, as it resembled a snake curling around all the Southern states east of the Mississippi and strangling them.

At the same time the Yankees would march south from Washington to Richmond, Virginia. By taking the capital and starving the rest they would force the Rebels to surrender.

'That's right, Mr. Jeffreys. They have their damned blockade up and down our coast. Though we got runners who get through, the Yankee's grip is tightening. We cannot manufacture ships enuff to break it on our own, we have to hope you British will break it to get our cotton.'

That old cotton argument again. I could have told him that Britain would not go to war with the United States to give employment to a bunch of mill hands in Lancashire, but I didn't.

We jawed a little more, then the Governor yawned and bade me good night, saying he would be busy for the next few days but I was welcome to make free of the estate, and would I do him the honour of accompanying him to a fellow planter's home next week where there would be a goodish crowd meeting for dinner. I thanked him and accepted, of course. Had I known what I was letting myself in for I would have leapt over the verandah and given the hounds one bite and a running start.

The Confederate objective was simply to survive. The longer they avoided defeat, the more they sickened the grieving mothers and exasperated taxpayers of the North. The South hoped the North would tire of the expense in blood and gold, kick Lincoln out and leave them be.

The North had to attack the Southern capacity to feed itself, and defeat its armies wherever it encountered them. The South had to keep the North at bay. It could do this by defending its capital and keeping open the Mississippi and its connections with the western Confederate states. The western states reached down to neutral Mexico, where the Confederates could import war materials and transport them east, so they had to prevent the North splitting the Confederacy in half down the Mississippi.

The Confederates had another important string to their bow. They still hoped optimistically that the European Powers would recognise them as a new country, use their navies to break the blockade and maybe go to war with the United States.

Incidentally, this was how the thirteen original colonies won independence from Britain. We were too busy keeping the French off our backs to give the colonialists our full attention, so they won their precious independence by default. But you try telling the Americans this; they think they beat us on their own, and won't admit they would never have achieved it without the help of the Frogs.

That's by the by, the point is that after a rip-roaring start, the Rebels were losing the war on all fronts, and it seemed to me they would have to surrender soon, or suffer starvation and total collapse. And the sooner they faced facts, the sooner I could go home.

I had a pleasant week making myself comfortable and resting up, reading the newspapers, roaming the grounds and generally becoming my own man again after all my troubles. The Governor's household ate heartily, despite the food shortages that were gripping the South, for his wife managed domestic affairs well. Seeing further than most, the Governor had set aside a few acres to grow staple foods against a protracted war. He cultivated rye, rice and corn, along with a large vegetable garden beside his orchard, where he had beehives for honey. Also chickens, and I even managed to pot a wild turkey which raised a cheer in the kitchen.

The following week we crossed the river into Mississippi State and drove several miles along the banks to dinner at Orange Grove, a plantation owned by a man called John Burnside.

It was a splendid establishment, erected in typical Southern splendour, columns on plinths, statues of athletes and high, ornate ceilings set in a veritable earthly paradise. I would hardly have been surprised to see the inmates dressed as Roman senators. This was the South all over, of course; Greek philosophy and Roman arrogance, with the Negroes safely out of sight, sound and smell, damn your eyes.

There was a fair number for dinner. The local worthies, fellow planters and a liberal smattering of Confederate officers, all epaulettes and finery. And there were ladies present too. This was a pleasant surprise, for now that I was at last back to my finest Tommy trim, my lower organs were telling me it was about time they came out of purdah. Well, I'd suffered almost constantly since landing on these shores, and surely I was entitled to a little fun for a change?

Once again I was impressed by just how welcome everyone made me. After a quiet word from the Governor, Burnside took me around the dinner table, introducing me individually to all, as the esteemed Mr. Jeffreys from the London *Times*.

'Not only a distinguished writer for the most important newspaper in the world,' insists Burnside, 'Mr. Jeffreys leaves us in no doubt as to where his sympathies lie. He is a man for the South, and when he finally gets to file his reports back to England, we shall have some honest reporting for a change.'

'Heah heah,' pipes up one of the assembly.

'So I want you all to make our guest at home. Give him a true Southern welcome.'

And would you believe it? They did, with three cheers and a tiger. Not that I was listening, much, for there was one woman at the table whose appearance cast all other thoughts from my mind. Among the old biddies, wives and grass widows sat a glorious specimen of young womanhood. Middle twenties, I would guess, long dark hair, prominent bouncers over slim frame and a bright complexion that reminded me strangely of my Julie. She would make a handy substitute.

'Mr. Jeffreys,' continues Burnside, 'this here is my niece, Miss Cora Cooper. She's come down from Kentucky to escape the Yankees and is residing here for the time being.'

This was the best news I'd had since landing on these shores. As I took her hand gallantly, the sparkle in her eye told me she welcomed a diversion from plantation life. Unmarried too, so no inconvenient husband to cuckold.

'Pleased to meet you, Mr. Jeffreys,' says she in a chirpy sing-sing voice. 'A newspaper man? How exciting, you must tell me all about it. I would like someday to write for a newspaper myself.'

The entourage haw-hawed at this, saying when she found a husband, running her home would keep her too busy to write, less'n the newspaper wanted new recipes for the table.

Coming from Kentucky, she can only have known rustics like those assembled here. Well, man of the world Tommy would be happy to educate her in the ways of newspapers, and much else besides.

'Only too pleased to be of assistance, ma'am,' says I, running my finger through my whiskers, and she gave my hand a secret extra squeeze before releasing it, whilst looking me straight in the eye.

My loins tingled as Burnside took me to the next guest. Call me arrogant, but I can spot on the instant when someone lusts after a spot of old Tom, and the squeeze confirmed it. The important thing now was, how to get her alone? I knew I must tread warily. Southern gentlemen take a dim view of their nieces bounding into the bushes with whoever takes their fancy, and tend to redress the matter with shotguns. This would need careful handling. Burnside, or Uncle John, as I now thought him, doubtless took his duties as guardian seriously, chaperones and the rest, so I must await my opportunity. Experience told me to have faith in my amoral star, keep my wits about me, and chance would provide. Other guests included a Mr. Kenner and a Mr. Forstell, but I cannot remember any other names. Well, I had something more important on my mind.

The meal was excellent. Turkey, goose and poultry with superb vegetables, washed down with a most excellent wine from Burnside's own cellar, a cellar lovingly tended by a white-haired old Negro who fussed over the bottles as though they were his own.

After the meal we drank the health of the South with mint juleps, and struck up conversation.

Crops had been poor this year, apparently. There had been something of a drought, which surprised me, as I had spent most of my time here soaked to the skin. Plenty of water upriver, though. The Yankees had broken the levees and flooded out riverbank homes in Arkansas. This led to a fine old rant about how the North made war on civilians and tried to deprive them of their land and crops and property.

Mentioning property turned the talk to the Negroes. It seemed that the war and the fact that slavery was one of its causes had made them harder to manage than usual.

'Yessuh,' says one fellow. 'T'aint nevah seen sech uppity Niggahs than I have this year. Talk of war and ee-mancipation has riled them up like they done sat in the beehive.'

'That's true,' agrees another. 'Freedom talk unsettles them. Blacks are savage brutes by nature. We have civilised them some, but their civilisation is only skin deep. Scratch the most educated Negro and you will find a primitive savage.'

'Things are fine,' says an older man, 'so long as the authority of the white master is unchallenged. When the Negro knows his place he stays there, and is all the happier for it. But once that control is questioned, like now by the Yankees, he reverts back to his natural savage condition.'

I learned that the blacks didn't always bow down to the Massa. There had been local uprisings throughout the century, well before the war.

As early as 1811 slaves rose up in mass revolt here in Louisiana, marching down River Road towards New Orleans, burning plantations and crops, capturing weapons and ammunition, and killing two whites. It took the militia, vigilantes and a unit of United States Army troops to put them down. Sixty-six slaves were killed in the revolt, others tried and sentenced to death. They were shot then decapitated, their heads placed on poles along the River Road as a warning to other slaves. Still revolts broke out from time to time, though smaller, and the Louisiana planters were forever concerned about it happening again.

'My drivers ain't nevah bin so busy like this season. The Niggers have bin workin' slow, breakin' tools, injuring animals to get a rest, fakin' sick and stealin' like the Lord ain't watchin'. Nevah seed nuffin like it.'

'Whipping's what they need,' says another.

The women flushed a little at this, save my little popsy, who shot me a delightful grin that made me drop my fork.

'Have you ladies enjoyed your meal?' says Uncle John. The ladies took the hint and withdrew, Miss Cora shooting me a passing look that said "Well? The ball's in your court now." By gum I was in good spirits as the menfolk shifted up the table. How to get Miss Cora alone? For a man of my experience, this should be a breeze. Not tonight though, tonight was just the overture. As we old thespians know, it will all be alright on the night. #Note_15

Chapter Sixteen

'Whipping, that's what these ornery Negroes need, and ain't I just the one to give it 'em? Trust me for that.'

With the ladies withdrawn, the men began telling each other how to deal with uppity Negroes, each outdoing the other. Whippings were the standard punishment, the only question was how many lashes and how strong. They considered twenty lashes a reprimand, sixty a fair reward for malingering, and whipping till unconscious for backchat. Women as well as men; even pregnancy did not save women from the rawhide. They were made to lay face-down across a hole in the ground where they placed their belly, so as not to hurt the valuable unborn slave child, and *driver, flog away!*

I am not easily shocked but whipping pregnant women was a shade raw, even for me. It must have shown in my face, for presently Uncle John changed the subject and brought me into the conversation.

'Well, Mr. Jeffreys, you were in New Orleans when it was taken. Would you be kind enough to tell us about it?'

I didn't really want to, being preoccupied with more important matters, but a guest has certain responsibilities. Especially one who's backside is hanging out of his trousers, so to speak. I was reliant on the good offices of these people, so I strove to give them their money's worth.

'There wasn't much the true patriots of New Orleans could do. Once they had got past the forts, the Yankee ships anchored in the middle of town, and it was a case of surrender or they'd blast the place to kingdom come. The people are as brave as any Southerners, but resistance would have been suicide. This way, when your army returns, there will still be a city worth fighting for.'

This satisfied them, and after a few slow balls asking where I had been since my first visit to Cahabanooze - exploring the South for the *Times*, says I - and how I escaped the Yankees in Nawlins, they turned to other war talk. First they damned the Confederate State government for its craven abandonment of Baton Rouge, allowing the

255

Yankees to sail one hundred miles up the Mississippi and walk in without a fight. They spat tobacco juice on the tablecloth in anger at the dastardliness of the Yankees. It seems some Rebels attacked a rowboat containing a Yankee naval officer and the Yankees bombarded the town in retaliation.

Occupying New Orleans, then up the Mississippi was, of course, a step towards splitting the Confederacy in half, *a la* the Anaconda Plan. With the Federals steaming down from the north to threaten Memphis, this was another link in the chain. When the two forces met, the North would have succeeded in splitting the South and victory would be within their grasp. Or so it appeared.

The talk turned to Shiloh, where all agreed that the South threw away their chances by letting the Yankees regroup (I may have hinted that I was there, you know how drink carries your tongue), then on to the Battle of Pea Ridge in March. This was a Rebel defeat, which worried them more.

The Confederates under Major General Earl Van Dorn had tried to outflank an advancing Union Army in northwest Arkansas, the next State up from Louisiana and Mississippi. The Federals managed to fight them off. Van Dorn then made a second foray with more success, capturing Elkhorn Tavern and the Tanyard area. The Federals counter-attacked and their artillery forced the Rebels to retreat, abandoning the battlefield. The battle cost the Rebels 4,500 men, and the upshot was that the Union now controlled Missouri. This was closer to home than the planters cared for, and to me looked like another nail in the South's coffin.

It didn't, to my disappointment, lower the dinner guests' will to fight.

'We cannot submit to the unprincipled, greedy grasping, self-righteous, heathens of the North,' says one over his cigar.

'And we nevah will,' agrees another.

'Them godless Black Republicans reckon they can rule us jes' because they have industry. They impose tariffs to protect their own kind, their factories and profits, and the rest of us kin slide.'

'They think they can stop us spreading west and taking our slaves with us. But slaves are our property, and if a man cannot take his property with him wherever he chooses, then something is mighty wrong. And we are gonna put it right.'

'They believe because they have the banks, the factories and the population, that this gives them the right to tell us how to lead our lives, but what they don't have is civilisation, culture, liberty or settled order. Well we have all those things, and danged if we will give them up just to satisfy the ledgers of the New York counting houses.'

This was the general thrust of their argument. The North were heartless money-grubbing merchant Scrooges who would fill the Garden of Eden with smoke-belching factories and grimy tenements. The South were cultivated philosophers who valued beauty, music and wisdom in an unchanging world. Charles Dickens would have loved 'em. But what about slavery?

'We have slavery, they have tyranny. Slavery is ordained in the Bible, tyranny is man-made. I know which I prefer.'

'Heah heah.'

'And however many setbacks we face, we will win through in the end. Why? Because we have God on our side, and because one Johnny Reb can whip ten Billy Yanks.'

'What say you, Mr. Jeffreys?'

I agreed wholeheartedly, of course, adding that the South should give the North a taste of its own medicine.

'We should invade the North and surround Washington,' says I, brandishing my glass. 'That'd teach the buggers.'

This raised a cheer as I expected. I said it to keep in with the hotheads in the room. The Rebel officers called out to me approvingly, all British Bulldog and be-damned. I little knew that before long the Confederates would attempt this very manoeuvre. Or that I... well, my involvement will keep till later.

Talk continued in this vein for a little longer, then we joined the ladies. I had been considering how to get better acquainted with Miss Cora, and came up with a winner.

'I wonder, Mr. Burnside, can you tell me will I be seeing you at Sunday service?'

'Why certainly, Mr. Jeffreys. Pleased to learn you are a good Christian gentleman.'

'I try to be, Mr. Burnside, I try to be.'

I was delighted to see Miss Cora approach with a broad innocent smile.

'Well Mr. Jeffreys, I shall be attending of course, and look forward to seeing you there. If you have time, perhaps you can teach me a little about the workings of your newspaper.'

I'll teach you more than that, thinks I, spirits soaring as she winked at me behind her uncle's back.

'I should be delighted'

So it was settled. I set this down as a piece of advice to those who come after me; never underestimate the good that may come from religion.

There was general talk for a while, and presently the Governor announced that he must be getting back home.

Uncle John insisted we toast the South and all who sail in her, so to speak. We obliged and gave an *hurrah-boys* for the Confederacy, seriously on their part, and the evening came to an end. This was a relief, for their talk of battles to come and their inevitable triumph was sending me to sleep. Behind the bluster, it was clear that the Rebels were losing all ends up. East coast, Border States, the Mississippi River under threat, south in New Orleans, and even far west. My old pal Colonel Baylor's dreams of a Great Western Confederacy had crumbled. In true Confederate style, they had whipped the Yankees at a place called Glorieta Pass, but at the same time lost their supply wagon train and had to retreat back to Santa Fé, and eventually concede New Mexico and Arizona to the Union, or more likely, to the Indians.

I had won my own strategic victory, which was the main thing. Miss Cora and I would discuss the newspaper business - and other matters arising, I hoped - on the Sunday, and I would play it from there.

As I raised my glass to Confederate victory, I pondered just how long these outnumbered, outgunned and out-supplied dreamers could resist the men, money and muscle of the Union. Not much longer, I was certain.

I spent my time relaxing around the grounds of the Governor's estate, counting the days until worship.

Plantation life is slow, and I could quite understand why the South was resistant to change. Every day the same, stifling heat punctuated by the occasional Armageddon-like thunderstorm. The drivers herded the slaves to the fields before the Sun was far above the horizon, and set them to their tasks. These varied according to season and crop, but for most of the year they toiled from dawn to dusk, women and all. The older women, too worn out for productive work, looked after the children, who at least had a better time of it than the children of our own poor folk. Children were encouraged to play all day, building their strength for when they were old enough to work the fields themselves.

Southerners would claim that the climate was too hot for white folk to toil, so the Lord created black slaves for this task, but it seemed to me that white labourers could do the work just as well if put to it. The difference is, of course, that white labour would want paying, whereas the blacks work for free. The average adult slave, the Governor told me, produces about £140 worth of sugar per year. The cost of keeping blacks is negligible, so why pay Irish or other labourers and lower your profits? He set aside one field for growing corn, the staple of the Negroes and livestock, and supplied a roof over their heads and enough clothing to keep them decent. As I mentioned earlier, house slaves had by far the better arrangement, being visible much of the time. They were given good quality clothing or livery, so as to look presentable to visitors.

The plantation owners controlled most of the wealth and political power in the South, despite their low numbers, but they and their families were kept busy running their estates and had little time for regular socialising. Their social lives consisted of visiting other plantations or travelling to the nearest big towns, which for Louisiana meant New Orleans and Baton Rouge (both temporarily out of bounds) and other towns, where they attended balls, concerts, operas, and plays.

The master oversaw the slaves in the fields, while the plantation mistress ran the household, managing the upkeep of all plantation buildings and the production, purchase, and distribution of food and clothing. They tended to have many children, although the Governor only had one to my knowledge, and would insist on occupying themselves with embroidery and dressmaking, as though they couldn't afford the finest Paris could supply.

The womenfolk spent their husbands' money on refinements and the trappings of civilisation. They purchased fine furniture, tableware, artwork, clothes, and jewellery, all from Europe, which they showed off to friends and the wives of rival planters and business associates. Some men kept houses in New Orleans, where they vacationed after the harvest, as a change from plantation life.

With the war getting nearer, casual trips around the countryside were discouraged, so I could not invite Miss Cora out for a picnic. Not that we'd be allowed to picnic unchaperoned anyhow. My best bet was to meet her at divine service, and discover if it were as truly divine as I hoped.

Sunday finally arrived, and along with the Governor and his wife, I crossed the river and drove to the church. The reverend gave us a fine holy harangue about how the Yankees were doing the work of Satan, going against God's Word in the Bible that slavery was a natural condition for the black man, and we all reverently hollered in agreement.

We filed out, with much handshaking and how-de-dos to the Governor's friends in the flock, and in due course we met up with Uncle John and his party.

'Hello there again, Mr. Jeffreys,' says Miss Cora, 'I hope you have time to give me that talk on life in a great newspaper.'

I'd be better qualified to give her a talk on life in a great brothel, but no matter. Nothing untoward could happen in the grounds of a church, so nobody raised objections when I offered to enlighten her whilst strolling under the spreading trees down to a small brook, babbling near the entrance to the church drive. Arm in arm, most respectfully, I steered her beyond the congregation and under the trees.

'Why Mr. Jeffreys,' cries she, all fluff and innocence. 'You walk so fast. Do all Englishmen hurry so?'

'They do when they don't have much time,' says I, easing slightly. We passed out from sight and sound of the church, and I led her off the path into a conveniently secluded spot, shaded by bushes.

We sat down on the soft grass, and Miss Cora opened the batting. I can still remember her long dark tresses spilling out from under her Sunday bonnet, birds twittering and various tropical insects buzzing below us beside the brook ...ahh, dry your eyes old Tom. If you tried it today the only thing stiff would be your arthritis.

'So, Mr. Jeffreys, tell me about how come you work for a powerful newspaper like the London *Times*?'

'Well now,' says I, 'you need to have the eye to spot a story, the nose of inquisitiveness and the ear of understanding.' Also the buttock of exaggeration, but never mind.

'And you have these things?' She leaned forward, looking into my eyes. I know a cue as well as the next fornicator.

'Of course, let me show you.' I slipped one arm through hers and stretched the other around the back, pulling her towards me. She didn't resist, and in a trice we were fully embraced. By George, this was more like it. The fortunes of war cannot be all bad when they bring forth refugees like Miss Cora. Almost worth starting a war for.

'Cora? Are you heah honey?'

Blast. It was her aunt, or step-aunt or whatever she was. Uncle John's wife. Miss Cora broke off our embrace and looked towards the sound. Surely they could not be leaving so soon? They and their neighbours must have heaps to catch up on, like how the crops are doing in the drought or who has the best Negroes or something equally interesting. But no. It seems they were leaving church early, blast 'em, and to blazes with my fun.

'I must go,' whispers Miss Cora.

'Not yet,' gasps I, shouty-whisper. 'Five minutes will do....'

'Miss Cora!' the voice was more urgent now. She sat up, dashing my hopes.

'I must go.' She smiled. 'And you, too, Mr. Jeffreys'. She stood up and raised her voice.

'Thank you for your advice on newspaper work. Most informative.'

Cheeky young minx. I buttoned myself up disappointedly, but with grim assurance that this was but the first round. The return match would last a little longer, or my name wasn't George Jeffreys, or rather, British Tommy.

We stepped cautiously through the bushes back to the path and I escorted her into view of the remaining churchgoers. She turned her head and with her parting shot, taunted me with promises of love's labours found.

'See you next Sunday, Mr. Jeffreys. Perhaps we can have a little longer after service so that you can teach me some more about the world of newspapers.'

And off they went, leaving me feeling like a child robbed of his Christmas present.

The next few Sundays were no better. Whether Uncle John sniffed the wind and caught a whiff of Tommy's lechery, or simply Southern custom that prevented guardians from leaving an eligible belle without a chaperone, I had no better chances to renew my amorous acquaintance with Miss Cora. Scholars of the immoral act will understand that being so near and yet so far had an infuriating effect on me. I wanted to board and scupper Miss Cora like I wanted my next breath. She was pretty, in a fresh, country girl way, not a patch on some of the beauties of my carnal acquaintance, but she was in my thoughts constantly. There was only one way to get her out of my system. Patience, old Tom, I told myself. She was willing, I knew; it was just a matter of time and place.

I settled down to life on the old plantation. It beat the alternative, which was taking my chances with the war, but as a way of life it was little better than a luxurious prison. I spent my days taking walks around the estate, occasionally bagging a turkey for the pot, or relaxing in my rooms while the Governor took care of business. Most evenings I took dinner with him and his wife, enlivened once or twice a week when they had guests over, or dining at the villas of other plantation owners.

Plantation small-talk aside, the overriding topic of conversation was naturally the war, and would you credit it? After being pounded on the ropes all year, losing New Orleans and then a month later after a great river battle, Memphis, the South got their second wind. Johnny Reb began showing Billy Yank what good leadership, fast marching and suicidal bravery can do. The South ripped the initiative from the North and left her floundering.

The North's Anaconda took a good kick in the unmentionables when they were repulsed at Vicksburg, that great bastion of Southern power on the Mississippi. With Vicksburg in Rebel hands, the North could not split the South, leaving her able to import food and military supplies from the Western Southern states and Mexico.

Nearer to Washington, Confederate General Thomas "Stonewall" Jackson - *Old Jack* to his men, between you and me certifiably insane - rang rings around the Federals with a tiny force in the Shenandoah valley, marching this way and that and generally making the Yankee General "Commissary" Banks look like the rank amateur he was. Fear multiplied Jackson's numbers and he was rumoured to be marching full on Washington. This scared the pants off the Northern political classes, and forced Lincoln to keep troops back that were meant to help besiege Richmond, thus saving the Confederate capital from capture. The South, which had known little but bad news all year, were enthused to greater exertions. They redoubled their will to fight on, and all talk of a humiliating surrender was forgotten.

I said Stonewall Jackson was insane? Well, he would not eat pepper because it hurt his left leg, nor bend down in case he squashed his innards, and would hold his right arm above his head to maintain bodily harmony. He was deeply religious, refusing to write or fight on a Sunday. If the godless Yankees forced him to break the Sabbath by fighting he would desist the first day he could to atone for his sin.

Despite, or possibly because of his lunacy - when one of his units ran out of ammunition he told them to resist cannon with bayonets - he was a damned fine general, and his men worshipped him. Not my type at all.

Meanwhile, an unremarkable Confederate General charged with defending hard-pressed Richmond got himself shot at the Battle of Seven Pines, and President Davis had to find a replacement fast. The battle itself was a draw, but convinced Union General McClellan (hopeless, but popular with his men because he hardly ever fought, unlike Stonewall Jackson who was popular with his men because he never stopped fighting) that the Rebels were too strong to attack again in a hurry. The new man appointed by Davis had spent much of the war digging defensive trenches, and was thought to be an old slowcoach, a stick-in-the-mud and an unadventurous commander. His name?

General Robert E. Lee.

You can read all about the tactical genius of the new Confederate commander in the books. Charged with defending Richmond against Union forces that outnumbered him at least two to one, he embarked on a series of outrageously daring manoeuvres that outthought and outfought the invading Northern armies, sending them scurrying back to the warmth of Washington. (Had he won at Gettysburg the following year, a battle in which I played a small but vital part, he would have won the war for the South, and deserved it too, but I'll have much more to say about this in its proper place).

His first great action is known as the Seven Days' Battles. Typical Lee, he attacked McClellan's 115,000 strong Union army with a force of just 85,000. After a week of outwitting McClellan, failing to destroy his army completely by a whisker (and bad luck as Stonewall Jackson arrived late), Lee removed the Yankee threat to Richmond. With Richmond safe, the Confederates would fight on.

General Lee's brilliance probably prolonged the war by about two years. He was offered charge of the Union forces just before hostilities began, but declined, preferring to serve his native Virginia. It would have been better for the South had he accepted the Union post, then he could have wrapped up the war in six months and saved countless Southern lives. Try telling this to a Southerner if you wish, but you'd best have a swift horse handy.

So while I lazed and gorged in comfort, the war turned in the Rebels' favour, leaving me no nearer to getting home and no closer to giving Miss Cora a damn good lecture on newspaper production. I was randy and bored, an unwelcome combination, and determined that next Sunday I would attempt to produce an issue or perish in the attempt.

The only problem, as usual, was how to escape her watchful uncle and hawkeyed aunt. I wracked my brains to come up with something, but short of setting fire to the church, I was stymied. But where there's a carnal will, there's a way, thinks I, its just a matter of steely resolution.

As events turned out, I needn't have schemed so deeply, for unbeknown to me, others were scheming too.

If attending religious service regularly brings you salvation, I was well on my way to a seat at the Good Lord's top table. Once again I accompanied the Governor and his entourage to church. A larger group than usual this time. Joe Roberts, the Confederate Lieutenant who had introduced me to the Governor was visiting on leave, and had brought with him four brother officers. He was the Governor's nephew, of course, and his friends shared my accommodation in the guesthouse. They were red-hot secessionists, and their enthusiasm for continuing the war to Southern victory whatever the sacrifice nearly drove me to the bottle. If the country wasn't so damned dangerous I would have considered striking out on my own, and leaving them to it.

However, one has to make the best of a bad job, so I donned my Sunday finest - the Governor had kitted me out with a wardrobe - and joined the congregation. The sermons were more cheerful latterly, broadcasting news of the South's great victories and how, with God's help, the Yankees would soon bow the knee to the inevitable. Then everyone could get back to lording it over the Negroes and making an honest dollar selling cotton to the English, as ordained in the Bible. He went on the say that the European Powers must surely recognise the South any time soon, now that we showed them we were a force to be reckoned with. So with the Good Lord, General Lee and Europe all batting for the South, victory was only a heartbeat away.

When the parson had simmered down, the congregation mingled outside as usual, and in due course I met up with Miss Cora. I was pleased to notice she wore her winning smile as though especially pleased to see me.

'Why hello again, Mr. Jeffreys. You are looking quite the dash today. It was a lovely sermon, was it not? With any luck we will have peace in time for Christmas. Good to see you. I say, have you heard the news?'

I managed to get a word in edgeways.

'What news?'

'Didn't you know?' She slipped me a knowing wink, 'Your host Governor Roman, as I am told to call him, has kindly invited my uncle and aunt and me to stay for a few days at his establishment.'

'The deuce he has!'

'My aunt will be my chaperone.'

'Of course.'

This was marvellous, and just the thing to make up for my disappointments up till now. What an opportunity to discuss newspaper production in the comfort of my room. I could do myself far better justice there, too. I may not have much pride, but there are some areas where I believe I can always meet the deadline. But stay; I no longer had the guesthouse to myself. Joe's blasted officers were sharing with me. Why, I fumed inwardly, were they sitting around the jolly old plantation, sipping mint juleps and gorging themselves on poultry and sweetmeats when there was fighting to be done? Shirking, I called it; they should be out in the fields sharing the suffering with their men. I could take care of the home front.

Still, *nil desperandum*, as we carnal scholars say. With Miss Cora on the strength for a few days an opportunity to get her amongst the magnolias was sure to present itself. All that remained was to sort out the military tactics.

'When may we expect you?'

'Thursday. We shall stay until Saturday. Uncle John has a splendid overseer, who can look after the plantation for a few days.'

'Of course he can. What else are staff for? I shall expect you on Thursday, then,' I gave her a discreet nudge and a leer, 'and we can continue your education.'

She winked, warming my nether regions, and we went our separate ways. What the church needs to boost attendance, in England too, is a few more Miss Coras. On that religious theme, I hummed a jolly hymn all the way home.

Thursday could scarcely come too soon. While planning my campaign to invade and conquer Miss Cora, I took stock of Joe's inconvenient friends who were cluttering up my guesthouse. The four of them were well-spoken and polite, though quiet, and unlike most Confederate officers I'd come across, were not forever discussing the war. They were all educated, at least one had been to West Point, and clearly came from well-to-do families. They were all too serious minded for me to really get on with, unlike many British officers who when off-duty would carouse with bottle and bawdy songs. Upstanding Southern gentlemen the four of them, so I doubted they would oblige me by looking the other way should I invite Miss Cora in for a nightcap. Accordingly, I scouted out a hidey-hole for us, and came up with a deuced clever one.

There was a laundry lean-to at the back of the house which contained enough fresh linen and blankets to kit out a hospital. House-slaves cleaned and pressed during the day, but were of course packed off to their quarters every evening. It would be deserted, and if a few blankets were ruffled in the morning, they would put them right without troubling the Governor's wife. A furtive reconnaissance established that it was not locked at night, so all that remained was to take Miss Cora for a stroll in the garden, and dive in.

Thursday night was a frost. Uncle John, his wife and Miss Cora arrived as promised, but the aunt declared that the journey had tired her out, and she was sure Miss Cora was tuckered too.

'It will not do to overtax yourself, my dear,' drones the harridan, 'an early night tonight and perhaps we will both have our strength back tomorrow.'

The dragon was built like an all-in wrestler, by the way, and looked no more tired than a sailor on pay day, but Southern etiquette dictated that her word was law, so with a coquettish moue at me, Miss Cora followed the old bat upstairs to their rooms. It was a horny old Tom who turned in later that night. I'd have to contain myself until tomorrow.

The following afternoon they made up a party to look around the Governor's plantation, as though one slave farm looked any different from another. I didn't go, having had my fill of watching Negroes toiling in the sun, and occupied my time reading the latest newspapers brought along by Uncle John. The South was winning all ends up, to judge by the editorials, and I began to wonder if they really could win recognition after all. Not that I cared one way or the other, much, but the sooner it ended, either way, the sooner I could shake the plantation dust from my feet forever.

Not until I had rattled Miss Cora first, and my hopes rose as I saw the party returning. A few hours of repose, then dinner, followed by an evening stroll in the garden. Aye, that was the agenda. And the war could go hang.

Dinner started early. Fine by me, of course, and we chomped our way through the numerous courses in short order. There was quite a crowd; the largest gathering I had come across since I took up residence. The Governor and his wife, Uncle John's party, Joe and his four officers, plus a smattering of local worthies and their wives. No competition for Miss Cora though, with her bouncers on display in her low-cut dress, the jezebel, and my buttocks ached as the ladies withdrew. Some of the usual war chit-chat, thinks I, then its heigh-ho for the laundry room.

'How do you see the war ending, Mr. Jeffreys?' asks Joe.

There was only one answer to this. 'With a Confederate victory, to be sure.'

The table agreed, and one of them pumped me on when England would recognise the South.

'Just as soon as the South convinces the world that she cannot be conquered. Should you take Washington, then that will be the proof of it.'

Heah heahs around the table, and they settled down to more optimistic bragging about how the Confederacy

269

would eventually spread all the way below Mason and Dixon's line to the Pacific coast and down into Mexico. Humbug, to be sure, but it kept the table happy.

Not before time we joined the ladies, and I was pleased that there was such a crowd, as it made it a simple matter to buttonhole Miss Cora and suggest a quiet stroll in the grounds. Her aunt and uncle had seen us together many times by now, so my suggestion raised no comment. I had let it be known I was unmarried and it crossed my mind that they may have considered me a good catch for their niece. Certainly they had never objected to us chatting alone together after church. Well there was no chance of us making a happy couple - my wife would not have approved for a start - but I wasn't going to dash their hopes, it would not have been polite.

'What a splendid evening, Mr. Jeffreys,' says she, as I escorted her casually into the garden. Indeed it was, the fresh cool of the evening was the perfect antidote to the heat of the day, and the sky was cloudless with sparkling stars.

'A bit chilly, don't you think? We had best take shelter in case it rains.'

She laughed high-pitched, and squeezed my arm.

'Are you cold, Mr. Jeffreys?'

'Dashed cold. But never fear, I know a cosy little hideout where we can take shelter.'

I must impress upon young fellows who come after me that the secret of winning a campaign is seizing the moment. Without waiting for an answer, I steered her gently off the main path and ushered her through the bushes round to the back of the house and the lean-to,

'Ooh Mr. Jeffreys, whatever is in there?'

'Shelter. Come on Miss Cora, before the lightning strikes.'

She giggled at this.

'Why Sir, I do declare your desire is not shelter but concealment.'

The modest Southern belle, you see. She was happy to accompany me, but for form's sake had to pretend to be taken unawares. Let them keep their modesty, says I, so long as it does not get in the way of the action.

I slipped the door latch, and manoeuvring her steadily by the arm, took her forward. With the moonlight streaming in through the windows I saw packs of blankets neatly folded on low shelves, and while Miss Cora sniggered demurely, I bundled them onto the floor to make an instant mattress.

'Mr. Jeffreys, I believe you are trying to seduce me.' She said it with a twinkle, so I pressed home my advantage by taking her in my arms and kissing her strongly, full on the lips. She let me keep the initiative for as long as two seconds, then responded like a wildcat.

'Gimme!'

These country girls are deuced strong. Its all that tussling with their numerous brothers I suppose. Grappling like a stevedore, she squeezed me in a bear hug and pressed forward forcefully, catching me off balance - all fourteen stone of me - and causing me to fall backwards, her on top, flat onto the makeshift mattress.

Nobody catches me out twice. In a moment we were rolling from one side to the other, lips firmly pressed together, only breaking briefly for gasps of air. Preamble over, I made for the meat.

'Oh Mr. Jeffreys!' cries she, and I had to put my spare hand over her mouth to stifle her Southern squeals while I dived into her top hamper with the other. She got over her sham decorum quickly enough - they always do - and joined in like an Irishman on Saint Patrick's night. The blankets rustled to a flurrying of crinolines, boots and trousers, and as I pulled her to my side I leered down along at her trim body glistening in the shafts of moonlight. Brrr! This was the place to be; all thoughts of war, plantations and bloody Negroes forgotten, I climbed aboard and felt her soft, suppleness give way as I plunged in greedily.

She clung to me like a limpet, let out a breathless sigh and clasped her legs around my heaving torso. A moment to adjust and she was away, gripping like a champion jockey. By gum, it came back to me, all I had been missing this past year, and I strove to keep aboard, recalling that it's *my* pleasure that counts, and plunging away as though my life depended on it.

At last we reached the winning post, and she unclamped me and let me fall off, exhausted but satisfied.

Not for long though, ten minutes of polite fumbling and she was crying for more. I was out of practice, but thought of the honour and glory of old England, and did her proud once more.

'Why Mr. Jeffreys,' whispers she when we were done, 'You still haven't told me about life in a British newspaper.'

Trust a woman to come up with such nonsense at this moment. It reminded me of my own dear wife, spouting imbecilities whilst engaged in the carnal act. I shushed her to silence, as we were right up beside the house, and I hate to think how much noise we had made during our grappling. She asked me questions about my supposed newspaper career, while I mouthed quiet endearments and wondered if I could manage a third bout without breaking anything.

Suddenly she stiffened, and I heard voices from the open window next to the lean-to.

'Who comes here?' says a voice, one of Joe's officers by the sound of him.

'One who is true to our cause.' This was the Governor.

'How is he known to be true?'

'By the recommendation of a tried Knight.'

'Can he then be trusted?'

'Such is our belief.'

'But should he fail and betray us, what then?'

'He will learn the penalty soon enough.'

'Advance.'

What in Hell were they talking about? It sounded like a meeting of the secret nine. Not something that concerned old Tom, you may be sure of that.

I turned to Miss Cora to see if she could enlighten me.

'What's all that about?'

She grinned knowingly 'Why, Mr. Jeffreys, don't you recognise those words?'

'Of course not, why should I?' I was baffled, and not a little alarmed. It wasn't just the sinister words, but Miss Cora's reaction to them. The hairs began to prickle on my neck, and it wasn't from lust.

'We had better go back to the house, Colonel Armstrong, before folk wonder where we got to.'

She was right. Whatever was going on, it would not be improved by them discovering the Tommy way of cementing Anglo-Confederate relations. We disengaged, and I began climbing back into my clothes. Suddenly it hit me.

'What did you just say?'

'I said we must return to the house.'

'No, after that. What did you call me?'

She laughed. 'Why, Colonel Armstrong. That's your name is it not?'

'No. Well yes.' She was staring at me like a I was a Negro she'd caught in the pumpkin patch. 'But... I mean, how did you know?'

'I have known all the time, Colonel. George Jeffreys the great newspaperman!' she tittered as at a good joke. 'You see, my father is a Copperhead.'

I wondered if I had heard right.

'A copperhead?'

'Yes Colonel.' She was no longer laughing, instead looking me clear in the eyes with the gravitas of a Methodist in a brewery. 'A Northerner who supports the South, and is not afraid to aid her in her fight for freedom.'

The facetious thought occurred that the South needed brains, not copperheads, but I kept mum.

'And I am my father's daughter, Colonel.' She finished adjusting her clothing, straightened up the fallen blankets and made for the door. 'Come, they will be expecting us.'

'But...' I cudgelled my wits to understand what was happening. One moment I had been galloping away

273

without a care in the world, now it seemed I was in the midst of some deeper than damnation gang of... gang of what? 'But you haven't explained how you know my name. And this isn't the North. What are these Copperheads doing here?'

Oh, you'll find out everything soon enough. And we folk here are not Copperheads, exactly.'

'Then what are they - you - then?'

'We go by various names. Mutual Protection Society is one. Some say Freemasons. We are best known as the Knights of the Golden Circle.'

Chapter Seventeen

I bar all secret societies. Some of them are harmless enough, Guy Fawkes plotters with dreams above their ability, but others know what they are about, and spin a web that is damned dangerous for any harmless souls caught up in it.

The Knights of the Golden Circle was a dangerous secret society par excellence, and hadn't they snared poor Tommy just? With hindsight I should have followed my best poltroon instincts and saddled my horse and fled for the hills. Being caught by surprise, and having just completed two exhausting gallops I was not thinking clearly, and let Miss Cora lead me meekly to my fate.

She took me to the Governor's office, where she was the only woman present. In front of me stood the Governor, with Joe and his four officers, all changed into civilian clothes. 'Here is the Colonel Armstrong,' she announced portentously.

The Governor spoke up.

'Those who would pass here must face both fire and steel.' He addressed me direct. 'Are you willing to do so?'

Oh sweet Jesu, here we go again. More fanatics. I attract them like parliament attracts windbags. Miss Cora nudged me.

'Say aye,' she hissed.

'Aye ...or rather, yes, of course.' What else could I say?

The Governor smiled.

'Of course you are ...Colonel. Please sit down.' He waved me to a seat and turned to Joe. 'Pour Colonel Armstrong a drink, if you would be so kind.'

Miss Cora stood behind my seat, leaning on the backrest, while Joe thrust a drink into my hand. The office was decked out with the usual fittings, and with the six men and one woman looking at me, I could only take my drink and learn what fate and the confounded Knights had planned for me this time.

'Colonel,' says the Governor, 'the time for pretence is over. When you came here the first time, Joe here told me your true identity, and how you helped our Southern forces in California and Arizona. Your mission to Fort Fillmore for the General is known to us, as is much else besides. We didn't ask questions, and were happy to go along with your charade as a London newspaperman' - standing behind me, Miss Cora gave my shoulder a squeeze; she was enjoying this, the little trollop - 'but now we need your help once more.'

I thought they might. So the blasted General had put his spoke in once again. Doubtless he had got word to Baylor about my true identify and supposed heroism. That would explain Baylor's eagerness to thrust me into the firing line at every occasion, blast him. And presumably Joe had known all about my VC-winning past when he hornswoggled me into visiting the Governor the first time. My reputation had bitten me on the buttocks once again. And all I could do was sit still with a bold expression, stomach knotted, and wait for the blow to fall.

'Colonel Armstrong, we of the Golden Circle are one with the Confederate States of America in wishing to defeat the Yankee invasion of our soil. To this end we are raising funds to purchase arms, other military supplies and ships. Especially ships.'

The others nodded in agreement. Well, if they wanted a donation, I still had my Yankee dollars borrowed from the snirp back in New Orleans, but somehow I guessed they wanted more than that.

'Now, Colonel, my friends and I are not short of money. Indeed, we can be counted as wealthy men. However, while the war lasts, Confederate currency and Southern real estate carries little weight outside this country. And we cannot export enough cotton and sugar to finance our purchase of warships due to the blockade.'

He sipped his drink. 'We need gold, Sir. Gold to purchase warships for the Confederacy. When we have it we can transport enough to purchase our immediate needs aboard a small, fast ship that will beat the blockade and reach England.'

A suspicion was growing like a worm in my gut. To forestall it I asked the obvious question.

'But do you have the gold?'

Joe interrupted. 'We do... and we don't.'

Well that was plain then. I saw they were expecting something more from me, so I tried a hopeful long-shot.

'Well if you have, once you get it to England, you will need someone to arrange matters. I suppose you want me back there immediately to set up such an arrangement?'

This took them aback. After a moment, the Governor replied.

'Not exactly, Colonel. We have agents in England who can handle that side of the business. They have ways and means of commissioning warships and purchasing supplies. What they lack is the wherewithal to pay for them. I regret to say,' he added with a frown, 'that your British shipbuilders have taken advantage of our plight. Knowing that we need warships urgently, and because your government will not allow us to buy ships openly, they have raised their prices beyond what is just and fair.'

Well done old England, thinks I. Good to know someone is making a dollar out of their crazy war. Besides, if the French have at us again, do you suppose the Yanks will sell us ships on the cheap?

He glared for a second, as though I was stuffing my pockets with Rebel gold, profiteering personally while widows starved, then collected himself.

'Our people have amassed a cache of gold bars upriver in Memphis. You do not need to know how. They have them safely hidden, but are unable to move them without assistance. Do you understand?'

I was beginning to. And with my neck-hairs tingling I could see what was coming; Tommy and five Rebel officers strolling about Union-occupied Memphis with a wheelbarrow full of gold bars, whistling for a carriage to take us hundreds of miles east for transportation to

England. Well if he thought I was going to tote half a ton of gold through a country ablaze with warring armies, run the Union blockade and set up shop in England buying guns and ships (illegally) for his beloved Confederacy, he had got the wrong man.

I couldn't say this, of course, so I sought plausible grounds for turning down his appalling scheme before he pronounced sentence. Ahh... got it. But first the soft soap. I took a deep breath to steady my voice, looked the Governor straight in the eye and gave him the reply a true supporter of the South would give.

'Sir, your magnificent news fills my heart with joy. Once that gold is in London, why, you'll have ship-builders queuing up by the dozen to build your warships. This is a great day for the South, and if there is anything I can do when I'm back in England...'

The room smiled and one of the officers - the West Point man - hear-heared.

'We are sending the gold to our agents in Liverpool. Thank you Colonel; that is just the reply I expected.'

He switched off the smile and donned his serious face, and with dissolving spine I awaited the inevitable.

'The gold is not in Liverpool yet. It is hidden somewhere in Memphis. Our first task, therefore, is for a small group of patriots...' he glanced meaningfully at me, '... to collect it from under the noses of the Yankees. Then we of the Golden Circle can arrange its safe transportation to our agents in Liverpool. They in turn will place orders with British shipbuilders and in time we will break the blockade and in so doing, win our freedom from the Black Republicans of the United States.'

Is that all, I wanted to shout. Easy as that, eh? And you can just conscript any innocent bystander - small group of patriots forsooth! - into your lunatic schemes without so much as a by-your-leave. But of course I swallowed my fears and kept a straight face. By the grace of God I had a face-saving card to play. One which would allow me to reluctantly bow out from his appalling proposal.

'Sir, you flatter me with your confidences, 'deed you do. And nothing would give me greater pleasure than to help you in your noble mission.' I frowned, then continued, 'but alas, it cannot be.'

That shut them up, but only for a moment.

'What do you mean, it cannot be?' cries the Governor, while the others looked on in concern.

I sighed audibly, like a man struggling with his emotions, then let them have it both barrels.

'You see, Governor, though my heart lies with the South, my duty lies elsewhere. I am a British soldier, Sir, and my oath is to Her Majesty Queen Victoria. I took leave of absence to help the South in any small way I could, but I have been away too long, and I must return home to my country. But have no fear...' I raised a hand to forestall his explosion '...I can do more to promote the Confederacy in the councils of England than anything I might achieve here. These brave officers,' I looked around at Joe and his lads, 'are more than capable of the mission with which you have charged them. Why,' I raised a modest smile, 'I would just be in the way.' I shook my head sadly, a man torn between conflicting loyalties. 'I was going to mention this to you after your house guests had left. And then thank you for your boundless hospitality and...' I stifled a choke, '...and ask for your blessing.'

I sat there like a Christian regretfully spurning the chance to grapple with the lions in the arena because he has souls to save elsewhere. My repose did not last long. A brief silence while they took in my refusal - for that's what it was - then Joe and his officers rounded on me.

'But we need you. We cannot get to the gold without your help,' says one.

'You mustn't turn us down, Colonel,' adds Joe. 'We need you to help us get this gold to where it can do the most good.'

'Surely Colonel,' pleads the next, 'England can spare you just a month or two longer.'

I put my head in my hands like a man in torment. I was too, wondering why they thought me so important to their crackpot plans and what they would do if I refused to budge.

'Gentlemen, please don't think its not my heart's desire to be alongside you, bearding the Yankee devils in their Memphis lair, but duty to my homeland calls, and as I say, you are more than capable of winning through without my feeble efforts.' That last bit was the truth, at any rate. 'But my country needs me. From your newspapers I learn that France is on a mission of conquest to Mexico, and Europe is in a state of flux. Who knows when Britain might need all its defenders once more?'

This was true, too. While America was busy beating the blazes out of itself, Mexico had suspended debt interest payments to Britain, France and Spain. Well you don't stick out your tongue at the Great Powers and hope to get away with it. Before you could say Shylock, we sent a joint expeditionary force to collect what was ours. Britain and Spain just wanted their money - plus interest - but Napoleon used it as an excuse to try and conquer the whole country if you please, especially the silver mines. When we discovered Napoleon's empire-building intentions, The British and the Dagoes about turned, leaving the Frogs to get on with it. Lincoln fumed at this European invasion of continental American soil, but was powerless to intervene being up to his neck in the Confederate rebellion (I shall relate my involvement with Emperor Maximillian and the rest of the Mexican nonsense later on, if I'm spared).

I donned my most noble expression.

'When the trumpet sounds, I must be there to answer. As soldiers yourselves, I am certain you will understand.'

Well, I'd turned them down, but with good - I hoped - reason. Now to sit stern and serious, and see how they took it.

The Governor had not spoken yet. He was looking thoughtful, stroking his chin, as though weighing things up. Finally, to my surprise, he broke out into a smile.

'Why Colonel, we understand completely. We sure do. In these troubled times you want to get back to

England to serve your Queen Victoria as quickly as you possibly can.'

'That's it precisely Sir,' says I, relieved.

He smiled some more, while the others looked on, mystified.

'You want to get back home right away? Then I have some good news for you.'

I doubted it. That smile held trouble. He beamed at his nephew, all Uncle Pickwick and bedammed.

'See to our glasses, Joe. We got some figuring to do.' Joe fulfilled the order while I sat there, wondering why the Governor was so ominously pleasant. I had told him the mission was a non-starter, at least as far as I was concerned, but he was as jovial as a monk in a convent. It wasn't canny, but I could only thank Joe for the drink and await the Governor's words.

'Everyone fired up? Good. A toast, gentlemen, and lady.' This to Miss Cora, who hadn't so far said a word about my hurry to be home. 'A toast to Good Queen Victoria and victory to the South.'

When we had hurrahed and downed our drinks, the Governor at last got the point.

'Colonel, you want to get home to England as quickly as you may. We want you to help us locate the gold hidden in Memphis. Well,' he grinned, 'You will be as pleased as I am to learn how we may achieve both'

I sat numbed to the core as the officers looked from the Governor to me and back. Miss Cora squeezed my shoulder again, but I was too preoccupied with the madmen in front of me to enjoy it.

'We do not need you to help us transport the gold to England. You have another part entirely to play.' He paused to refresh himself while I waited, torn between hope and fear. Could he want me, perhaps, to go ahead to England as a herald, and prepare his agents for the arrival of a shipload of gold? That would be the best news I'd had all year. Of course, once safely over the horizon, I would go to ground in London and sit out the war in safety. I remembered enough of my Bible classes to recall that John the Baptist once had a similar heralding mission and came to a sticky end.

He leaned towards me, glass in hand.

'You see, Colonel, our agent in Memphis has the gold in his safekeeping, but we don't know exactly where. When the Yankees occupied the town he sent us a message saying he believes they suspect him of being a Confederate agent, so he dare not risk sending further messages to us. Certainly not about a consignment of stolen gold. We need someone to make contact with him and discover from his own lips where he has hidden it.'

And it took no divine inspiration to know who that someone was. Nor did it escape me that he had let slip the gold was stolen. By George, I have been dispatched on some harebrained errands in my time, but this beat all. I was to trawl the streets of an occupied city, whistling down every back-alley seeking a spy whose cover was half-blown already. The whole scheme was insane. I must slide out somehow or other, but with all eyes on me I should have to tread warily.

'But I don't know Memphis,' I stuttered. 'I mean, I am honoured by your faith in me, but as a stranger... why, I could seek your man for weeks without success.'

'You need have no fear of that, Colonel. You will travel to Memphis with Joe and his brother officers. They will bring you to the outskirts and send you off with full directions to the house of our agent. We also have a password that you will say to him to prove you are with us.'

He had it all down pat, blast him. Even a secret password, probably in Latin. I tried another tack.

'The town is occupied by the Yankees, as you say. Doubtless they will stop and question anyone found in the streets, and demand of them their business. As an Englishman I will attract suspicion. How will I explain my presence?' A thought crossed my mind. 'Why, they will like as not conscript me into their army.'

Joe and the boys registered concern. Careful, old Tom, thinks I, in a moment they will be questioning my loyalty to their blasted cause.

The Colonel brushed aside my concerns. He was positively grinning, and it occurred to me that it must be quite fun sitting in your magnificent estate, sending other folk out into the world to carry out your cracked schemes.

'Quite the opposite. As an Englishman and a neutral you have the advantage over the rest of us. Don't you see? Nobody will suspect that you are connected with our organisation. When asked, you are simply an Englishman caught up in a war that is no concern of yours. All you wish for is to journey north to New York and a fast boat home. You can even use your real name. In fact,' he took another pull at his glass to celebrate another bright idea, 'it is best you do. The Yankees want to keep in with the British, and if you pose as a Northern supporter they will speed you on your way all the quicker.'

'Not if they conscript me.'

He ignored the interruption, or more likely didn't hear.

'They will be running boats up the Mississippi into Yankee territory, and you can catch a ride on one of them. You will be in Washington, rather, in no time. Then...' he paused as though he had something to add, but thought better of it. 'Then on to New York and a ship to England. This, Colonel Armstrong,' he gloated, 'will not only strike a bold blow for the South, but get you home to England and duty to your Queen Victoria quicker than taking your chances on breaking the blockade on a Southern boat.'

A ray of hope dawned as it occurred to me that I would be alone in Memphis. My spirits soared as I realised that Governor had given me the way out. When Joe and his brother fools waved me goodbye on the outskirts of town, I would simply go to the levee and cadge a boat north, without bothering their Southern spy and his gold at the end of the rainbow. Joe and the rest could wait for me outside town until the Yankees found them, or they died of boredom. By the time they suspected I was not returning I would be deep into the Northern States and could snap my fingers at the Knights of the blasted Golden Circle, the General, the Governor and all the rest of 'em,

283

'They won't conscript you, Colonel,' says a voice from behind my shoulder. It was Miss Cora. There was a girl I was rapidly going off.

The Governor laughed.

'That they won't. You see, you will not seek our agent alone.'

My spine tingled. What was coming this time?

Miss Cora left off leaning on the back of my seat and joined us around the table.

'Colonel, Miss Cora is accompanying the party. She will pose as your wife. Recently married. Even the Yankees won't split you up from your darling wife to join their army. They will wish you well and escort you to the first northbound boat.'

I nearly told them I was married already, but bit my lip as I recalled that as George Jeffreys, I had claimed to be unwed. Did they know my true self, the valiant British Tommy, was already spoken for? Best not mention the fact to five Southern gentlemen and a feisty Southern belle who had just finished a two-round bout with me.

'In case you're fretting about the cost of a wedding ring,' drawls Miss Cora, who was a sight too clever for my liking, 'I brought one along right handy.'

Of course she had. I remained silent. Well, what could I say?

She gave me a shrewd look.

'Perhaps the Colonel is concerned for my safety?'

'Indeed I am, ma'am.' By gum, I grasped eagerly at this straw. 'I cannot risk the safety of a good Southern lady amongst those Yankee mercenaries.'

'Your concern does you credit, Colonel,' says the minx, 'but you need have no fear.'

She reached into the recesses of her costume and pulled out a derringer. God knows where she had gotten it from; it wasn't there earlier or I should have noticed.

'I got me a full-grown gun too, Colonel, with my bag. I am a Kentucky gal, brought up with brothers and can handle a gun as well as any man. I shall be as safe in Memphis as I would be in Richmond.'

284

'So you need not fret on that score,' adds the Governor. The self-satisfaction oozed out of him, and with a sick feeling in the pit of my stomach I saw that I could not protest any further. When they've got you by the essentials the only thing to do is agree keenly with whatever they say and look big about it.

'When do we start? It will be an honour to take Miss Cora along to Memphis as my... wife.' For a fleeting moment it crossed my mind how having Miss Cora as my temporary partner might not be all sacrifice. After all, as my wife she could hardly refuse her (acting) husband her wifely favours, could she? Aye, you may think it hardly the right time to consider my loins, but we old soldiers know to take our pleasures where we find them. Who knows what tomorrow might bring?

'In a day or two. We dare not risk travelling by river from here. You, Joe and the other gentleman, and Miss Cora, will travel to Memphis. Joe will give you both the password for our agent, along with directions to his home, then you and your... wife will enter Memphis, meet our agent and discover the whereabouts of the gold. You will return to an agreed rendezvous and impart the necessary information to Joe, then go back to the town, find a riverboat and head together for Washington.'

Something didn't make sense.

'Washington? No boats to England from there. You mean New York.'

The Governor paused.

'New York in due course, Colonel.'

'We travel to Washington first,' insists Miss Cora seriously. 'Then you may travel on to New York. I shall stay behind in the Yankee capital.'

This was getting murkier by the moment. I couldn't make head nor tail of it. The Governor explained.

'You see, Colonel. Once we know the location of the gold, we need to get it out and safely away to England. Miss Cora is going to Washington to arrange matters, and you shall travel with her as husband and escort. You can no longer use your assumed handle of Mr. Jeffreys of the

London *Times* as that name is linked with supporting the South back in Arizona. You will travel as Mr. and Mrs. Armstrong.'

What in Hades was he talking about this time? It was beyond me. Beaten, I sat waiting for enlightenment.

'We have friends in Washington. The Knights have supporters throughout the North. Some in high places. One,' he hesitated for dramatic effect, the old thespian, 'is a United States senator. He is what is known as a Copperhead; a man who hails from the North but is loyal to the South. You and Miss Cora will meet him in Washington, identify yourselves with the password, and Miss Cora will tell him the Knights' plan. Put simply, the senator will authorise a ship to sail from Memphis to New Orleans carrying the gold. This cargo will be placed on an ocean-going vessel and sent to England. Washington will think it sails for the North, but what they won't know is that it is destined for our agents in Liverpool. Joe and the other gentlemen here will arrange matters.'

I threw in my last card.

'But Memphis is nearly four hundred miles away, with enemy forces in between us and them. That's a long, dangerous ride...' I found inspiration '...to take a woman.' Appealing to their Southern chivalry, you see. But I might have well saved my breath.

'We ain't riding all the way, Colonel,' says Joe. 'We are going up the Miss.'

'With the Yankee gunboats besieging Vicksburg? We should have to sail right through their siege and out the other side if we hope to reach Memphis this side of Christmas.'

Joe's officers were looking at me hard-eyed now, and I realised that I was overdoing the protests. One of them spoke up.

'Begging yore pardon, Governor, but it seems to me Colonel Armstrong ain't none too keen to help us.'

'Hush your mouth, Sir,' says Miss Cora, 'why Colonel Armstrong is only saying what a good soldier should. He's asking all the right questions an' making sure

286

we all have the right answers.' She turned to me. 'Ain't that so, Colonel?'

Damnation she was right, and enjoying every minute too, the troublemaking harlot. A good soldier should always ask the obvious questions, to ensure everyone's obvious answers were the same. Not that that was any consolation. If she hadn't befuddled my senses with her wanton galloping, I'd have leapt astride my horse at the first inkling of Knights' nonsense and been by now in the next county.

'That is so indeed, Miss Cora,' says I, all condescending gallantry. 'My apologies if I gave the impression I was anything less than eager to add my little weight to your grand cause, but a soldier's job is to ask the right questions before the battle, to avoid having to ask them after defeat.'

Had I been born to a lower station in life, it is my belief I would have made a first-class actor. How I have managed to keep a straight face when presented with the most outrageous proposals while my bowels dissolved is a talent seldom seen outside the top playhouses. This was another one, and had he spotted my deadpan performance, Shakespeare would have cast me in the role of Macbeth before you could say curtain up. This latest maniac, backed by his crazy Knights, expected me to beard their spy in enemy-occupied Memphis, direct Joe to where the stolen gold was hidden, pop along to Washington with Miss Cora, contact a traitorous senator and stand by while they arranged to smuggle it from Memphis to Liverpool. And all I could do was sit there, clutching my drink, and mutter that it was a deuced serious business.

'So it is agreed? You can serve our cause and get back safe to England quicker than you could from a Southern port. Your hand on it.'

The Governor put his paw to me gimlet-eyed while the others looked on. I met it across the table and we shook vigorously.

'Well Governor,' says I with a death's head grin, 'when you put it like that, how can I refuse?'

287

Chapter Eighteen

We departed first light two days later. My respect for the Knights had grown enormously as the Governor mapped out his plan for getting Joe, his four brother officers, Miss Cora and her new, temporary husband, safely to Memphis. With the Knights' organisation greasing the way, the Governor, or somebody, had it all planned out to the tiniest detail. The Lord alone knows how they managed to keep their infernal organisation in such working order in the midst of a war, but they did, and any hope I had of sliding out the moment Joe's back was turned vanished like the buffalo in Winter.

One point I should mention. I had been a little surprised when the Governor ordained that Miss Cora and I should travel as man and wife. Southern gentlemen might pup their Negro slave girls whenever it took their fancy, but the South frowned on any untoward familiarity with respectable white women. Touch a planter's daughter - or niece for that matter - and the usual outcome was a shotgun wedding if you were a suitable catch, or a shotgun blast if you weren't. So it was no surprise when after he had finished going over his plans, chilling my blood in the process, he drew me aside for a quiet, *locum* fatherly chat.

'Colonel Armstrong, I send my good friend's niece along with Joe's party with a heavy heart. In fact, I opposed it all along, but Miss Cora is... ahh, a strong-willed Southern woman, and if I say her nay she would up and follow you notwithstanding. She is trusted by the Knights, and was set to go straight to Washington to see the Senator, but she has persuaded me that travelling as your wife will enable both of you to pass through Memphis and on to the Yankee capital without hindrance. Only for such a serious emergency as the one facing the South would I permit a lady to travel under such conditions.' He glanced back to ensure we were alone, and lowered his voice. 'Of course, Colonel Armstrong, I know I can rely on you to behave as a gentleman...'

Warning me not to play my role of new husband too literally, I could see. If only he'd known we had already started rehearsals. I donned a puzzled expression, followed at just the right interval by one of shock.

'Sir, I can assure you I have nothing but the highest regard for Miss Cora, and am full of admiration for her courage and devotion to the cause. We shall play the parts assigned to us, to be sure, but I am not so dead to honour, as I trust, to regard our roles as any more than a regrettable necessity. I... I...' I stammered a bit for effect, 'I am horrified at any suggestion, Sir, of impropriety... I am the product of an English public school and a Christian upbringing.'

'My deepest apologies, Colonel,' says he, flustered for the first time since I had known him. 'Please forgive me. That darling girl is in my care, entrusted to me by her uncle, and her safety and ...ahh, honour, are my first concerns.'

Then why are you sending her on a mad mission into enemy territory, armed and fitted up with a bogus husband, I wanted to shout. Instead I looked stern and gripped his paw in mine.

'Your concern does you credit, Sir. Please rest assured that no harm will come to her. I will protect your sweet charge whatever the cost. She will be as safe with me as though I was... well, as though I was her real husband.'

That settled the matter, and we adjourned to the dining room to rejoin the others. The supper was probably delicious, but I had no taste for it.

The journey as far as Vicksburg was uneventful, and I shan't weary you with it. You may find it hard to believe that we could travel hundreds of miles through a country at war and call it uneventful, but you need to understand that the South covers a vast area, and the war at this stage was just a few bloodstained specks on a huge canvas. Unless you were unlucky you could journey great distances without encountering any trouble.

I said uneventful, and in this I include my relations with Miss Cora. I don't know if the Governor had had words with his nephew, but Joe ensured that whenever we camped, the loving bride and groom found themselves planted as far apart as possible. So no events there, neither.

With Joe as our guide, we skirted around Baton Rouge - Miss Cora, I was not surprised to discover, was an excellent horsewoman - and on the second day fetched up at the Eastern bank of the Mississippi where there was a fast, light boat waiting to take us up the river towards Memphis. I had formed enough respect for the Knights by now not to be surprised at this either. This long stretch of river was still in Rebel hands, and we travelled unchallenged past the heavily fortified Port Hudson, through Natchez, past Fort Gibson and Grand Gulf, and on upwards towards Vicksburg. We arrived at Warrenton where we alighted for the last time and made camp.

Nearby Vicksburg was the South's Rock of Gibraltar, the key to control of the Mississippi. A formidable bastion, protected to the rear by impassable mosquito-infested marshes and virtual jungle. The town itself was built on the hills above the river, guns trained on any traffic below. Federal naval forces had been engaged in a half-hearted siege for some months, but nothing to trouble the defenders. Yankee boats were still sniffing about however, so we had to make our way overland from Warrenton, leaving our vessel behind.

Next morning we rode towards the town, making our way cautiously along narrow paths and over spongy marshland. I agreed with Joe that the Yankees could not hope to march an army through this morass. It was guarded too, as we discovered when we were challenged by Confederate pickets, demanding to know our business.

Joe told them who we were, and they escorted us back to a camp just behind the town. The Knights clearly had influence here, for in no time Joe had squared accounts with the Rebel authorities and we were given leave to enter Vicksburg and continue unmolested.

'Right,' says Joe. 'We can relax here for the day. Get cleaned up and make yourselves presentable.' This was to the newlyweds. 'The dangerous work begins tomorrow. We'll ride north a spell, to where we have a boat waiting. We will probably pass Yankee boats steaming down to fire on Vicksburg, so we may be challenged.'

You can imagine how I felt about this. Should we be taken by the Yankees, they would never believe that I was not here of my own free will. They would hoot at the notion that I was here through a series of misunderstandings, and nothing would persuade them else-wise. I would be just another British fool who meddled in their affairs and backed the wrong side. Nor could I expect any assistance from the British Consulate in Washington. Prime Minister Palmerston, the old rogue, had ordered that the British keep well out of it, being neutral, and any Brit who took up Blue or Butternut colours was on his own and liable for court-marshal on return to England. The Yankees would lock me up in a prison cell and throw away the key.

I put such thoughts out of my mind and accepted Joe's invitation to bathe, brush up my clothes and generally get the stench of the Mississippi out of my bones. Later that afternoon we took a turn around the town, where I cast my soldier's eye over its towering fortifications and agreed with the townsfolk that the Yankees would have their work cut out breeching them. Storm Vicksburg? Wellington wouldn't have fancied it above half. It was built on hills up to 300 feet high, so steep they had to cobblestone the streets to allow men and horses to grip. I thanked the Lord I was not involved in the siege on either side. If only I had known the future. Ah well...

Joe insisted we move the following evening. With a Rebel escort we circled up river to beyond the city past the Yankee besiegers, and boarded a new Knights' boat, Memphis bound. Too small to take our horses, we left them with our grateful escort. We travelled on by night through Yankee-held waters, my nerves jangling at every sound. I protested that we were sure to be stopped by

Yankee patrol boats but Joe and the Knights had our story ready for inspection.

'Should we be stopped,' says Joe, 'you and Miss Cora...' he laughed, 'I mean, you and Mrs. Armstrong are newlyweds on your way to Memphis and then on north up to Cairo, then maybe along the Ohio River or north by train and finally to New York and home to England. Me and the boys are riverboat men you have hired to take you to Memphis where you can travel on in safety.' He glanced at his comrades. 'We are fleeing the South due to our Northern sentiments and intend to join the Yankee army at Memphis, after we set you right.' He frowned. 'They'll believe us easy enuff; there's traitors aplenty in Tennessee, specially the mountainfolk.'

The others nodded in agreement. It seems the glorious rebellion was not as universally popular in the south as I had thought.

An objection occurred to me.

'They may just conscript you on the spot.'

'They won't do that, Colonel. The Yankees aren't as desperate for men as we of the South. They'll let us progress on up to Memphis and see you safe on a Cairo boat.' He laughed. 'And we will... just as soon as you and Mrs Armstrong return to our meeting place with the whereabouts of our gold.'

It seemed pretty thin to me, but then devil-may-care operations are not my cup of tea, exactly. Well, whether it worked or not, there was one person determined not to find himself caught twixt bluecoats and butternuts, and devil take the hindmost.

'Belay there.' The Yankee patrol boat loomed out of the Mississippi mist. As my loins tightened with funk, our crew obeyed the order and presently it pulled alongside. Several Union officers backed by soldiers holding lamps stared down at us.

'Who are you and what is your business?

'Hello Captain,' says Joe looking up, 'are we glad to see you. We're on our way to Memphis to enlist in the Union Army.'

'Where are you from?'

'Most of us are from Tennessee, but we have an Englishman and his new wife on board. We are escorting them to Memphis where they will travel on up to New York and then home to England.'

The Captain grunted suspiciously and ordered several of his men to board us.

When they had accounted for our numbers, with several curious glances at Miss Cora, the Captain peered down and addressed Joe.

'You the leader?'

'Kind of. May I talk to you Sir?'

'Come on up.'

Joe ascended the rope ladder and joined the Captain on the patrol boat. There was a stage-wait while the Union troops told us to rest easy until the Captain decided what to do with us. After what seemed an interminable time, though it cannot have been more than ten minutes, Joe and the Captain reappeared. They were plainly on far better terms now, and the Captain told his men all was well and they should return to their stations.

'Thank you Captain,' says Joe. 'Much obliged to ye.' They shook hands and Joe leapt back down into our boat.

'All's well,' cries he as the patrol boat began drawing up its rope ladders and made to depart. We cast off upriver, and he addressed his fellow officers and the newlyweds, chuckling merrily.

'Well that was a stroke of good fortune and praise the Lord.' He pulled out a paper from his pocket.

'This here's a passport from the worthy Captain, requesting all other Yankee patrol boats allow us on our way to Memphis.'

'How come?' asks one of his fellows. Joe grinned and fished out a small object from inside his jacket.

'On account o' this.' He opened his palm and, mystified, I saw that it contained a small, five-point copper star.

'What's that?'

'This, Colonel Armstrong, signals that I am a member of a certain organisation. When I showed it to the Captain he knew that his higher duty, above that to the Black Republicans of Washington, was to help us on our way.'

My heart pumped violently as I grasped the risk he had taken with our - more to the point my - neck.

'But how did you know he was a supporter of your ...organisation?'

'Once I guessed he was a Kentuckian, I dropped a certain word into my speech. He responded with the appropriate answering word, so I knew I could trust him.'

It was a hot and murky Mississippi night, but my blood froze at this secret tokens and passwords nonsense. I've had much unwanted experience of coded messages, funny handshakes and signs, and I know all too often it ends up with a stiletto in the back down some dark alleyway. Worse than that, it confirmed that the blasted Knights of the water closet were not confined to Southerners. I knew Miss Cora was meeting with a Northern Senator who was ready to betray his country by helping its enemies ship gold to England, but discovering that Union patrol boats could be captained by traitors unmanned me completely. I had a half-formed plan to desert Miss Cora and her desperate gang of treasure seekers first chance I got, but I now knew I daren't run or peach to the Yankees in case I crossed the path of another confounded spy. One thing was certain sure; I couldn't trust a single person in this benighted country. If I betrayed this gold-hunting mission, word would get back to the Knights for certain, and where would poor Tommy be then?

Luckily, for I hate to have to take swift action unless I'm facing immediate danger, all I had to do for now was sit tight in the boat and let Joe take the strain. Resting up by day and moving upriver by night, we were stopped twice again by patrol boats but on each occasion Joe presented his pass and we were allowed to travel on without hindrance.

In due course we reached the outskirts of Memphis, and tied up our boat in a backwater a couple of miles short of the city. Joe and his boys would return to it once they had the information they sought, the information, sweet Jesu, that Miss Cora and I were here to obtain.

'Right Colonel,' says he. 'We'll set up camp tonight and you an' Miss Cora can make your way into Memphis tomorrow. Me and the boys will give you forty-eight hours to return, allowing for hold-ups, then we will come looking for you.'

'Don't you fret none, Joe,' pipes up Miss Cora, 'the Colonel and I will be back the same day, then we'll return and catch a steamer up to Cairo. Easy as pie.'

I wished I shared her confidence. But when I thought about it, there seemed little chance of coming adrift as long as we did nothing foolish. She was a cool hand, this Miss Cora, and I told myself that our task was none too onerous. Simply stroll into town, the happy couple, make enquiries as to the next northbound steamboat, pop in to see an 'old friend' for a chat, and heigh-ho back to Joe and the boys for coffee. The only dangerous part, so far as I could see, was contacting the Knights' agent. If he was being watched, we might find ourselves asked embarrassing questions. Well I'd cross that one when I came to it, possibly at high speed. And Miss Cora could fend for herself. She'd be all right; she was brought up with brothers.

In my time I have made my reluctant way along some evil paths. African jungle and Afghan canyons spring to mind, but for sheer dust and grime the trek into Memphis beats them all.

Miss Cora and I bade Joe and the others goodbye and walked the two miles into town, coughing and spluttering every time the breeze stirred. Clinging hot dust flew into our eyes, noses and clothing, and even when the hot breeze dropped the dust was so thick we had to wade through it like so much dirty snow. By the time we arrived on the outskirts of town we resembled nothing more than a pair of scarecrows that had been left up in the attic. I confess I may have complained to Miss Cora.

'We are lucky,' says she. 'Had it been raining we would have been wading through two feet of mud.'

'How can we walk through town in this condition? We are liable to get picked up for vagrancy.'

She looked at me and grinned.

'Why Colonel, that's no attitude for a dashing hussar of the Great British Empire. And fear not, the good folk of Memphis have seen dust before; As Mr. and Mrs. Armstrong, we can take a room in a boarding house and make ourselves respectable.'

This sounded like an excellent idea, and I cheered up on the instant. There is something about danger that makes me incredibly horny and though Miss Cora was at present looking as unsightly as sin, underneath the dust I knew the meat was all present and correct. If there was one job I fancied above half, it was scrubbing down her finely honed body and making it fit for inspection. Mad says you, given where we were, but as students of the depraved will agree, beauty is in the eye of the holder.

'Capital notion,' agrees I and gave my dusty maiden a squeeze to settle the thing. 'Lead on.'

She gave me a peculiar look, as if surprised at my sudden change of mood, and together we found a suitable boarding house. The concierge barely looked at us twice, but accepted our Yankee dollars for two night's stay and showed us to a room and bath.

'Ladies first, Colonel,' says Miss Cora, after the Negro boy had filled the tub. I noticed that in common with most things American, it was far bigger than it needed to be, and just what doctor Tommy ordered.

'Of course,' says I, the perfect gentleman. Had she known me better she might have locked the bathroom door, or then again perhaps she mightn't. Filled with amorous anticipation, I disrobed while giving her just long enough to settle in, then bounded through, holding a towel for form's sake.

'Colonel!' she squealed. Gad she was a picture; soaked and slippery, her bouncers peeking above the suds like two babies' heads. I felt a fellow feeling for Mark Anthony, who once had a similar experience with Cleopatra.

'Colonel be-damned,' says I, drooling. 'Stand by to repel borders.'

And before you could say Nelson, I had dropped the towel and plunged in alongside.

'I'll soon rub the dust off, now which leg wants to be first?'

After a short protest to maintain maidenly honour, she joined in the spirit of the game like an admiral in a brothel, and in no time at all we had emptied about half the contents of the bath onto the floor. Just as well, for once we were clean we buckled-to still in the tub, and had the water level been any higher Miss Cora would have sunk beneath the plimsoll line.

In due course we were done, and I had just the strength to carry her back to our room, fireman style, and drop her, still dripping with soap suds, on to the bed. When she had caught her breath, for wrestling in the bath takes it out of one and we had been cooped up in a boat for days, she returned, blast her, to business.

'OK Colonel, fun's fun, but we have a serious task here. I know the way from the city centre to our err... friend's house, so we must first go to the city centre.'

Full of zip after our water sports - like I always say, there's nothing like a good gallop to put a fellow in best fighting trim - I wasn't having this.

'Not at all, young Miss Cora. First off, we find the next riverboat north to Cairo. Once we have tickets, our *bona fides* are established should any inquisitive Federals demand to know our business. Why, we are neutral British citizens travelling north and of no interest to anybody. Then, knowing how much time we have before embarkation, we visit your friend.' A clever thought sprang to mind. 'Better still, you visit him alone. Two of us will attract attention. Also, as he does not know us, together we might scare him off. A woman calling on her own will not excite attention.'

'Why Colonel, how gallant you are.' She fixed me with a stern eye. 'You think a single young woman calling on a man will not attract attention?' She ran her hand through her wet hair, distracting me somewhat. 'We will attract less attention walking two-by-two, and don't worry about us frightening off our agent. We of the Knights don't run from shadows, nor from a newlywed couple.'

'Don't mention that name here,' I urged. I'd formed enough respect for the blasted Knights never to wish to hear of them again, even from their own agents.

'All right Colonel. And don't you think of sidling out leaving me to do the man's work. We march together, y'heah?'

'Sidling out, damn you.' I was annoyed now. One thing we poltroons fear above all, and that is finding our poltroonery discovered. 'I'm offering to keep guard just outside. That's the more dangerous job, so less of the sidling out.'

She looked at me deadpan, and spoke quietly.

'A girl can learn a lot about a man when she makes love to him, Colonel. And what I've learnt is that you are none too keen on this here mission. Left to you, we would just jump on the next riverboat and leave Joe and the gold go hang.'

Wasn't she right though? How they do it beats me, but I've lost count of the number of women who deduced my true character just by a quick roll in the hay. I've never found *their* true character in *flagrante delicto*, as we classical scholars say, but maybe that's because I am concentrating on the action and have no time for character assessments. Nor should they, the selfish brutes. Meanwhile, Miss Cora had given me a nasty scare and it was my job to put her straight.

'My dear Miss Cora, how can you possibly think such a thing? My heart is with the South, and with you and... and Joe and the boys, and your magnificent organisation. If I sound cautious, well, that's just my army training, where we put hard, military logic before romantic adventure. And hard military logic says we should book the tickets first, to prove we are who and what we say we are, then visit your friend, with me protecting your back from just outside his place in case he is being watched. That's all. So please...' I gave her my most winsome Tommy smile and stroked my hand gently through her hair, 'forgive me if I seem cautious, but as we say in England, better safe than sorry.'

If women can deduce a man's personality by jumping into bed with him, they can be fooled by smooth words, a polite squeeze and a bonny expression.

'I'm sorry Colonel for doubting you, it's just that this mission is vital to our cause, and I guess anything that seems to hinder it looks like treason or cowardice.' She smiled at last. 'Will you forgive my doubting you?'

'Why Miss Cora,' says I, torn between relief and lust. 'Whatever for? You are doing your duty as a good soldier should. And speaking of duty, you have marital responsibilities you know...'

What with one thing and another it was well into the afternoon by the time Mr. and Mrs. Armstrong sallied forth into the Memphis dustbowl once more. After some persuasion, in bed and out of it, she had agreed to do things my way. With this in mind we made our way to the riverside in order to obtain passage on a boat to Cairo.

The atmosphere this time was quieter and less frenetic than my last visit. Then it had been a Confederate city preparing for war, all the talk of States Rights and how Yankees can go burn in Hell. Now it was at peace, albeit the peace of the quietly conquered. The despised Yankees had arrived in force, obliging the loyal Southerners, or traitors depending on where you stood, to mind their Ps and Qs. Beneath the surface, tensions might be as fraught as ever, but trade continued, and we strolled past stores, warehouses and imposing civic buildings bustling with men, women and Negroes hurrying about their business.

Nobody paid us the slightest heed, and my nerves settled as we mixed in with the shoppers crowding the streets as though the war was a distant dream. I wondered how the recent occupation by Federal forces might have changed things. At first glance, apart from the blue uniforms instead of grey, and the discreet change of flags and bunting from the stars and bars to the stars and stripes, there was not a whit of difference. Even the saloons stayed open, and did a roaring trade by the sound of them. If the Memphis citizens resented this Federal invasion of their secessionist soil, they had the sense not to show it, most of the time. Memphis was open for business as usual.

'Curse them Yankees,' Miss Cora fumed, 'I was here last year and every window you saw had a State flag hanging from it. You bet they are kept safe for when the Yankees fly from our forces, just you wait and see.'

'Keep your voice down,' says I, concerned. 'We are neutral, remember? And you are my wife coming to England and take no interest in politics. You understand?'

She shot me a most unwifely look, but praise the Lord, confined her remarks to commenting on how the shops were busy and folks were getting on with their lives.

For a city recently taken in battle, there was no sign of damage from fire, cannon or looting. I later learned from Billy Russell that Memphis was a centre of contraband for both sides, so both sides left its infrastructure in peace.

In fact, this calm veneer was misleading. Underneath the surface, resentment of the invaders simmered dangerously. Since the Battle of Memphis in early June, when the Federal navy wiped out the Rebel fleet in under two hours, Memphis had been a city in chaos. Hundreds of the strongest secessionists - except the Knights' agent, rot him - flew south even as Union soldiers hoisted their flag over the post office building after the battle. These included bank employees, telegraph operators, physicians and other citizens employed in the day-to-day running of the city. Luckily their juniors rushed to fill in the gaps, and gain easy promotion, so commerce survived, as I thought it might.

As usual, it was the womenfolk who were most likely to show open defiance, bawling "Yankee", "traitor" and "coward" at any who showed Northern sympathies. John Company's loyal Sepoys suffered similar catcalling from the Indian women, though in both cases only when there were no regular soldiers in earshot. Miss Cora and I attracted no such vulgar attention, I'm relieved to report. Calling Miss Cora a Yankee could have had severe repercussions for all concerned.

Before seeking accommodation on a northbound boat, We found stables and hired two horses. I had no wish to wade through mud and dust back to Joe's camp, and besides, if things went adrift we might need to light out at speed, though this was a notion I did not care to dwell on.

Leaving the horses behind, along with a ruinous sum of dollars for the hire from Miss Cora's purse, we strolled on down to the broad esplanade alongside the river and sought a boat to Cairo. After several false starts, for regular shipping had not yet recommenced following the fall of the town to Federal forces, we found just what we were looking for.

'You wanna ride up to Cairey?' says a likely looking boatman. 'Waal, I'm going that-a-way myself. If'n you kin hold out till tomorrow morning reckon ah kin oblige ye. Fer a small consideration.'

'Thank you. That would be fine, Mister...'

'You kin call me Jim. Jim Travis. Pleased to meet you Suh. An' you, ma'am,' he doffed his cap. 'Of course,' he slipped us a sly grin, 'by rights I must fust get permission from the military authorities. That may take awhiles.'

'We don't have time,' snaps Miss Cora. 'My husband and I must get to England as soon as possible.'

'Waal, in that case...' He winked. 'Guess it will be a mite more expensive.'

Miss Cora paid him half his exorbitant fee, the balance to be handed over on arrival in Cairo, and pocketed the scrawled receipt. So far everything had gone smoothly, but the riskiest part was upon us.

'OK husband,' says Miss Cora determinedly, 'now let us return to the town centre so I can find my bearings.'

We duly backtracked back up to the centre, and after a moment or two to study, she bade me accompany her towards the poorer part of town, near to the railroad.

With the townsfolk going about their business, we ambled invisibly between the respectable shoppers and working men, past the shops and buildings with the roll of heavily-laden wagons, the rattle of omnibuses and general bustle of commercial life. Turning east we left the main avenue and meandered through alleys and narrow streets to the bohemian quarter. We passed by dancing saloons, gaming rooms and similar dives populated by Negroes and whites of the lowest stamp, and craggy toothless women. My back-hairs once more tingled.

'This way.' Miss Cora, who seemed to have the homing instincts of a Scotsman seeking a pub, took us meandering through the back alleys until we reached a tiny cul-de-sac.

'The man we seek lives in the third house.' She pointed to a peeling door in a narrow, terraced tenement. Good luck to him, thinks I. The wide open spaces of America to live in, and he chooses a slum better suited to Glasgow or Paisley.

'Wait here and keep an eye out for Yankees,' say she. 'I shall return as soon as I may.'

With that she marched forward and after quite some knocking, the door opened. Miss Cora disappeared inside, leaving me prey to some disloyal thoughts. Should I run? I couldn't while Miss Cora was free and full of ginger. I had no wish to get on the wrong side of the Knights, and besides, I was a sight safer travelling with her than alone. A refugee is one thing, a respectable married couple quite another. So as long as things remained quiet, my best option was to stay and keep guard. On the other hand, one sniff of the Yankee authorities and Miss Cora and her spying colleague could look out for themselves.

After what seemed an age but couldn't have been longer than two or three minutes, the door opened and Miss Cora emerged. Once glance at her flushed features told me she had the information she sought. Now to collect our horses from the stable and get back to Joe and the boys.

'You live here Mister?'

I almost screamed as a voice behind me called out crisp and clear. Glancing around, my throat filled with bile as my worst fears were realised with a vengeance.

Four men stood behind me, well dressed in civilian togs with a businesslike manner all over them. Where they appeared from was a mystery to me; they probably spied us entering the back-streets and recognised us as imposters, not reeking of gin and poverty.

I froze. I'm not often stumped, but I couldn't for the life of me come up with a reasonable excuse to be where I was. Saying I lived there would be laughed out of court. Luckily, Miss Cora, approaching rapidly, replied for me.

'He is protecting his wife, *Mister*, as you will discover if you try laying a finger on either of us.' She arrived at my side and linked arms.

The men were not impressed. Appraising us - a most uncomfortable feeling - they stared suspiciously.

'And who might you be Miss?' asks the leader.

'Mrs. George Jeffreys. And this here's my husband.' She pointed to the new wedding ring on her finger. 'We just got wed and we are on our way to New York and England. My husband is English, I just called in on my cousin to say goodbye.'

It sounded plausible, but these Yankee police types don't flatter easily. Stony-faced, the leader addressed me direct.

'You let your wife do all the talking? That's no way to start a marriage.'

His mates haw-hawed at this, and I felt resentment bubbling underneath my fear.

303

'Maybe its time you did some talking yourselves,' says I with a confidence I did not feel. 'Who are you and why are you asking us our business?'

One of them turned to the leader.

'Well he's English, anyhow.'

'Reckon he is at that. Don't prove a thing though.' He turned to me.

'We are Federal officers, and the man your good lady wife just visited is someone we have an interest in. So we are gonna take you back with us and ask you a few more questions.'

'What for?' cries Miss Cora. 'We are free people going about our business. You have no right to detain us. Leave us be.' She tried to push past the lawmen but they held firm.

'Not a chance, ma'am. You and your husband are coming along with us.'

I could have told her you cannot argue with law enforcers. They would take us back to their headquarters and question us until kingdom come if they didn't like our answers. We couldn't fight against four armed men - well *I* couldn't anyway - so there was nothing for it but to go along with our captors. We faced prison, if not worse. I cursed myself for letting myself get roped into the Knights' lunatic schemes yet again, but what choice did I have?

Well if I'd given up, there was someone who hadn't.

'I said you both are coming along with us,' repeats their leader.

'The Hell they are! Long live the South, yee-haw!' A scream like a wolf's howl from an upstairs window accompanied a rifle shot and the lawmen's leader staggered backwards, clutching his chest before falling into the gutter. The others stared at him uncomprehendingly for a split second, then clutched the wall for cover. One of them loosed off a shot back at the window.

And where was Tommy? I stood still for one heartbeat as I realised that Miss Cora's agent had taken a hand. That was all I saw, for with our assailants distracted I shook off Miss Cora and flew away along the alley quick as knife. Round the first corner I flew, and with the sound of gunfire behind me, I raced through this alley and that, heedless of the occasional drunk or general flotsam of humanity idling by.

Breathless, I turned one more corner, into a busier thoroughfare, and stopped to collect my wits. That was our mission scuppered to be sure. They would rustle up reinforcements and kill the agent to avenge their leader, and Miss Cora would find her pretty self on a charge of assisting in murder, to say nothing of spying. They'd probably hang her, and if they caught up with me she wouldn't hang alone. What to do? I daren't steal one of the horses we'd hired. Horses were like gold-dust with both armies commandeering them for cavalry and pulling wagons and cannon. Steal a horse and you'll have half the country after you. My best bet was to lie low somewhere outside of town, then sneak back tomorrow and catch the boat up to Cairo. They'd have put wanted posters up by then, but they knew nothing about me so barring bad luck I should be safe enough. To be sure, I hadn't the cash to pay Jim Travis the balance for the trip, but I'd worry about that when the time came. Sufficient unto the day, as the gospel says.

There was a chance that the agent and Miss Cora - who was armed - might kill all four agents, which would be most satisfactory, but I dismissed this as deuced unlikely. Then again, if Miss Cora started saying it with bullets and was killed in the mêlée she couldn't give away anything about me. Harsh, you may say, but Tommy comes first. Thank the Lord she had called herself Mrs. Jeffreys, probably by mistake, but who knows? If the U.S. authorities got wind that Tommy was up to his old tricks it would be the Newgate hornpipe for me and no error.

On that depressing thought I struck warily through the streets to the outskirts of town.

Chapter Nineteen

I have slept out in the woods as a hunted man more times than I care to remember, and this occasion was no different to the rest. Swearing at the fates that I was too old to be living like a vagabond, I found a quiet neck where I was unlikely to be disturbed and crawled into the bushes. Once settled, I studied my situation and concluded calmly that there was nothing for it but to try and board Jim Travis's boat on the morrow. To be sure, I ranted inwardly, damming all the inconsiderate bastards who had brought me to my present sorry state, from Lincoln down, but ultimately I knew there was nothing for it but to trust to heavenly providence and judicious knavery to see me through. Praying I wouldn't snore, I managed to sink into a wary slumber until the sun's rays brought me back to unhappy consciousness.

Finding a stream, I made what toilet I could, and presently threw back my shoulders and marched confidently - on the outside at any rate - back down into town.

I half-expected Yankee police officers and detectives to be combing the streets on the lookout for me toting nooses - hiding under the stars stimulates the imagination wonderfully - but to my immense relief, I was able to mingle in with the morning shoppers, workers and layabouts without attracting a second glance. Reassured somewhat, I sauntered down to the riverside where my boat out of Memphis was, I hoped, waiting for me.

It was. I spotted Jim on deck, berating a black boy who was loading sacks on board and being damnably sloppy about it, to hear Jim's curses. The sheer normality of this gave me courage, and for the first time since yesterday's shootings I saw the way out. There were a fair number of folk noisily going about their riverside business, too busy to take heed of me, so consigning my soul to the Lord I made my way down to the boat. I felt my heart race and my body shake with fear and excitement as I forced myself to amble casually past the small sheds and around

306

the bales and boxes and general detritus alongside the landing bays. I'd have to explain Miss Cora's absence, of course, but dissembling has never been a problem for me. I'd say that some of her cousins had arrived to see her for the last time before she travelled to England, and they would take her up to Cairo in a few days. I was travelling on ahead to conclude private business matters before arranging transportation back east. Say the word *business* to an American and they will swallow any tale, no matter how unlikely. Pity about Miss Cora, thinks I, for she was a good mount, but she involved herself in politics and since when has any decent person benefitted from that? Aye well, she died the way she wanted, fighting for the South.

'You cowardly snake!'

I nearly puked with shock. Emerging from behind a shed just in front of Jim's boat, Miss Cora stood glowering before me.

'Where in Hell have you been, you stinking rat?'

So she had escaped, and here she was full of vim and mischief, looking ready to knock me to the ground. Thank heavens she wasn't holding her gun. You'll think it inappropriate, but for a moment I forgot my fears as I contemplated another bout in the bathtub. Strong women have that effect on me. I stood numb while she fumed and I massaged my heart back into position. Eventually I composed myself enough to reply.

'Why Miss Cora, thank the Good Lord you escaped. I have been at my wit's end trying to discover what had become of you.'

She wasn't having this.

'The Hell you was. Why you ran off faster'n than a polecat up a tree. If'n I wasn't packing a pistol I'd be dead now.'

'So you killed them all?'

'Me an' my colleagues. I didn't have time to tell you, but our agent wasn't alone. He had another true Southerner with him and between the three of us we sent them Yankees to Hell.'

She was flushed with anger, but I detected a quiet note of satisfaction as she related her tale. Pride in a job well done.

This was marvellous news. Dead men can't bear witness. We were in the clear! Now all that I need do was convince Miss Cora I hadn't run out on her yesterday and we could travel on as husband and wife, with all that that entailed.

'Why Miss Cora, that is the most wonderful thing I have ever heard. And to think, I spent the night worrying about you, and wondering how to complete our mission. And all the time you were safe and well.'

'Don't try to hogwash me, Colonel. You ran like a stinking yellow-belly.'

'Yellow belly nothing,' says I, all injured innocence. 'Your man fired from his window to cover our escape, sacrificing himself for the mission, so I took advantage as a soldier should. That's what he wanted us to do.'

'*Our* man, Colonel, or had you forgotten?' But her expression showed doubt. Clearly she hadn't considered that running away might have been a sound military tactic for the good of her blasted cause. Can't imagine why; its something *I* always consider right off the bat.

'I thought you were right behind me. As soon as I realised you were not, I backtracked, but it was too late. I could only pray to the Good Lord that you were OK.'

'Then why didn't you go back to tell Joe and the boys?'

'And lead the Yankees to their camp?' God it sounded lame, but it was the best I could do at short notice. 'Who knows how many men they have plastered around the town?' Which brought me to the main point. 'It's not safe to linger. Let's get onto the boat now and get out of here.' I gave her my Tommy grin, 'we can kill Yankees together another time.'

She was still angry, but I could tell she was slowly coming around to believing my story. By the time we got to Cairo we would be resuming life as man and wife.

'Don't you want to know if I got to Joe with the whereabouts of the gold?'

'Well did you?' Not that I cared, but one has to show willing.

'Oh I did, Colonel, rest assured. Joe knows where the gold is, and soon a certain senator in Washington will be sending a ship down to help him dispatch it to England.'

'Why that's glorious,' says I, all patriotic fervour and bedammed. 'Once the gold reaches England your folk there will be able to purchase ships to break the blockade.'

Before she had time to reply, a welcome voice cut in.

'There you are. I was jes' bout to leave without ye.'

Jim stood before us, parading a smile that said he was more than happy with the money Miss Cora was paying him. 'You ready? You don' seem to have much baggage.'

'We travel light,' says I, looking meaningfully at Miss Cora. 'Come on darling, we mustn't keep the gentleman waiting.'

'We'll be right with you,' says she calmly to Jim, 'you go on ahead.'

Jim shrugged and returned to the boat, and Miss Cora addressed me for the first time today in a civil voice.

'Colonel, do you give me your solemn word that you absolutely thought I was right behind you when you ran?'

'Why darling...'

'And you thought our agent was sacrificing himself so we could escape and get the gold to England?'

'But of course... the mission is more important than any of us.' Jesu the things I say.

She sniffed. 'Well Colonel, the mission is well on course to succeed. Next stop Washington.'

But not for long, thinks I. I'd be on the first train north. Quietly I congratulated her on her destruction of the Yankee detectives, and for once meant every word.

'Now let's get on board ship before any more Yankees turn up.'

'If they do, Colonel, they'll go the same way as the others.' She gave me a keen look. 'As will anyone who gets in the way of the mission.'

It took us three days to get to Cairo. During that time Miss Cora melted a little, and we conversed on friendly terms. She removed a cloud from my horizon by telling me Joe and his boys were none the wiser about my running away. She told them we got split up in the mêlée and she would seek me out at the riverside in the morning. Damned sporting of her, but of course she was the one who insisted I travel along as her husband, so she could hardly tell the Knights I'd jumped ship at the first squall. Not without looking a fool. Anyhow, relations between us improved as we chugged up the Mississippi. Using an apple as a cricket ball, I even raised a giggle or two from her, demonstrating how to bowl overarm. Much to the crew's amusement, I prevailed upon her to try for herself. I had to hold her *in-situ* as it were for like all women, she could not throw overarm without overbalancing, but daren't take a husband-like squeeze with the rabble watching. No chance for after hours net-practice neither; the boat was far too small for privacy, and we slept separately on deck. Patience, Tommy me lad, thinks I, from Cairo to Washington we'll resume married life. I'd considered my safest route and decided it was best to travel with Miss Cora to Washington after all, and catch the train onwards to New York. I'd no wish to beard her tame Senator in his Washington lair, so as soon as we arrived in Washington 'twould be time to go our separate ways, preferably when she was asleep. This being the case, it was only fair to give my temporary wife a few happy memories for posterity's sake.

On the third morning we reached Columbus, then two hours later Jim Travis grabbed my sleeve and pointed ahead. That's Cairey,' says he. I looked ahead and spotted the Stars and Stripes waving from a lofty staff at the angle of low land formed by the confluence of the Mississippi and Ohio rivers. I'd passed briefly by Cairo ten years earlier, and as we neared the town I could see that the war had not been kind to it. It boasted a large hotel, rising far above the levee of the river, and a church and spire to remind the traveller that Cairo had not always been this desolate, and a line of shanties and small houses, the rooms and upper storeys just visible above the embankment. The founders had envisaged a thriving metropolis, situated as it was where the rivers meet, and had established the Southern terminus of the Central Illinois railroad. It was to be a great trading post, you see, but with the war killing river trade stone dead, Cairo was now a semi-deserted wretched looking slum, rather like London's Isle of Dogs on a drizzly night in November.

Miss Cora paid off Jim, and after a brisk farewell we left the boat and proceeded to the hotel. The hall contained a number of officers in United States uniforms, and I was disconcerted to find that the lower part of the hotel was set aside for use by the U.S. military. Not for myself, you understand, but Miss Cora bristled like a cat in a dog show, and I fretted she might say or do something rash, landing poor Tommy back in the mire. Fortunately she kept her counsel, and presently we found ourselves in a tiny room disconcertingly reminiscent of a dungeon, with a window looking out on the two rivers lined with sheds and huts, terminated by a battery.

'Look at them,' says she, staring down through the window, 'damned Yankees invading our land and helping themselves to our property like we was niggers or Indians.'

'Fortunes of war, my dear,' says I, kicking off my shoes and falling back on the single bed. 'Never you mind, just remember we are merely passing through, and have more pressing matters to consider.' We did, too. Well, *I* did anyhow, and seeing that Miss Cora was in no mood to resume conjugal duties just then, I summoned a Negro waiter and ordered dinner for two, then moseyed on along to the hall to inquire about ways to travel east. Here we struck lucky, for it transpired there was a steamer leaving up the Ohio River past Cincinnati for Pittsburgh that very night. Miss Cora was delighted.

'Pittsburgh is less than two hundred miles from Washington,' says she. And about three hundred from New York, thinks I. Five days - nights - to Pittsburgh, then the Baltimore and Ohio train to Washington DC, then on to New York. I would wave a reluctant farewell to my latest temporary wife and strike out for the *Empire State*, as New-Yorkers called their town. Would Miss Cora set her blasted Knights after me? No, I couldn't credit that. She had other fish to fry in Washington. Besides, I had formed quite an affection for Miss Cora, and I believe it was mutual, if you will forgive me saying so. She hadn't mentioned my running out on her again at any rate, and seemed to want to believe my story even though reason rebelled against it. And besides, I had got her this far, hadn't I? Through the danger areas and with the secret whereabouts of the gold? Once we passed Pittsburgh she was as safe as the bank. All we had to do was take a train east to Washington where I'd light out for New York and Home, and I'd snap my fingers at Lincoln, the Knights, Johnny Reb, Billy Yank and the rest. And not before time. I hadn't seen a cricket match since leaving China.

I'd travelled this way before, and the Ohio River held nothing but nightmares for me. This time, I assured myself, it would be different; no unexpected flights to upset my digestion. And, I am relieved to say, it was.

'Well Colonel,' says Miss Cora as we entered our stateroom, for she seemed to have unlimited funds, 'I suppose I'll have to believe you about that time in Memphis. Here we are, just a hop, skip and jump from Washington.' She beamed happily. 'Don' wanna tempt providence, but it looks like the Lord is shining on our mission and that's a fact.'

Capital, thinks I. We'll be dancing the sailor's hornpipe in no time. It was five nights to Pittsburgh and I intended to enjoy every one of them.

'Less talk of the mission,' says I cautiously, 'but you're right. We'll pass Cincinnati in no time and then on

312

up to Pittsburgh. A train to Washington and you can conduct your business in safety.'

'Our business, Colonel.'

'That's right; our business to be sure. Then, duty done, I'll be off to New York and England to speak up for our cause there.'

I sailed over her words, but they were an uncomfortable reminder of what lay ahead. I didn't dare show myself in Washington political circles. They're a nest of vipers at the best of times, and somehow I doubted they'd calmed down in the midst of a civil war. I was known to some there (including Lincoln himself, by all that's holy) and the last thing I needed was to be spotted hobnobbing with a Senator doubtless already suspected of traitorous intentions. At the very least Lincoln or his top thug, Secretary of State Seward (who also knew me personally and loathed the English like the pox), would inform Palmerston and little Vicky of my behaviour, and God knows what might come of that. Knowing the Yankee government, they'd most likely hang me as a British spy and declare war on England. No, thinks I, distracted by Miss Cora adjusting her clothing and making herself at home, come what may, when she plots treason in the very seat of government, she'll do it without me.

A thought occurred.

'What will you do after you have finished your... ah, business?'

'Me? I have a few things to do, Colonel. The Senator is not our only true friend in Washington. I have others to see, powerful wives and,' she looked away for a second, 'other women, who have information the South will find useful. They'll arrange safe passage back to my own country.'

Well I knew Washington society had divided loyalties, and Lincoln couldn't so much as fart without the South knowing about it, but if I needed any more persuasion that Washington's hive of intrigue was no place to linger, Miss Cora had just supplied it. My bowels quaked at the thought of Lincoln's chief detective Pinkerton

313

(another man who knew me personally and would recognise me in a coal cellar at midnight, and with no love for me neither), unveiling a massive Rebel conspiracy with Tommy slap bang in the middle. By God I knew all the top dogs, didn't I just? And all with fangs ready to bite lumps out of poor Tommy's arse. On reflection it might be better to abandon Miss Cora before we reached town.

But there's a time for everything, and top of the agenda was boarding the gorgeous apparition with whom I was sharing a stateroom - no wonder the Confederacy was short of funds - and who was now excusing herself to take a bath, informing me with a flirtatious wink that this time she was locking the door.

'So no bushwacking me today, eh Colonel?' says she, laughing through the door as she turned the lock and - big mistake - removing the key from the keyhole.

'Have no fears, my darling wife,' laughs I. 'I'll stand guard outside.' With that I summoned the steward to furnish me with the spare key.

Time passed quickly, as it always does when you are in the lap of luxury with a bouncing beauty to fill your nights. We kept to our stateroom a fair bit, but escaped at mealtimes to enjoy dinners of pre-war sumptuousness. The South was running short of food in some areas, Miss Cora informed me over a feast that could sink a rowboat, due to the poor harvest and shortage of white men on the farms, being off fighting the war. The sooner the dammed Yankees - she kept her voice down, to my relief - took the licking that was coming to them and crawled back behind their own borders, the sooner meals like ours would be available to all her countrymen. Oh aye, I agreed through a mouthful of prime beef, then added for mischief, all except the blacks and the poor whites. She bridled at this, I don't suppose people put the point to her all that often, and replied evenly.

'The poor whites, as you call them Colonel, can have all the food they want if'n they're prepared to work. And we give the slaves everything they need and they bless us for it. We took them out of the jungle, dressed them decent and taught them the value of honest labour in the eyes of the Lord.'

It was all one to me if they dressed them as clowns and taught them the value of honest juggling in the eyes of the matinee crowd, but she was only saying what almost everyone in the South believed; the Negroes loved the massa and were happy in their bondage. It seemed to me then, and still does today, that any president less stubborn than Lincoln would have let these recalcitrant Bible-thumpers go their own way and rejoiced to lose 'em. Why he wanted to keep the South is beyond me. He should have dropped it like a rattlesnake and snaffled Canada by way of compensation. Still, that's politicians for you the world over. Looking at our own crowd growling at Germany today, it just shows what most decent folk know; politicians will be the death of us all.

We halted at Cincinnati to drop off and collect passengers and goods, then started out on our last lap. Miss Cora and I were the perfect travelling companions, all talk of what had occurred in Memphis happily forgotten. How trivial it all seemed now! I am a natural actor, having acted the hero all my life, and I had pretended Miss Cora was my wife for so long I almost believed it.

Finally, on the fifth day, we arrived at Pittsburgh. Here our luxury travelling ended. Pittsburgh is the vilest, most smut laden, noisy, rank, slum-infested example of modern civilisation the world has ever known. And with citizens to match. It was an industrial centre for the Union, producing metal coffins for the army, amongst other less ominous products. There was money about the place though, for the blackened factory chimneys belched out their rank fumes constantly, engulfing the city in perpetual smog. I was relieved we were just passing through; I'd sooner take a holiday in Birmingham.

Somewhat disorientated after our soft living aboard the riverboat, we traversed the uneven streets to the railroad station, a'throng with grubby, sickly-looking factory hands, mothers and their squirming brats all

315

streaked with soot and grime. Oh aye, and the occasional high-sprung carriage conveying some greasy factory owner on his way to the bank. Vans and drays rattled along, shaking the wretched brick tenements as they passed by and heaps of slag and broken brick all around gave the impression of a vast manufacturing city from Hell.

For a wonder we were not assailed by the usual gangs of rowdies, Irish and Germans and the like, who normally infested such American industrial towns in the sixties. I learnt later that they had all gone off to the war, and let's hope they got what was coming to them for interfering in other folks' business. For those remaining behind, labour shortages ensured that wages were high and the manufacturers' order books were choc-full of government contracts. It is not hard to make money out of a war if you know how to go about it, as who knows better than I.

Here our luck took a knock.

'Train to Washington?' The station master shook his head. 'Ain't no train to Washington today, nor tomorrow neither.' It seemed the war had disrupted the regular service, and indeed the line had been closed earlier in the year for fear of Rebel interference.

Distraught, Miss Cora insisted we must get to Washington as quickly as possible as her sister was ill with the fever there, and she and her new husband needed to minister to her. How could we get there quickest?

'Yore best bet is to take a hotel here for a day or two and try your luck then. Or you can see if there's room on a coach going south to Maryland and mebbe catch a train to Washington somewhere thereabouts.'

My neck hairs tingled at the mention of going south, but Miss Cora was all for it. Poring over the station master's map, it seemed we could travel to Meyersdale, just north of Maryland, or somewhere similar, and take the train from there. It wasn't perfect, but I had no wish to linger in Pittsburgh; my stomach couldn't take it.

'That's settled then,' says Miss Cora to the station master, who must have felt for our marriage seeing the woman calling the shots, but she held the purse strings, you see. 'Will you please make enquiries as to whether there is a coach going to Maryland any time today and is there room to spare for us?

There was a coach, but I would have said that there was no room for a pigmy, let alone a great hulk of a fellow like me. That didn't worry the coachee, who took our fares and shoe-horned us in to the carriage anyway. Lucky we had no luggage, had I been travelling with my real wife we would still be loading her bandboxes to this day.

The coach trundled southwards alongside the rail lines, stopping at several hamlets and way stations along the route. We slept overnight in a crowded station's waiting room, just spread out any old how. I was too boneshaken from my day in the coach to even think of reminding Miss Cora of our marital vows, but there was no privacy anyway.

I won't bore you with the travel. It was a bind as such journeys usually are, and cramped solid to boot. We passed several more small stations and hamlets and were heading for the Maryland border and, I hoped, a train to Washington, when a jarring screech from below and a loud cursing from above informed us our coach had split a wheel.

'Everybody out,' yells the coachee, while he and his mate set about repairs.

We filed out obediently, into the fresh late summer evening, upset to lose time, but happy to be able to stretch our legs. We'd stopped in a gentle valley with sparse cottages dotted about in the distance, smoke trickling gently from their chimneys. It was an idyllic view, farmland with a little brushwood and forest and a nearby picture-postcard cottage with a picket fence and the warm orange glow of a roaring hearth flickering at the windows. Not quite England, exactly, but with the stars twinkling above the view conjured up memories of home and safety.

This made me think of my life in London. Beer and hot pies and Bow Street's Cyder Cellars, and billiards in the Haymarket, and St John's Wood where the better-class whores kept things lively, and my wife doing the social rounds of respectable society, and I think; Tommy me lad? You've been through more than any God-fearing coward ever should. Time for home and England old son. Surely, this is the last lap?

'Don't nobody move! We got twenty rifles covering ye. Stand still and do nothing foolish. One move and yore dead men.'

Chapter Twenty

As Tommy finds himself on the business end of the gun barrel once again, you may be wondering how the war was getting on.

Despite losing New Orleans, the top and bottom of the Mississippi and failing in the far west, the Confederates were in the ascendancy. At the second battle of Manassas, 50,000 Rebels under Generals Longstreet and Jackson whipped 75,000 Yankees under Union General Pope. Braggart Pope claimed his headquarters were in the saddle, prompting a rare joke from General Lee who said Pope's trouble was he had his headquarters where his hindquarters should be. Lincoln sacked Pope and re-hired McClellan (he'd sacked him earlier for general uselessness in the Peninsular Campaign where he'd sat on his arse in the rain while the Rebels consolidated their defences). McClellan was a ditherer who would have made a first-class drill sergeant but who made my old Crimean commander, the late unlamented General Raglan who could never remember if we were fighting the Ruskies or the Frogs, look like Napoleon.

Flushed with success, and knowing that the South had to win quickly or be ground down by superior Union wealth, numbers and equipment, Lee had decided to invade the North. He couldn't conquer it, of course, but taking the fight to enemy soil would allow the Virginia farmers to get on with gathering the harvest and simultaneously put pressure on the Yankee government to sue for peace. Also the Rebel soldiers were in sore need of clothing and footwear, and Maryland could furnish them with both.

The Northern public were growing restless, with inflation soaring and the body count growing - the second Manassas was a bloody mess - and voices were calling for a crusade against slavery to produce a cause worth fighting for, as if freeing the slaves would make anyone happy apart from the liberals. Lincoln didn't dare declare emancipation for fear of alienating the border states, especially Kentucky and Missouri (and turning their fifty thousand bayonets over to the Rebels), but with Lee's troops crossing into Maryland and inviting the populace to join him, Lincoln might well lose them anyway, and with them the war.

The Confederates even engineered an uprising by the Santee Sioux in Minnesota, promising the redskins recognition as equal to whites, if you please, votes an' all. You can imagine how long after the war *that* would have held. But it achieved its purpose, gripping the Yankees by the ankle from behind while they were occupied wrestling with the Rebels in front, while at sea the blockade still had more holes than the Armada, with Confederate ships such as the *CSS Florida* sailing through it to land supplies in Alabama right under the Yankee navy's nose.

Further west, the Confederates were pushing into Kentucky under Generals Kirby Smith and the much overrated Braxton Bragg, and meanwhile England and France were beginning to notice supplies of cotton were running low. The South still hoped for European intervention, with their agents politicking away in the European citadels. Southern victories in Maryland and Kentucky might well convince Palmerston and the Frogs that the Confederacy was here to stay, in which case they'd be tempted to support the South as victims of Northern aggression (and secure their cotton while they were about it).

The Border States saw much guerrilla activity, with bands of Rebel irregulars (and out-and-out criminal gangs masquerading as Rebels) carrying out raids on farms and homesteads, and attacking trains, tying up Union forces urgently needed elsewhere. Attacks on the railroad increased as the war progressed, but even in September 1862 just the fear of attack meant you had to watch your back.

The guerrillas who had ambushed us were, thank the Lord, disciplined Confederate troops who happened upon us by foul luck whilst returning to their base.

There were about a dozen of them, butternut-clad hard-bitten ruffians but with an air of military efficiency about them, and they obeyed their officer, a lieutenant, without question. Any fears I had about being shot out of hand (and you may be sure I was full to the brim with them), dissipated as the lieutenant called us to order. They rounded up the passengers, Tommy and Miss Cora with the rest, and the coachee and his mate, and told us the lay of the land.

'Sorry to break in on you like this, folks, but we are at war and war makes god-fearing people do strange things. You of the North have to realise that you are invading our lands, trampling our crops, stealing our property and killing our sons. We of the South want nothing but peace, but we won't stand idle while you bleed us dry. So beggin' your pardon, but we aim to relieve you of your valuables as slight recompense for the trouble your mercenaries have caused, then set you peacefully on your way.'

'But I'm with the South! Hurrah for you boys, Dixie forever!' cries Miss Cora in a voice to stop a train. Her eyes had shone on seeing Rebel troops get the drop on her hated Yankees, and I had to usher her to the back to prevent the other passengers seeing her grins. Now they turned to us as one, shock and hatred in their eyes. Whatever happened next, this was the end of our coach ride, and New York and escape were as far away as ever.

I could have kicked the bitch. Here we were, about to suffer a light robbery and then be released unharmed, for I believed the Rebel officer, and little Miss Dixie has to go and shoot the works that she, and by implication her husband, were for the South.

'With the South are ye?' exclaims the lieutenant while his boys hooted. 'Wa'al in that case we won't take your valuables by force, but accept them as a kindly donation to the cause you support.' He grinned at his men. 'That right, boys?'

The boys hooted some more and said sure thing; they were rightly grateful for the donation.

'Now,' says the lieutenant, growing serious. 'My men will pass among you and accept your valuables. Don't try fool 'em you're travelling with air in your pockets as they'll search you if they suspicion you're holding out on them. The quicker you hand over the goods, the quicker we can all be on our way.'

On our way *where*, thinks I, as the robbery began. What would happen when the Rebels departed? Sure as shooting, the fleeced passengers would take out their spleen on us. Damn Miss Cora! Could I disown her? No, we were travelling as man and wife, and if I didn't look sharp, we'd hang the same way.

All too soon it was our turn.

'Right ma'am,' says one of the boys good-humouredly, 'if you are truly for the South as you claim, you won't mind making a contribution to our cause.'

'Not at all, soldier,' replies Miss Cora. 'Let me check my bag.'

'Allow me,' says the soldier, not laughing now as he snatched her bag from her and began rummaging roughly through it.

'Why lookie here!' hollers the soldier exultantly, 'seems this Southern supporter is doing right well out of supporting the South but residing in the North.'

With that he produced a wad of Yankee dollars as thick as your arm.

'Hundred dollar bills. Fancy!'

'Let me see this,' says the lieutenant. All eyes were on us as he strode up and took the wad. Turning to us he looked at me quizzically. 'This is a heap of money for your wife to carry about her person. Guess she rules the roost in your house.'

I suspected he fancied himself as a bit of a comedian as his boys laughed and tittered at my discomfort. But Miss Cora wasn't fazed.

'Lieutenant, I must speak to you in private.'

'Bet she must,' haw-hawed the soldier while his mates held their ribs with mirth. They've little respect for rank, these irregular outfits, and to keep order the officers must earn the men's esteem. Even then they talk to their

322

officers as equals, hence the ribald noises and witticisms at his expense.

'You wanna talk privately in the bushes with her, Lootenant? Why you just go on right ahead. We won't tell yore wife none, trust us for that, haw haw.'

The lieutenant cursed them good-naturedly, told them to get on with shearing the passengers and turned back to Miss Cora.

'Ma'am, we don' have time to stand here and chew the fat. You got something to say, say it.'

'Very well Lieutenant.' She lowered her voice so she was barely audible above the sound of our passengers' grumbles, horses chaffing and jingling at the holdup and general hubbub. 'I am a Confederate agent travelling to Washington on the authority of senior government men. This man here is my escort. You hinder us at your peril, and calamity to the South. We can no longer travel with this party as they know we are with the Confederacy, so you will have to escort us to where we can strike out for a railroad station on our own.'

You can imagine what I thought of this. Senior government men, begad. The lieutenant was impressed too. His eyes widened and he looked from Miss Cora to me and back again, doubtless thinking that the secret service ain't what it used to be. Finally he found voice, albeit quietly.

'What's that you say ma'am? You some kind of spy for the South? A woman agent? All due respect ma'am but d'you expect me to believe you?'

She reached into the recesses of her costume and produced a small badge, a five-pointed copper star.

'This mean anything to you, Lieutenant? Or should I say Lieutenant Nuohlac?'

The god-forsaken Knights again. *Nuohlac* was *Calhoun* backwards, after John Calhoun, their spiritual inspiration. He believed slavery was good for everyone, and that the South should not concede an inch to the Northern emancipators. Happily dead, his name reversed was a sacred password among their more cracked members, which was all of 'em, in my opinion. I should have known they'd turn up soon enough. Americans bar our royalty and maintain that the British aristocratic system keeps better men down, but for sheer nepotism the Knights have got it all sewn up. They make the freemasons look like a ladies sewing circle.

The lieutenant goggled at the star for what seemed an age, and then chided her gently.

'We don't say that name outside the Temple ma'am. And kindly keep your voice down.' He glanced at me. 'Him too?'

'No, but he is my escort to Washington. An Englishman but in full accord with our aims.'

He gave me an austere look then turned back to Miss Cora. 'We'll take you with us. I need to present you to my captain. He'll know what to do for best.'

'He one of us?'

'Yes ma'am.'

'Very well, we shall go with you and meet with your captain. He'll understand the importance of my reaching Washington.'

She looked back through thin eyes at the coach's passengers and crew.

'Lieutenant. Those people know I support the South and will be aware that you have taken us with you. Best if you kill them all; dead men tell no tales.'

Even I was shocked. And to think we had been buckled-to like a pair of stoats for near on the past week. The lieutenant was shocked also. He blanched, then replied icily.

'No ma'am, we are soldiers not murderers. Let them think what they will. Sides, we kill a party of unarmed civilians - ladies too - an' we'll have the whole State on our tails. Confederacy's reputation in tatters as well. No, we'll leave them safe and sound, and get you back to our captain.'

He seemed anxious to get us off his hands and responsibility as quickly as possible, and who could blame him? Plainly a well brought up Southern gentleman, where women knew their place, Miss Cora's callousness must have shaken him to the core. Or was that why she said it? I felt a new respect for her.

'One more thing, Lieutenant,' says she. 'Hand me back my money, if you please?'

'Move out men. And deepest regrets, folks, for taking your valuables, but our needs are greater than yor'n. S'long.'

With that we saddled up, Miss Cora and I on two of the horses that had pulled the coach - they took the others too - and made our way into the gathering dark.

Once I'd climbed back into my wits, I decided that things could have been worse. True it was confounded bad luck to run into a Rebel raiding party, and Miss Cora could have saved us a lot of trouble by keeping her Dixie tongue firmly in her mouth. Then again, without her patriotic moonshine they would have robbed us blind and left us penniless, miles from anywhere without even the coach to take us further, being unhorsed. This way we kept the money, and the Rebels would see us safe to a railroad station far ahead of the coach party, so we should be set fair for Washington right enough.

After an hour or so in the saddle, leaving us somewhere on the border between Pennsylvania and Maryland, we arrived at a remote, empty farmhouse. The lieutenant called a halt, and cantered down the line alongside us.

'OK Mrs. Armstrong,' says he with a smirk, 'or whoever you really are, we are gonna halt here, a little way from our main camp while I figure how best to play this. I am under orders not to bring anyone to our camp, for fear of discovery, even someone as important as your own good self.'

'I must see your captain right away,' snaps Miss Cora. 'I must get to Washington as soon as possible. We cannot waste time here while you go figure.'

'Now ma'am, no need for raised voices. We are s'posed to rendezvous with some scouts hereabouts to learn of any Yankee troop movements, and then report back. We have orders to await them at this spot.'

'With the South crying out for guns and supplies?' She stamped her foot like an only child refused a treat. 'We don't have time to wait here for some scouts who may not even show up. I demand you take me to your captain right away.'

Give me a woman who knows her mind. The Good Lord himself couldn't have faced down Miss Cora with the wind in her fair sails, and neither could the lieutenant. The upshot was that he agreed to split his forces, half a dozen under a sergeant to remain here - along with your faithful correspondent - and await the arrival of the scouts, the rest to escort the lieutenant and Miss Cora to the Captain.

'Take care now Colonel,' says she as they made ready to depart. 'We'll be on the road to Washington in a couple of shakes.'

The rest of us settled down in the farmhouse, kindling a small fire in the fireplace and sharing their rations, for which I was most grateful. I was at last properly at ease for the first time since leaving the riverboat. The butternuts had accepted me as a friend of the South and afforded me respect without asking too many questions, assuming I was wound up with their intelligence folk.

Just when I was beginning to wonder when Miss Cora would return, a guard rapped smartly on the door and told us there were horses approaching.

'Must be the scouts,' says the Sergeant. 'Take cover anyhow, 'case its Yankees.' They scattered outside, prepared to open fire if was a Yankee patrol. I stayed put, and peeked through the kitchen window, ready to flee to the woods at the first sign of trouble.

As the riders approached, their leader gave out a cheery halloo.

'Home from home, boys,' cries out a broad Dixie voice. 'Any soup in the pot?'

Then it was hail-fellow-well-met, as a score of Rebel scouts pulled up at the farmhouse.

Relieved, I straightened up and returned to the main room, taking the opportunity to refresh my coffee cup and toast my backside over the hearth, for the evening carried an early autumn chill. I was alone but could hear the voices from outside clearly. The leader of the scouts was asking my sergeant for the latest shave. I heard the sergeant give a few details of their raids, then ask what news the scouts may have.

'Well Sergeant,' the leader raised his voice, 'guess we have news for you. That we do.'

Something about the way he said it alerted my neck hairs. It wasn't canny.

'What noos is that, Sir?' asks the sergeant.

'This news...' there was a silence pregnant with menace. I was alert on the instant, ready for anything. '...tell 'em, boys.'

Gunshots rent the peaceful night to smithereens. Rifles and six-shooters loosed their deadly loads simultaneously at close range targets who were dead before they hit the ground. The clamour resounded through the woods and the house like demons banging steel plates in Hell. Perhaps twenty shots fired in ive seconds, leaving seven men dead without so much as a scream between them.

It stopped as quickly as it began. There was no gloating or curses.

'Only seven,' says their leader laconically, 'too easy really. Still, spread the bodies around, boys. When the rest of the Rebs return, we want them to think these here wuz killed by Yankees, not their own fellows.'

Bushwackers! Dressed as Rebels. That's how they got close up. Bile gorged up to my throat and I shook with fear. They'd shoot me on sight, and were bound to enter the farmhouse any second. I couldn't flee with them immediately outside; they'd spot me on the instant and run me down or shoot me from behind. I must hide, but as I stole silently from the main room, footsteps clumped through the door and a voice behind called out in surprise.

'What in Hades?' shouts the voice. 'Hey William, there's another one of 'em here. Hold hard stranger. You're going nowhere.'

I couldn't run. He'd have me in the back before I could make two paces. I turned reluctantly around to see a young fellow dressed in Rebel grey, levelling a Sharp's carbine at my stomach.

'Another one?' says the voice outside. 'Well shoot him.'

'He's not in uniform.'

'Civilian? OK, hold him there, be right with you.'

'I'm not with them,' I babbled, 'they held me prisoner. I am a British officer. They took me against my will.'

'You just be quiet mister. You'll get your chance. Hey William.'

Just at that moment a young man glided gracefully into the room, his belt stuffed with two Colt navy revolvers. He eyed me curiously in silence. I stood stock still, knowing his next words would either save me, or be the last I heard this side of the pearly gates. Finally he spoke.

'What's your story?'

'My story? I was travelling from Pittsburgh to Washington when these fellows kidnapped me. I'm a British officer and they decided to take me, for ransom they said.' A desperate thought occurred. If I could persuade them I was a valuable prisoner they might take me for ransom themselves. That would keep me alive, for now at any rate. Couldn't see Palmerston brassing up much cash for me though, but time enough for that. 'I'm Colonel Armstrong of the British Army.'

'A British army colonel? Long way from home, aren't ye?'

He grinned merrily, and at once I noticed his features. He stood over six feet with a deep and powerful chest above a slim waist, legs sloping gradually down to surprisingly small feet. Here was a man who would turn heads anywhere, a quiet, thoughtful face with youthful dignity all over it, light moustache over thin lips, roundish jaw, cheekbones slightly prominent with a mass of fine dark hair spilling over his shoulders. Soft hands, and his eyes were as gentle as a woman's. A more peaceful-looking person you never did see, yet he'd just murdered a group of Rebels in cold blood. Oho, thinks I, here's another of them.

'Sir you must believe me. These Rebels took me from my coach several hours back, near Meyersdale Pennsylvania. They said they would keep me prisoner until the British or the U.S. government paid my ransom.'

'That a fact?' He stroked his chin thoughtfully. 'British army officer you say?'

'That's right.' I nodded. 'Colonel George Armstrong.'

Some of his associates came in and began to help themselves to dead men's coffee. They were relaxed but alert, and leaving me to their leader and his friend with the rifle. A cut above the average bushwackers, I wondered fearfully who or what they were.

'Seen much action?'

Most of it over my shoulder, thinks I. Aloud I agreed.

'Indian Mutiny, China, the Crimea. One or two skirmishes elsewhere...'

'Medals?'

'The Victoria Cross, among others...'

'Thought so. You look like a man of action. Tell me Colonel, this here war of ours. Whose side are ye on?'

This was a facer. The wrong answer could mean a bullet.

'As a British officer I am of course neutral...'

'Stow it Colonel. Are you for slavery or agin it?'

Something in the way he uttered the word *slavery* showed me my next move. With my heart beating fit to burst my ribcage, I went for broke.

'Slavery is an abomination. I oppose it with all my heart and soul.'

He looked me in the eye, held it a moment like he was weighing me up - most disconcerting - then turned to his fellow with the rifle. 'You kin lower that now, Jack. Colonel Armstrong is our guest.' He held out his hand to

329

me. 'William Haycock at your service. Reckon we just got time for a coffee and then we'd best be on our way.'

I blame myself. When William Haycock asked me had I any military experience, I could have told him I was in charge of the latrines, or shoeing the horses or washing the uniforms or anything away from the sharp end. But no, even as I looked down a rifle barrel, I couldn't resist saying I'd seen enough action for a dozen men and won the VC to boot. This was the worst thing I could have said, for it told Haycock I was the ideal man to help him strike a singular blow for the Yankees, dragging me into the mire once again.

They weren't bushwhackers but something far more dangerous. Haycock and his gang of marauders were jayhawkers, U.S. army irregulars dressed as Rebels in order to infiltrate their ranks, obtain information and spread a little mayhem and murder when it suited. They had nearly finished their shift, as it were, when they chanced upon a Rebel scout, learnt the rendezvous from him - I didn't care to ask how - and sallied up for a bit of fun on their way to matters more urgent.

'We are on our way east, Colonel,' says he as we cantered away from the farmhouse and its grisly memories. 'Word is Lee is marching north and we are going to rejoin our army, get back into blue uniforms and stop him.'

Good luck to you, thinks I, and I'll cheer you on from my berth in a London-bound ship. Once we joined the Union forces I could travel to Washington unhindered, and cadge the fare home from Lord Lyons. Nothing would be too good for the great Colonel Armstrong.

'Course,' adds Haycock casually, just as I was beginning to relax, 'we may take a swipe at Lee's boys afore we git there.'

I didn't know it then, but the cunning young bastard had planned all along to take what he called a swipe at Lee's boys. He had his plan, but not the means to carry it out. Not, that is, until I blundered along.

We rode east for three days, spotting no military, friend or foe, and camped out on the third night after crossing the Potomac. As I snuggled into my chilly blanket I hoped that by this time tomorrow I would be sleeping in a sound bed. With luck we would meet the Union forces that were lurking around here somewhere, before Haycock had a chance to spar with any invading Rebels.

Despite his sorrow-seeking valour, I found myself liking William Haycock. He was a likable man, random murders always excepted, with a merry twinkle in the eye and always ready for fun, but he would as soon fight as eat his breakfast, and such fellows are best avoided, likeable or not. I'd shake his hand, wish him well, then turn north to safety first chance I got.

'Coffee Colonel?'

Haycock himself woke me before dawn, having brewed up the coffee while I slept.

'One of our scouts just reported back. Seems Lee has camped out at Frederick, Maryland, but he's likely to move afore long. Where he goes we follow.'

This was bad news at any time. If the enemy are ahead, its time to sound the retreat, if you ask me. But there was worse. He took a pull at his coffee then turned to me.

'Colonel,' says he through a wide smile, 'we're gonna have us some fun today.' Somehow I doubted it. 'I got me a plan that will rock those damn traitors back all the way to Dixie.'

It seemed to call for something, so I hear-heared and agreed those Southern traitors deserved all they got.

'They sure do. An' they're gonna get what's coming to them, right enough.'

So long as it didn't involve me, I was happy for this amiable lunatic to grab some glory punishing the Rebels.

'Yes Sir,' says he. 'We're gonna hit them right where it hurts. And do y'know the best of it?'

'Go on... '

'We could never have brought it off without you.'

I nearly spat coffee all over him. Without me? What the devil did I have to do with it?'

'You see Colonel, we been mixing with Rebs these past months, and it is easy as falling off a log. They got no organisation, no Sir. We cud just wander through their camps and no-one pays us no heed.'

'Military incompetence the world over,' says I, wondering where this was going.

'Anyhow, it seemed to me that instead of just strolling through their camps with our ears open, mebbe we should be doing something more practical.'

'Like what?' I waited for the blow to fall.

'Assassination, Sir.'

I had to resist spitting once more. Clearly the fellow was cracked.

'I bin seeking a volunteer to walk with me through the Rebel camp, find us a top general in his tent, and stick it to him. And anyone else in sight. Trouble is,' he frowned, 'in a big camp t'would take us a while to find the chief's tent, and even the Rebs would suspicion a couple of raggedy scouts wandering loose seeking out the General.' He mused for a moment while I digested his words with growing alarm.

'No Sir, t'aint no good two scouts asking directions in the Rebel camp. But...' he grimaced at me, a fearful sight, 'an English Colonel? That's a horse of a different colour.'

'I don't follow you Sir,' says I, following him all too closely.

To my mounting terror, Haycock explained that he wanted a couple of brave idiots to stroll through the Rebel lines up to their field headquarters, if you please, and slit the throats of the Rebel high command. Even Lee himself. What had prevented him carrying out this madness before was that the Rebels might wonder why he was asking directions to where their generals roosted, and what excuse could he give? Until I came along.

'You see, Colonel, you are a British officer keen to get the lowdown on the Confederate Army and it's generals so's you can tell your government back home if'n they are worth supporting. The Rebs will do anything to accommodate you British, 'cos they hope the English fleet will break the blockade to get their cotton.' He laughed knowingly, like a fox with the key to the hen house. 'Why, the seceshers will be falling over themselves to speed you to Lee's lair, or at least the nearest senior general. Me? I'm the guide appointed to take you through to the Rebel lines.'

Aghast, I hid my face with my coffee cup and tried to think how I could talk him out of his suicidal plan without him seeing the truth; that the whole crazy scheme frightened me to death. Even as I quaked I knew it was no good. He had it all in hand. We would tool over to the Rebel camp, politely enquire the way to headquarters, beard Lee and his aides in his tent and slit their throats. I had to stop him without him seeing my fear. I'd heard enough outside the farmhouse not to be in any doubt what he would do if he knew I was shirking through funk.

'But assassination? That's hardly gentlemanly behaviour for a United States soldier, surely?'

'Not gentlemanly? Colonel, this is war. Do you suppose you British were gentlemanly at Lexington?'

This was some skirmish between the British and the Americans during their idiotic war for independence. It seems that the British looted a house or two for essential supplies and executed a few traitors, but had the Americans stayed loyal to the Crown in the first place they wouldn't have had their civil war and Haycock and Tommy would have been safe at home. And so would thousands of American boys now rotting under fresh battlefields. That's by-the-by, the point was that Haycock wasn't the type to fall for the *gentlemanly* argument so I'd have to think of something else.

'Anyhow, we'd never get near Lee's tent. Do you think he has nothing better to do on the eve of battle than give interviews to foreigners? At best they'd pass me off to a flunky, at worse they'd string us both up as spies.'

He tilted his head and looked at me sideways, as though doubting my courage, so I added, 'not that we should forget the idea for that reason. If there's the slightest chance of success we should take it. Trouble is, William, we'd be throwing our lives away for no cause.' I sniffed, manly-like, and looked him in the eye. 'I've seen enough of you these past few days to know that its men like you we need to fight this tyranny of slavery, and to do that you need to be alive and free.' I nodded solemnly, shut up and looked noble.

He paused for a moment, as though weighing up my remarks, then to my dismay burst out laughing.

'Why Colonel, if that ain't the finest piece of moonshine I ever did hear. You worrying about me gitting myself killed? Why, I see yore plan. You want to ride over the hill your own self and do the job without me. Old England grabbing the glory eh? Well you just fergit about that. We's going together, you old dog. We're gonna ride up to that Rebel camp, talk our way to Lee's tent and slit a throat or two. Then we'll stroll on back through the camp, mount our horses and skedaddle like we're chased by the devil hisself. That's what were gonna do, right after breakfast. Hey Jim,' shouts he. 'Gimme some civilian clothes, I'm the Colonel heah's guide.'

I lay frozen in fear while the man in front of me chuckled happily and called for more coffee. What could I do? Once again, through the most infernal luck and my own bragging under fire, I was in the clutches of another maniac who thought I was as mad as he, and devil to be done about it.

Had you told me that nearly twenty years later, he and I would spend all night carousing around a western town and enjoying every minute of it, I would have spat in your eye. But it's true, so help me.

A grand fellow, William Haycock, if you can stomach his habit of causing trouble wherever he hangs his hat. Why the man could bring mayhem to a monastery. He's dead now, but the world still remembers him by his extravagant yet appropriate nickname, Wild Bill Hickok.

Chapter Twenty One

Springing his insane design on me just before breakfast did nothing for my appetite, but it did mean I had scant time to spend brooding on the terrors ahead. More often than not, when assorted maniacs tell me of their intention to thrust me face-first into the stew (I've encountered a score or more, my martial whiskers attract them like Chinks to opium), they give me a few day's notice, shredding my nerves before we have even left the pavilion. Wild Bill, on t'other hand, barely gave me time to finish my coffee, then it was a case of saddle up and let's go meet whatever fate, that old whoreson, has in store.

I had no chance to bolt as we rode towards the town of Frederick, twenty or so Union spies and one reluctant British officer seeking (God help us!), General Lee's Confederate Army of Northern Virginia. Hickok's boys were escorting us most of the way, and I had to pretend to be as eager as them to spill Rebel blood, or face them spilling mine. Bill (after the war he went back to his real name, so far as I know, of James Butler Hickok) explained that we would break from them when we approached the Rebel encampment, and mosey on ahead, leaving his boys to make their way without us back to Union lines.

While humouring Hickok's bantering, for the thought of slitting Rebel throats had put him in good spirits, I cudgelled my wits to find a way out.

There was none. As we trotted out of some woods onto open land, I went as far as I dared, assuring Hickok I couldn't wait to sink my teeth into Rebel necks like Varney the Vampire. But, I wondered, might the Rebels avenge their dead general by hanging local citizens in reprisal? Also, the hunt would be up for any Yankees in Rebel uniforms. Would his boys be OK? Hickok laughed my fears to scorn.

'Johnny Reb won't take it out on local folk, Colonel. Jeff Davis and Lee want the good people hereabouts to join them in Lee's crusade agin the North. They won't anyhow, I reckon, but hanging some won't 'xactly help persuade them.' He looked around at our escort. 'And don' you fret none about my boys; why, they'll be back across the Potomac and sinking toasts to their own bravery afore the Rebs find they've been burgled. Haw haw.'

You can't reason with an enthusiast, so I soon gave it up and concentrated on the danger ahead. Bill and I would be safe enough until our escort departed near the Confederate position, wherever that was. What then? Could I betray him to the Rebels? No, I wouldn't dare and besides, he'd peach on me too, and we would hang together. Even if we lived, Bill would know I'd betrayed him and his blasted emancipation cause, and he'd find a way to do me down. Of that I was certain.

No, betrayal was out of court. What then? I was in a fearful funk; certain death if I backed out, almost certain death if I didn't. Though my liver has a yellow streak as wide as the Mississippi, I keep my wits about me when in a corner. For now I must go on and see what lady fortune has in store for me. After all, I've got away with it all my life.

'Hold it boys.'

One of our scouts came galloping over the hill ahead, waving his hat to attract our attention.

'There's something up yonder. Fall back to the woods.'

I didn't need telling twice. Nor did Hickok's boys, damn 'em, for I might have had the chance to ride straight through the little copse just behind and on to New York, or Timbuktu, or anywhere away from these gun-toting hellhounds. As it was, we all reached the copse together and obeyed Bill's order to dismount and prepare for anything.

'Johnny Reb is jes' over the hill,' announces our scout breathlessly as he pulls up in front of Bill.

'How many?'

'A whole damn army. And they're sitting still.'

Bill beamed at me. Then turned back to the scout.

'Then that's it. Good hunting lad, now go rein in the other scouts and we'll be parting our separate ways.'

I stood helplessly by while we awaited the return of the scouts. What could I do? And any hope that I could tap Bill gently on the back of the head the minute his men rode away was scuppered by Bill ordering them to stay where they were for an hour, in case we had no joy.

'Right men, Colonel Armstrong and I are off to teach the Rebels that nowhere is safe for a man who breaks his oath. You fellers wait heah one hour and if'n you don' see us agin, ride north. Jus' one more thing...'

And blow me if he didn't walk around and shake hands with every man-jack of them. Maybe, thinks I, after the war he wants to run for president.

The men watched us ride on ahead, towards the hill behind which the Confederate Army were making camp.

I held the reins loosely as we cantered gently on, Bill jabbering excitedly but in full control, at my side. Eventually we breached the hill, and for a moment I forgot my fears as we saw General Lee's Army of Northern Virginia encamped ahead.

It wasn't the biggest array of force I'd seen in one place, by any means. Nor the smartest, for the Rebel soldiers had no bulging quartermaster stores to fall back on, nor the best armed. But for sheer brazen effrontery, it took the breath away.

Here at Frederick, Maryland, stood an army in open revolt against the United States of America. Bold as brass, shaking its fist at the founding fathers, the Constitution and the nineteenth century with its telegrams and iron ships and factories. They stood proud, shouting at the modern world, "here we stand; the past, alive and armed, confronting you for our right to live as we please, in any century we choose, and bedamned to you". The sheer magnitude of the war came home to me in a flash. It was a trial of strength between the future and the past, and the past was winning.

Not that I cared. So as long as I had my money - and my wife Julie's pile - and status to fall back on, why, what matters the century? What mattered was, as always, British Tommy. And how would he come through this time?

'C'mon Tom,' cries an excited Hickok. 'Remember, you are a British officer curious to study the Rebels, and full of admiration for 'em. I am yore loyal guide, showing you the way.'

With that we cantered forward openly, until we met the inevitable challenge from a Confederate picket.

'Who goes there?'

A spy and an assassin, thinks I, but I left the parley to Bill.

'Are we glad to see you boys,' calls Bill, bright and sassy, 'we bin in the saddle for more'n a week, seeking friendly faces.'

'Git down from yore horses an' let's git a look at ye.'

We dismounted and led our horses to the copse that housed the pickets. An officer approached backed by pointed rifles from the bushes and demanded of us our business.

'My name is Haycock, mounted ranger from Arkansas under General Price, but slightly detached, haw haw.'

'You a deserter?'

Bill laughed the question to scorn as my spine turned to jelly at the word that likely meant summary hanging.

'Don' use that word agin, soldier,' says Bill, simmering down. 'No Sir. I am here under orders.' He waved at me.

'Allow me to present a distinguished officer all the way from Queen Victoria herself. 'This here is Colonel Armstrong of the British army, come to see how proper soldiering is done.'

This raised a titter or two, and the men appeared from the bushes and lowered their pieces.

'General Price ordered me to escort the Colonel here so he can see for hisself how the South will never be whipped by Lincoln's mercenaries and mudsills. An if'n the English want to take up our cotton any time soon they'd best sail right through the Yankee blockade an' we'll be right pleased to open the store.'

The boys hear-heared and sure 'nuffed, but the officer wasn't satisfied.

'You got written orders from General Price?'

'Written orders?' Bill snorted derisively. 'We bin travelling through Yankee territory, me an' a British officer. Course we don't got written orders. The Yankees would hang us both as spies. Now, you gonna let me take Colonel Armstrong to see the elephant or aren't ye?'

Of course the officer could hardly arrest a British Colonel, what with the secessionists desperate for European recognition, so after some hemming and hawing, he detailed a squad of his men under a lieutenant to escort us to the camp, leading our horses, where I would present my distinguished British rump to the first general we encountered and Bill would take it from there.

Our escort led us past the outlying units of the Rebel army by simply nodding at them, and it seemed to me that by putting on a bold front, a man might measure the length of the camp without serious challenge. My hopes rose as I wondered whether Bill would look the other way long enough for me to slip my cable. Give me half a yard start and I reckoned I could be through the Rebel army and out the far side before he could whistle Dixie. That's if the escort about-faced once they had delivered us to a senior tent, of course.

All too soon for me, we left the outlying units behind and reached the main body. 'Here we are, gentlemen,' says our officer, looking at us and pointing ahead, 'you are beholding the army that's gonna finish this war and bring freedom to the South.'

I doubted it, as we ambled through the rag-tag soldiery, clad in grey and butternut rags, an astonishing number shoeless, all wiry and looking like they hadn't had a decent meal in months, but then I considered what they had achieved so far. Two years ago the Confederacy existed only in the minds of a few fire-eaters and the Knights of the blasted Golden Circle, a gaggle of Southern States without industry to speak of, virtually no navy and outnumbered three to one. Yet here they were, eighteen months into a civil war, standing north of Washington and banging on the door of the United States, demanding recognition. Who was to say one more victorious battle wouldn't sicken the Northern citizenry to sue for peace? I would have done; anything to get these ornery bastards off my lawn, and let slavery go hang.

I shelved such philosophising as our escort hailed a colonel and asked directions to field headquarters. To my surprise the colonel did not demand our identities or insist on passes in triplicate - the Yankees would have done - but instead told us the way without demur. We pressed on, Bill leading his horse and swinging his free arm nonchalantly, calling out encouragement to resting troops as if he was taking his dog for a walk in the park, and eventually we found our objective. My heart beat like a jack-hammer as we approached a group of larger tents, near a well-worn path and obviously the heart of the Confederate Army. This is it.

'Well gentlemen,' says our officer, 'you have the honour of witnessing General Lee's H.Q. before mebbe the last battle of this war for liberty. One of these heah tents holds the best general and finest gentleman on God's green earth bar none.' He turned to me with a grin, 'if you English had been up against Lee at Waterloo, Colonel, guess you would all be speaking French by now.'

He saluted, ordered the rest of the escort to fall in, saying carelessly they hadn't got all day, and strode off.

They left us standing alone, just yards from the Confederacy's military elite. I had no time to marvel at the escort's sheer complacency - we may have been assassins for all they knew, and by the gods, one of us was - as Bill tugged me gently by the arm and pointed along the rows of tents.

'Come on Tom,' orders Bill, 'walk slowly along the line. We want a tent that's standing empty so we can make plans.'

Bile rose up in my chest and I found myself helpless to do anything but amble alongside, both leading our horses. I said we were alone, but there was no lack of junior officers walking to and fro carrying papers, and many enlisted men just loafing about the place, chewing tobacco and spitting. Cooking fires wafted their thin streams of smoke, swirling gently in the light breeze. We could hear the strains of *My Maryland* played on a Rebel whistle fluttering through the ether. It was disorderly order in the bright sunshine, and nobody minded us a button. Little consolation for old Tom, you'll agree, as Bill found a large tent plainly deserted with flaps open wide. Once he slit a general's throat - oh sweet Jesu, don't let it be Lee's - the loafers would be alert right enough then, and tear us limb from limb.

'Inside,' he hissed, and consigning my soul to the Lord, I accompanied him in.

It was a large, airy tent, almost homely, with boxes strewn about the sides, a sleeping area at one end with blankets and a small dresser, and a makeshift table in the centre strewn with papers, pens, inkpots, cigar box beside an ashtray overflowing with spent cigars, and a makeshift spittoon.

I stared anxiously at the bright entrance while Bill rifled their papers, waiting for an obliging general to happen by looking for a light. What if the entire high command turned up together?

'You worry too much, Tom,' chuckles he, peering through the paperwork like Cratchit. He was enjoying himself, first playing at assassins and now spies. 'If'n anyone comes in, why, you are a noble British officer seeking to meet the leaders of the great Rebel army of the Confederacy.'

They'll believe *that*, thinks I, when they find Bill poking through their correspondence. Most likely they'd hang us on the spot.

'Well for the love of women, stop reading their reports,' says I. 'If anyone shows up we want to be standing respectably at the entrance. Better yet, outside it.' And better still, a hundred miles away. But Bill wasn't listening. He'd stopped rustling the papers, and was holding one at arm's length, reading intently.

'Look at this,' cries he in a stage-whisper you could have heard in Washington. He held up a handwritten page to me. "Special Orders No. 191".

Probably the latrine rota, thinks I, but I dutifully obeyed and read the following heading.

Special Orders, No. 191
Hdqrs. Army of Northern Virginia
September 9, 1862

It began with some nonsense about banning people from Fredericktown unless they had business there, and arrangements for transporting sick and wounded. I shrugged dismissively, wondering who cared, but Bill bade me read on, so I did. "The army will resume its march tomorrow, taking the Hagerstown road... Longstreet to pursue the same... Major Taylor will proceed to Leesburg... Jackson's command will form the advance... "

That was enough. I stopped reading and stared into Bill's triumphant face.

'We've got 'em,' he almost panted, eyes alight with excitement. 'We git this to McClellan he'll lick them nine ways to Sunday.'

'What about killing Lee?' says I foolishly, for events were moving so fast my wits were shot.

'Fergit it. We gotta get this back to our army.'

Relief flooded over me like the Pope's forgiveness as Bill carefully replaced the rest of the papers where he found them and generally straightened up the table.

I was for getting out immediately, but trust Bill to keep calm. He was a bearcat for nerves.

'Hold on Tom,' it won't do to have this loose in my pocket. Pickets might search us.' He cast around the table.

'Got it,' says he, opening the cigar box and grabbing four cigars.

'No feller in his right mind would wrap General Lee's battle plans around his smokes. Guess we'll offer one to any soldier who stops us an' he'll let us pass.'

It was one to me if he stuffed the battle plans where the sun don't shine, but even in my heightened state I saw the sense of it. The main thing was to get out of here before someone cried *I spy strangers*.

'Come on Bill,' says I urgently. 'Time to move.'

'An' then some,' he laughed, placing the cigars and their guilty secret into an envelope and stuffing them in his top pocket, peeking out open to the world. 'I guess we'll take our leave by a different route. Wouldn't wanna meet our Rebel escort on the way back.'

To my amazement, nobody remarked upon the two scarecrows strolling from the tent like French tourists, collecting our mounts and melting into the grey and butternut throng. My amble through the Rebel army was the scariest experience yet in my sorry time in America thus far, acutely aware as I was that Bill carried a document poking cheekily out of his top pocket which would damn us both as spies should any one of the thousands of handy Rebels think to search us.

For a wonder we made it to the edge of the encampment without so much as a raised Rebel eyebrow, and as we speeded up past the outer lines, I permitted my spirits to rise. Could we make it? Could we bring the Rebel plans to the Union chiefs? By Jove, if we delivered Lee's army to the North I would be once again the hero! The man who saved the Union. Well, one of 'em, I suppose, but I fancied I would make more of it than could Bill. I'd praise his contribution, of course, and insist it was touch-and-go whether I'd have got the plans without his help, but folk would know it was me, daringly posing as a British officer on a fact-finding mission, that brought home the Rebel bacon. Tom old son, thinks I elatedly, you've won through again.

'Jest hold on a jiffy boys, where'd y'all be a-going in sech haste?'

It was an outlying picket. No surprise, of course, but that didn't stop my organs dancing the highland reel. I tried to look like a man on a mission, which, so help me, I was.

'Hello boys,' replies Bill nonchalantly, and went on to give him our cover story, updating it to say that British Tommy here had been most impressed after meeting with General A.P. Hill, and he, William Haycock, was now escorting the Englishman incognito back to the Yankee lines, whereupon he would travel to England and tell the Queen to break the blockade and invade New York pronto, or words to that effect.

A sergeant sniffed. 'Bin conversin' with Little Powell, have ye? You sure you ain't deserters?'

Damn fool question, but Bill was equal to it.

'Colonel Armstrong?' he smiled at me and the sergeant. 'Tell the good gentleman who you are.'

I took the hint. In my best British parade voice I introduced myself, giving rank, medals and antecedents.

'Sound like a Dixieland skulker to you? I reckon not,' cackles Bill. 'Truly Suh, I do.'

The sergeant's men guffawed at this, leaving him with no option but to go along with the joke.

'I guess you're right. OK, you can pass through.'

We thanked him, Bill saying he was a credit to the Confederacy, which I thought was hamming it up a little - trust Bill for that - and made to move on.

'Stay, though,' cries the sergeant. 'We'd best just check yore pockets first. You don' object?'

With no say in the matter, we cheerfully turned out our side-pockets and allowed one of his soldiers to pat us down. Lord knows what he hoped to find. The sergeant allowed us to put back our effects, including our guns, and pronounced himself satisfied.

'Well, looks like you gentlemen are on the square. Good luck on yore journey.' At last he noticed the bulge in

Bill's top pocket. I was wondering when he would; it stood out a bloody mile.

'What's that there?'

I froze. Bill looked down at his pocket as though surprised it was occupied, then chuckled.

'Why, that's just my cigars. Want one?'

With that he pulled the envelope out of his pocket, unfolded the wrap and selected a cigar.

'Here you are, Sergeant. A victory seegar. Think of me when you smoke it.'

He handed the cigar to the grinning sergeant and carefully folded the plans around the remaining three. Bill was right; nobody thought to read the cigars' wrapping paper.

'Thankee kindly,' says the sergeant. 'You take care now, y'heah?'

Bidding the sergeant goodbye, we walked painfully slowly ahead. After about fifty yards we were clear of the pickets and I suggested to Bill we get astride our mounts. I would feel a site safer with a horse under me.

'You're right. Guess we're clear now. Let's get going.'

'Hold it one moment,' cries a voice from behind. 'You two, with the horses.' We turned around and saw our sergeant back at the picket standing alongside an officer. It was clear as day that the officer had not credited the sergeant's account of why he let us pass.

'Come back,' cries the officer. 'I want to talk with you.'

'Time to go,' mumbles Bill calmly, which made one of us. I was ahead of him there. Before the officer had finished his words I had grasped my nag's neck and swung myself by main force astride her. She reared up in shock, and as I struggled to get her under control, shots rang out. Seeing us trying to flee, the damned Rebels were firing on us. A piercing shriek rent the air and as I mastered my steed I saw Bill's horse writhing on the ground.

'Tommy!' cries Bill. 'My horse is down!'

Without his horse, Bill was lost. He'd be captured or killed within minutes. Too bad, of course, but there was nothing I could do. Sharing my horse would slow us both down, and that was no good for Tommy. Pity about the battle plans, but my safety comes first. I made to spur my horse as he leapt in front of me.

'Fergit about me, I'm done fer,' shouts he, as I made to run him down. 'Here, take the plans and git them to McClellan.'

He thrust the wrap of cigars at me, and I instinctively clasped them to my bosom with one hand as I steadied the horse with the other.

'Ride Tom. Get those plans back safe.' He drew his gun and loosed off a shot at the Rebels, much good it would do, but I didn't need telling twice. Bill was sacrificing himself to help me escape with the battle plans, and it was up to me to deliver my side of the bargain.

I set off at a gallop through the brushwood, not daring to look behind. Thirty seconds of mad dash and I was clear away. Breathing heavily through shock and exhaustion, I slowed down to a lively canter and took stock.

Here I was, escaping the Rebel army with no sound of pursuit. I had got clean away. The Rebels had a masterly cavalry, far superior to the bluecoats at this stage of the war, but this left few horses available for steeple-chasing fugitive Englishmen across the fields. I was in Maryland, a State full of secessionists but nominally loyal to the Union, and barring bad luck I should be able to make my way to safety without hindrance. And I had the battle plans.

This raised a question of military importance. What should I do with them? If the Rebels found them on me it would mean certain execution. Then again, bringing them safe to McClellan would make me a hero. Hmm.

'Hey you!'

I almost screamed as a troop of Rebel cavalry crested a hill, about two hundred yards to my left. No time to ponder how they got there, I dug in hard and lowered my head, sending my mount racing in the opposite direction. The ground was soft, with trees spaced fairly wide apart, allowing me concealment without too much danger of a smash. In moments I cleared the trees and sped into an open field.

There was no sign of the riders behind. Perhaps they had not considered me worth chasing, but they had made up my mind for me about what to do with the plans. I daren't risk being caught with them, and with Rebel cavalry loose about the place, and the risk of my horse foundering, there was only one thing to do.

Crossing the field, I checked first that there was no-one watching me, then carefully dug the cigars in their guilty wrapper from my pocket and let them slip onto the ground. Whatever happened next, I was free of incriminating evidence. Pity about Bill's hopes of saving the Union, but after all, I was a hero already, with a Victoria Cross to prove it, and the extra adulation might have gone to my head. #Note_16

After a half-mile or so, I decided I was safe from pursuit, and slowed down to a canter to rest the horse. I was hopelessly lost, and now that my nerves had stopped rattling I realised I was ravenous. I'd not eaten since this morning and my stomach had begun to notice. I wondered if I dare risk seeking out a farmhouse or dwelling, and cadging a meal. Academic at the moment, as there were no houses about.

I was thirsty too, but at least I could do something about this. I discovered a small brook at the bottom of a glade, and moments later I'd dismounted and my horse was refreshing itself greedily. I bent down over the brook and did likewise, wondering if I should rest up here until I could take my bearings from the night sky.

'Hold it right there mister.'

It has always struck me as amusing that folk back home refer to America as the wide open spaces, where a man might lose himself in the peaceful wilderness. In my experience a man couldn't so much as scratch his backside without some interfering bugger or other levelling a piece at him and demanding to know his business. The place was full of 'em.

The heart-pumping shock at being jumped yet again vied with relief that I had jettisoned Bill's precious plans, and I looked round at the source of the voice that had challenged me.

Behind me stood a Yankee patrol. The realisation warmed me like a large brandy, and I made to rise. I was safe!

'Stay down mister,' says a lieutenant. 'Who're you, out here on your own? State your name and business. Look sharp now.'

Yankee military charm, I could tell. Staying low beside the brook, I replied.

'Am I glad to see you, Lieutenant. My name is Armstrong, Colonel Armstrong of the British army, and I am on my way to New York. Sorry about my appearance, but I've been chased by Rebels for the past hour or two.'

'A British officer? An' whose side are you on?' This didn't sound too promising. I couldn't see us sharing toasts at his regimental reunions. I'd learnt enough during my American odyssey to know that announcing yourself as British was no guarantee of a warm welcome. By and large, Americans like us British, but now and again you'll stumble across one who thinks it is still 1776, and hates us like poison. Just my luck to find a descendant of Paul Revere.

'I assure you Sir,' I protested, 'I am a loyal supporter of your Union.' And for some idiot reason, I added, 'in fact, I have the honour of acquaintance with your president, Mr. Lincoln.'

This caused laughter, and one soldier removed his hat and bowed, mock-graciously.

'Why, your majesty.'

'Quiet Mitchel,' chides the lieutenant. Turning to me, he added, 'Well Mister, maybe you're a spy and maybe you ain't. We'll see. We are returning to our unit, and we're taking you with us. Stand up; consider yourself under arrest.'

This was good enough for me. Once safe with their unit, I would convince their superiors of my *bona fides* and be practically home at last. In the meantime, I could look forward to a meal. Gratefully I joined their ranks, a private leading my horse, and we tramped back to their base.

They were soldiers of the 27th Indiana, making reconnoitre of the Rebel position. I cursed myself for disposing of Lee's battle plans, but it was no use moping over my lost chance for yet more undeserved glory. Best, I considered, not to mention it.

Their base was quite a distance and it was an exhausted Tommy who slumped down in the corner of the farmhouse which served as their headquarters. There, most of them were friendly enough and they gave me a much-needed meal, but my hopes of a quick release and a ticket to civilisation came to naught

'We cannot spare any men for escort,' says their colonel briskly, 'nor allow you to go free. If you are as innocent as you claim, you need have no fears. We want no trouble with you British, but I regret to say many of your countrymen have foolishly supported the rebellion, and we cannot take the chance of letting you loose. We will send news of your appearance here in our next dispatch to General McClellan, asking them to forward it to your Consul in Washington. Truth to tell,' he frowned, 'we have bigger fish to fry right now. Like a Rebel army a stone's throw away. We'll hold you here nice and quiet until we get orders from above.' He offered me a cheroot which I eagerly accepted. 'My apologies Colonel, but spies take the most unlikely guises and with the Rebels invading our land, damn their eyes, we dare not trust anyone.'

'I quiet understand, Colonel,' says I toady-like. 'You must do your duty. I give my parole I will not try to escape, and will happily await permission to travel in God's good time.'

I was happy to stay safe and sound under this colonel's protection for a week or two, by which time word would have gone to Lord Lyons in Washington that the great Tommy had come a'calling, and he would prevail on McClellan - or Lincoln himself, begad - to have me released, with a pound from the poor box for luck.

Had I known what the future held for me, I would have jumped through the farmhouse window and given him one clear shot of me running for the hills. #Note 17

They held me in the farmhouse cellar, mercifully dry and fairly free of rats, for about two weeks, but it was far from nice and quiet. Standing on bales and peering through a high slit in the wooden wall I could see Union troops arriving and marching off, cannon and wagons too, but nothing to let me know what was happening. I could hear spasmodic firing in the distance most days, which was all the more unnerving as despite my pleas, the gaolers told me little. I now know that the Rebels had taken the arsenal at Harper's Ferry (Just like me and John Brown two years back) and were shaping up to advance further north, but at the time it was all confusion.

Then early one morning I heard the beginnings of a most almighty battle taking place some miles away. My gaoler told me McClellan was engaging Lee behind Antietam Creek, near Sharpsburg. Cooped in my cellar, I had no way of knowing how the battle was progressing, or to the point, who was winning. I regretted all the more my panicky decision to lose Lee's battle plans, as the last sight I wanted to see was victorious Rebels knocking at my door. I concocted a story to give them, along the lines that I was a Southern supporter held prisoner by the Yankees, but I dreaded putting it to the test. Let Billy Yank whip Johnny Reb, thinks I, and let me get out of here and back to the world of sanity.

The next morning an eerie silence fell. Birdsong once more broke through and I recognised the signs of the aftermath of battle. But who had won? I called up above for news, but was told to hold my horses and I'd learn all when they were good and ready.

Over the next few days my gaolers informed me that they had won a great victory over Lee. They'd stopped him at Sharpsburg and he was fleeing with the remnants of his army back to Virginia. This was good news, as flush with victory, they might look more kindly on a stray

Englishman, and be inclined to let him quietly depart. They'd reported my existence to their superiors as promised, so I was looking forward to my release any time now.

In fact they held me for another two weeks or thereabouts. The Rebels, they told me, had crossed the Potomac and back into Virginia. Morale was high and my rations improved, but for the life of me I couldn't see what they were so flush about. It seems the armies had clashed nearby, no-one could take the upper hand, so Lee retreated back home. The Rebel army lived to fight another day. I wasn't to know it had been the single bloodiest day in American history. All the better for Tommy then, spending it in a cellar.

Finally, I had a visit from my colonel.

'Colonel Armstrong? Time to go.'

'Where?'

'Antietam. There's someone there who wants to see you.'

Puzzled, but relieved to get out of this hole in the ground and back in the sunlight, I took advantage of the colonel's offer to clean myself up and had a proper wash and shave for the first time in weeks. The colonel apologised but said he could not enlighten me as to who it was who sought my acquaintance.

'I am under orders to deliver you to Antietam, Colonel. That's all I know.'

They returned my horse, and under a strong escort, for there were rumours of Rebel raiders about the area, we rode near the Antietam battlefield, now happily quiet.

There they took me into a large house that had been commandeered by the Union forces as headquarters. I had hopes that they would introduce me to someone in authority who would give me a pass and set me on my way to New York, but instead they took me downstairs and deposited me in a dingy basement room and locked the door behind me.

Chin up Tom, thinks I. You are safe enough here in the middle of the Union army. All you need do is put up a bold British front to this peckerhead who wants to see you and all will be well. Stay though, he might be an admirer. As I have mentioned, the United States officers took soldering seriously, reading up on the campaigns of Napoleon and Alexander the Great an' all. Perhaps he wanted to shake hands with a genuine British hero (ahem), or compare medals. After I had languished for an hour or so, I convinced myself I had nothing to worry about; my troubles were nearly over. Wasn't I the optimistic fool, just?

Keys jangled and a minion entered.

'Someone to see you.' He looked back towards the cellar door. 'Come in, Sir.'

A brisk, no-nonsense man with a jutting beard much like Grant's strode in. He shook his head a moment, as though adjusting to the light, then stared at me long and hard. I returned the stare, you may be sure, and damn near leapt to the ceiling as recognition flooded in. The man standing before me I'd last seen in New York when he and his associates had bullyragged me into risking life and limb leading John Brown's gang of idiots in their disastrous attempt to rob the Harper's Ferry arsenal. Lincoln's head of the U.S. spy service, Allan Pinkerton.

'It *is* you!' cries he exultantly. 'When they told me ye were nearby I could'nae credit it. Rich man like yesel' for'eer gallivanting aboot the world seeking sorrow. Why, you pop up more often than a jack-in-tae box.'

With a jolt I recalled the Scottish brogue and the chip-on-shoulder attitude. I first encountered him many years ago back in Scotland, where he had headed a gang of uppity mill hands threatening the owners by demanding higher wages or shorter hours or some such nonsense. I commanded the local militia, whose job it was to keep the rabble in check. He'd never quite forgiven me, though his attitude softened after I did his bidding in the John Brown fiasco, not that I'd any choice. (Had I refused, William Seward - now Lincoln's thug-in-chief - would have peached to Queen Victoria that I had said "snooks" to Uncle Sam in his hour of need, and that would be the end of my military reputation and soft living.) To Hell with that; the question was, would his appearance here be good for me or otherwise?

'It'll nae do.'

'What will not do?'

'I cannae take ye tae the President looking like a scarecrow. You need a bath and a change of clothes, I'm thinking. C'mon man, let's get you cleaned up. We cannae keep the president waiting.'

Well this wasn't half bad. They wouldn't consider my appearance if they were intending to fling me in prison. But Lincoln! Why were they taking me to see the President? Wasn't he busy, what with the war and suchlike? Perhaps he wanted to thank me personally for past assistance, though knowing Lincoln, I thought that unlikely. Lincoln was one of the few men who had spotted me for a rogue from the off, and I doubted *he* wanted to compare medals. Then again, for some whimsical reason of his own, Lincoln liked me, and I him. Perhaps he was just curious to discover what I had been up to in his country while his back was turned, and would afterwards send me on my way without let or hindrance.

Pinkerton was deaf to my pleas for enlightenment, and after chivvying me into a quick bath while he sent for fresh clothes, he declared me presentable. He then led me to out of the building, and with a squad of troops - and some hard-hatted civilians, secret service thugs sure as breathing - poured me into a buggy.

'Whip up, driver.'

In no time flat we pulled up at a group of tents surrounded by any number of men in blue, the atmosphere light and pleasant, morale high after their supposed victory.

Pinkerton ordered me down - I was beginning to resent his peremptory attitude but there was nothing to be done - and his entourage, Tommy in the middle, followed him to one of the larger tents. Here he bade me wait, while he poked his nose through the flap and disappeared inside.

In due course he re-appeared, affable as ever.

'C'mon you. Time tae meet the President.'

I felt a thrill of excitement as I crossed the threshold into the large tent. Not just because I was about to meet the United States President, but in anticipation of meeting Lincoln once more. I was quite looking forward to it.

'Mr. President?' says Pinkerton, 'presenting Colonel Armstrong of the British Army.'

By God, here was Lincoln, tall, gangly and awkward-like as ever was, stooping slightly at the far side of the tent. His presence was both frightening - a wartime leader seeking your company? Safer to embrace a rattlesnake - and yet reassuring at the same time. Looking back today, I'll own that the United States was lucky indeed to have this beanpole as their leader. Anyone lesser and the American continent would have ended up with as many warring Statelets as ancient Greece. At the time though, I could have wished he'd stayed in Illinois, or run away to sea or blacked up and joined a minstrel troop.

He beamed at the sight of me, but addressed Pinkerton, and his first words froze my neck-hairs.

'You are convinced he's the man for the job? We'll only be able to try it once, you know.'

What job? Try what once? Jesu! Pinkerton nodded, rot him.

'I'm convinced, Mr. President. 'This mission is meat and drink tae Colonel Armstrong. Why, he didnae let us doon over the John Brown raid, an' he shan't fail us this time neither.'

'Hmm...' considers Lincoln, while I stewed helplessly, 'Colonel Armstrong was employed to prevent Brown's raid taking place. Remind me, was he successful?'

Keep talking Abe, thinks I. Tell Pinkerton I was a bloody disaster, and maybe he'll drop this mad talk of jobs and missions. For I was too old and ill-used to suppose this talk would lead to anything but poor Tommy with his backside in the firing line once more.

'T'was nae fault of Colonel Armstrong that Broon's raid took place. Ye've seen the reports. Forbye, Colonel

Armstrong is English an' precisely the man for this job. Nae wan better.'

No one better? If Pinkerton truly believed that, he was not fit to be chief of an escort, never mind the U.S. secret service. Intelligence my arse. And what's being English got to do with it? But it was too late now. Lincoln sighed, cracked his bony knuckles loudly, and smiled his familiar knowing smile down his eyebrows across at me.

'Very well, desperate times call for desperate measures. And now, Colonel Armstrong...?'

Continued in Volume two.

You have the opportunity to rate this book and share your thoughts on Amazon, Facebook, Google+ and Twitter. If you believe the book is worth sharing, will you please take a few seconds to let your friends know about it? If they find it enjoyable they will be grateful, as will I.

All the Best,

Barry Tighe

Notes.

Note_1: This was probably the brigantine *Venus* which in 1806 under Captain Samuel Chase took Charlotte Badger, an Englishwoman convicted of housebreaking, to banishment in Australia. Badger helped foment a mutiny, and so began her career as a pirate. By calling himself Charlie Badger, Armstrong's bucko mate may well have demonstrated a curious sense of humour.

See:
Charlotte Badger-Buccaneer – Author Angela Badger, Published by Indra Pub (June 2002)

Note_2: This may have been the Mexican gang leader known, appropriately, as Red Shirt. The records claim he was shot by a policeman while robbing a sailor who he had bludgeoned unconscious.

The crimps who operated along the waterfront of San Francisco would go to extreme lengths to supply sailors for a price to unscrupulous - and desperate - sea captains. The men delivered to their ships would be unconscious through drink, violence or drugs and appeared to be lifeless, so it was possible therefore to include a dead man or two among the crew. The crimps would sometimes include a dummy among the sailors whom they delivered. A suit of clothes was stuffed with straw and properly weighted, while the 'head' was swathed in blankets or scarves. They would sew a live rat into the 'torso' so its scrambling gave the impression of a man's chest breathing.

The Gangs of San Francisco - Herbert Asbury, Published by Arrow.

Note_3: *The Knights of the Golden Circle* was founded by George W. L. Bickley in 1854. Its object was to promote the interests of the slave-holding South, aiming to create a 'golden circle' consisting of Mexico, Central America, Cuba and the Caribbean as part of an expanded Confederate empire. It had extensive support - and intelligence gathering - among all parts of the United States.

John Wilkes Booth, the man who murdered President Lincoln was a member.

Crenshaw, Ollinger (October 1941) - *The Knights of the Golden Circle: The Career of George Bickley*
May, Robert E. (1973) - *The Southern Dream of a Caribbean Empire, 1854–1861*

Note_4: Asbury Harpending (1839–1923) was a Southern Supporter who did not allow his views to stand in the way of making money. Kentucky born, he made his first fortune mining in California and in Mexico in the 1850s. In 1861 he joined the Committee of Thirty, a clandestine organisation dedicated to seizing San Francisco for the Confederacy. After the war, he made - and lost - further fortunes, being involved in mining, real estate and railroads, as well as an innocent victim (he claimed) in the Great Diamond hoax of 1872.

In his memoirs (see below) Asbury Harpending gave the following account of the behavior of his colleague Edmond Randolph. Clearly he never did discover the part played by Armstrong.

"One of the most brilliant members of the early San Francisco bar was Edmond Randolph. He was a man of rare talents and great personal charm. Born in Virginia, a member of the famous Randolph family, he was naturally an outspoken advocate of the South. He was one of our Committee, and on terms of social and professional intimacy with every one of Southern leanings. He was on the closest terms with General Johnston and there is hardly a doubt that, purely on his own motion, he approached the General with some kind of a questionable proposition.

What happened at that interview no man knows, but Johnston's answer made Randolph stark crazy. He indulged in all kinds of loose, unbridled talk, told several of our Committee that he had seen Johnston, that the cause was lost and otherwise, in many ways, exhibited an incredible indiscretion that might easily have been fatal to our cause. No amount of warning was able to silence his unbalanced tongue."

Asbury Harpending, *The Great Diamond Hoax and Other Stirring Incidents In the Life of Asbury Harpending*, Edited By James H. Wilkins, The James H. Barry Co., San Francisco, 1913.

Note_5: This orator may well have been Thomas Starr King, whose oratory was claimed by the Union Commander in Chief, General Winfield Scott, to have 'saved California for the Union'. King held a rally at Market and Posts on May 11th 1861, under a banner proclaiming 'The Union, the whole Union and nothing but the Union', so Armstrong's words appear to have been remembered.

Dennis Evanosky & Eric J. Kos. Thunder Bay Press - *San Francisco Then and Now*. 2009 Salamander Books.

Note_6: The Confederate invasion of New Mexico was led by the Second Texas Regiment, Mounted Rifles, under Lieutenant Colonel John R. Baylor on July 23, 1861. They marched up the Rio Grande and made camp within six hundred yards - some accounts say two miles - of Fort Fillmore. Learning that the Union leaders had been informed of their position, the Texans altered their plans and instead of attacking the fort on the morning of the twenty-fifth, they crossed the river and occupied the town of Mesilla nearby. They were welcomed by Southern sympathizers.

Major Lynde ordered an attack which resulted in a indecisive skirmish. He then withdrew his troops to the fort. Next morning at the post Lynde gave orders to fortify against an attack. Later - possibly due to Armstrong mentioning how news of women and children losing their lives in defense of an unimportant outpost would play in the North - he gave the order to abandon Fort Fillmore and marched for Fort Stanton, 150 miles to the northeast. His junior, Captain C. H. McNally, later claimed that three hundred men could have held Fort Fillmore against three thousand attackers. They loaded wagons, buggies, and ambulances with military and personal supplies, and materials that could not be transported were ordered destroyed.

At 1:00 A.M. on July 27, 1861, the entire command, including the wives and children of five officers, evacuated Fort Fillmore, travelling along the Fort Stanton Road. Under a scorching sun, many of the infantry suffered severely with the intense heat and want of water. They finally came to a halt at San Augustine Springs. Meanwhile, Baylor ordered a detachment of soldiers to occupy Fort Fillmore and led his mounted troops in pursuit of the fleeing Yankees. He stated, "The road for five miles was lined with fainting, famished soldiers who threw down their arms as we passed and begged for water."

As the Texans approached the Union forces, Major Lynde, in despair, made a feeble attempt to place his troops in battle formation, but he soon requested terms of surrender. Lynde later wrote, "I could not bring more than 100 men of the infantry battalion on parade.... Under the circumstances... it was worse than useless to resist; honor did not demand the sacrifice of blood."

The departure of the Union troops gave the Apache Indians an opportunity to come down from the hills to plunder the settlers, as did Mexican gangs from across the border. Eventually citizens of Tucson voted to make Arizona a part of the Confederacy.

Note_7: Colonel Baylor was as good as his word when he agreed to keep Armstrong's involvement in his affairs a secret. Official records simply state that the sole survivor from the attack on the Apache camp was a Mexican guide.

Ray C. Colton - *The Civil War in the Western Territories: Arizona, Colorado, New Mexico, and Utah* [Paperback].

Note_8: As Armstrong recalls, Sibley spent most of the day in an ambulance, indisposed, he claimed, by illness. Others including Armstrong maintain that any indisposition was caused by alcohol. Colonel Green took command and it was his aggressive attack on Canby's center and left that won the battle.

    Canby meanwhile blamed the New Mexican volunteers for his loss but reinforcing his right while weakening his center and left was the real cause of the Union defeat. On Canby's right wing, Kit Carson's regiment of New Mexican volunteers saw only limited action but comported itself well. The volunteers were advancing and thought they were winning the battle. They were incredulous when Canby gave the order to retreat.

Kerby, Robert L. (1958, 1995), *The Confederate Invasion of New Mexico and Arizona, 1861-1862*, Tucson, AZ: Westernlore Press.

Taylor, John (1995), *Bloody Valverde: A Civil War Battle on the Rio Grande, February 21, 1862*, Albuquerque: University of New Mexico Press.

Note_9: News of Baylor's March 1862 order for the extermination of the Apache Indians outraged President Jefferson Davis, as Armstrong foretold. He removed Baylor from his post as Governor of Arizona, stripped him of his rank, and cashiered him from the Army.

    Baylor did not take this lying down. On December 29, 1862, he sent Major General John Bankhead Magruder, commander of the Department of Texas, an Apache shield, taken from a chief who Baylor had killed personally. The shield was decorated with a scalp, which Baylor's accompanying note described as 'a woman's fair tresses - those of a Miss Jackson, who had been murdered during one of the frequent raids.'

Some accounts claim the shield was also decorated with the scalps of infants, 'dressed like the skin of some animal, painted with bright colors and ornamented with beads.' Baylor insisted the shield 'be sent to His Excellency the President, to enable him to judge whether there is not some cause for the bitter feelings I, in common with the people of our frontier, entertain toward the Indians.' Magruder did not forward it on to President Davis, and instead persuaded Baylor to take back both his note and his "gift."

Baylor's Confederate Army career was not over. He enlisted as a private in a Texas cavalry regiment serving in the Galveston campaign of January 1863. Later that same year he won election to the Confederate Congress, where he served until the war's end, ceaselessly trying to obtain Confederate Government support for the recapture of Arizona from the Union.

Thompson, Jerry Don, *Colonel John Robert Baylor: Texas Indian Fighter and Confederate Soldier*. Hillsboro, Texas: Hill Junior College Press, 1971.

Allardice, Bruce S., *Confederate Colonels*, University of Missouri Press, 2008.

Allardice, Bruce S., *More Generals in Gray*, Louisiana State University Press, 1995.

Katheder, Thomas, *The Baylors of Newmarket: The Decline and Fall of a Virginia Planter Family*. New York and Bloomington, Ind., 2009.

Note_10: William Howard Russell of the London *Times* encountered much hostility from both the Northern and Southern newspapers. He remarks on this several times in his diaries, including this lament:

'In the South, the press threatened me with tar and feathers, because I did not see the beauties of their domestic institution, and wrote of it in my letters to England exactly as I spoke of it to every one who conversed with me on the subject when I was amongst them ; and now the Northern papers recommended

expulsion, ducking, riding rails, and other cognate modes of insuring a moral conviction of error ; endeavoured to intimidate me by threats of duels or personal castigations gratified and their malignity by ludicrous stories of imaginary affronts or annoyances to which I never was exposed ; and sought to prevent the authorities extending any protection towards me, and to intimidate officers from showing me any civilities.'
William Howard Russell - *My Diary North and South.* First published in 1863. Nabu Press.

Note_11: In fact the spelling was different. William Russell, *Times* correspondent, and railroad worker William Russel.

Note_12: See: Lieut. William Pittenger - *Daring and Suffering: A History of the Great Railroad Adventure.* (J. W. Daughaday, 1863). *Daring and Suffering: A History of the Andrews Railroad Raid,* by William Pittenger, with Introduction by Col. James G. Bogle, (Cumberland House Publishing, August 1, 1999.
Charles O'Neill - *Wild Train: The Story of the Andrews Raiders* (Random House, 1959.
Parlee C. Gross - *The Case of Private Smith and the Remaining Mysteries of the Andrews Raid* (General Publishing Company, 1963).
Russell S. Bonds - *Stealing the General: The Great Locomotive Chase and the First Medal of Honor* (Westholme Publishing, October 15, 2006.
Gordon L. Rottman - *The Great Locomotive Chase -The Andrews Raid 1862* Osprey Raid Series #5 (Osprey Publishing, November 2009.
Craig Angle, *The Great Locomotive Chase: More on the Andrews Raid and the First Medal of Honor* ([Rouzerville, Pa.: C. Angle, ca. 1992]).
Barry L. Brown and Gordon R. Elwell, *Crossroads of Conflict: A Guide to Civil War Sites in Georgia* (Athens: University of Georgia Press, 2010).

Stan Cohen and James G. Bogle, *The General and the Texas: A Pictorial History of the Andrews Raid, April 12, 1862* (Missoula, Mont: Pictorial Histories, 1999).

Stephen Davis, "The Conductor versus the Foreman: William Fuller, Anthony Murphy, and the Pursuit of the Andrews Raiders," *Atlanta History* 34 (winter 1990-91).

Charles O'Neill, *Wild Train: The Story of the Andrews Raiders* (New York: Random House, 1956).

Note_13: CSS *Louisiana* was an ironclad ship of the Confederate States Navy. Her construction was impeded by Confederate lack of shipbuilding resources as well as industrial action by the labor force. Whilst incomplete, she took part in the Battle of Forts Jackson and St. Philip, both of which fell to the North. She was destroyed by her crew to avoid capture.

Official Records of the Union and Confederate Navies in the War of the Rebellion, Series I, 27 vols.; Series II, 3 vols. Government Printing Office, 1894 - 1922. Scharf, J. Thomas - *History of the Confederate States Navy from its organization to the surrender of its last vessel.* Rogers and Sherwood, 1887.

Still, William N. Jr. - *Iron afloat: the story of the Confederate armorclads.* Vanderbilt University, 1971. Reprint, University of South Carolina, 1985.

Note_14: The *Trent* Affair was an international incident that nearly brought Britain into war with the United States. On November 8, 1861, under the command of Captain Charles Wilkes, the USS *San Jacinto* intercepted the British mail packet RMS *Trent* and removed two Confederate diplomats, James Mason and John Slidell. They had been bound for Great Britain and France to attempt to win European diplomatic recognition for the Confederacy.

The action was popular with the American press and public, but President Abraham Lincoln and British

Representative Lord Lyons sought a face-saving way out for the two countries. The South hoped the incident would lead to diplomatic recognition by Britain of the Confederacy and even war between the United States and Great Britain, leading to their independence. In Britain, public outrage at the actions of Captain Wilkes led to many calling for a full apology and release of the envoys under threat of war. The British government made such demands - their letter diplomatically softened by the Queen's Consort, Prince Albert - while it took steps to strengthen its military forces in Canada and the Atlantic.

Crisis was resolved after several tense weeks when the Lincoln administration released the envoys and disavowed Captain Wilkes's actions, but did not issue any formal apology. This compromise satisfied honor on both sides. Mason and Slidell reached Europe but failed to achieve diplomatic recognition. Their greatest contribution to the South was not as diplomats, but as hostages.

Thomas Grand Le Harris - *The Trent Affair: Including a Review of English and American Relations at the Beginning of the Civil War.* Nabu Press (April 1, 2010). Norman B. Ferris - *The Trent Affair: A Diplomatic Crisis.* University of Tennessee Press; 1st edition (1977).

Note_15: For a lengthy description of plantation life in the early days of the War Between the States, see: William Howard Russell - *My Diary North and South.* First published in 1863. Nabu Press (April 1, 2010).

Note_16: Armstrong has explained a long-standing mystery. When crossing a field in the vicinity of Robert E. Lee's army of Northern Virginia, Union soldiers from George B. McClellan's Army of the Potomac discovered three cigars wrapped in paper. On the paper surrounding the cigars was written the special orders 191 written by Lee giving details of his tactics for the upcoming battle. These details were for the eyes of his Confederate generals only.

Corporal Barton W. Mitchel and Sergeant John McKnight Bloss of the 27th Indiana discovered the plans when resting in a field just west of Frederick, Maryland, on September 13, 1862. They espied an envelope lying in low grass. Inside the envelope, wrapped in a piece of paper, were three fine cigars.

While Bloss sought for a light, Mitchel idly perused the writing on the wrapper. He discovered it was an official set of orders from General Robert E. Lee to his subordinate generals, detailing his plans for battle.

Bloss recognized the importance of the wrapper, and within hours the orders were in the possession of Major General George McClellan, commanding the Union Army of the Potomac.

One of his staff officers, who knew General Lee before the war, verified Lee's handwriting, and an elated McClellan realized he could use the knowledge to score an easy victory over the South's top general.

'Here is a paper,' he told an aide, 'with which if I cannot whip Bobbie Lee, I will be willing to go home.'

Despite the advantage, McClellan could not do better than achieve a drawn battle. Lee soon discovered that his plans were in the hands of his enemy and adjusted his tactics accordingly.

It is interesting to note that some accounts claim that the plans - and the cigars - came from Major General D.H. Hill, whose division had camped in the same field just days before the Indiana troops. Armstrong's report that William Hickok stole the plans from a little distance away seems more plausible, as three wrapped cigars in a field of Confederate soldiers would surely have not remained unnoticed for long.

Note_17: The knights of the golden circle buried secret caches of weapons, coins, and gold and silver bullion, mainly in the western states, though small caches were buried elsewhere. Much of the gold was acquired through robbing banks and troop payroll trains during the civil war. Also - with assistance from southern Copperhead sympathisers - from northern army military posts.

Though Armstrong does not mention it (as it no longer concerned him directly), it seems Miss Cora reached Washington and persuaded her Copperhead senator to assist in transferring the Memphis gold out of the country.

Certainly, orders from a high source in Washington soon afterwards produced a ship to transport an unnamed consignment downriver to New Orleans. It sunk in the Mississippi. The gold was never recovered.

Felix G. Stidger (editor) - *Treason History Of The Order Of Sons Of Liberty: Formerly Circle Of Honor, Succeeded By Knights Of The Golden Circle, Afterward Order Of American Knights (1903).* Kessinger Publishing, LLC (September 10, 2010)

Bill Westhead - *Confederate Gold: The Missing Treasure.* 1st Book Library (March 28, 2002)

Other Books by Barry Tighe

Spawater Chronicles

Over two thousand years ago the Romans came, saw and conquered   Britain.
They stayed for a few hundred years, give or take, until rising Villa prices, the ferociousness of the local lions and the quality of home brewed wine convinced them to take all roads back to Rome.
No Romans remained. Britain, both sides of Hadrian's Wall, became a Roman-free zone.
Except....

There was one little town where the Roman bugle-song anthem of retreat, 'Legitus Quickitus', was not heard. One town where the Romans and the locals, ears full of soap, were so busy splashing around together they missed the thunder of the departing last night chariots of fire. And as There were no cabs due for another 15 hundred years - and that's if you believe the cab office - the town's Romans decided to stay.

The town grew, thriving on the naturally occurring spa waters, nurtured by the river Fons and hardened by the combination of original Brits and Roman bath lovers. The last bastion of the Roman Empire, it is now a mighty town indeed. The town's name? Spawater, home of the legendary Spawater Baths.

The Spawater Chronicles are the tales of its citizens, and how they take on the world and win.

Books in the **Spawater Chronicles** series:

Volume One
Youth Market
Chickens versus television

Volume Two
Identity Cards
Nothing to hide nothing to fear?

Volume Three
Casino
Heads we win tails you lose

Volume Four
Gone Fission
It's a power thing

Volume Five
Vote Alison MEP
Booze cruise to gravy boat

Follow the Spawater Chronicles at:

http://www.facebook.com/CanWriteWillWrite

Http://www.canwritewillwrite.com

Also by the author:

Gieves to the Fore
Gieves and Wooster are back.

7294692R00215

Printed in Germany
by Amazon Distribution
GmbH, Leipzig